T0305295

CONTINUITY DESPITE CHANGE

SOCIAL SCIENCE HISTORY

Edited by Stephen Haber and David W. Brady

CONTINUITY
DESPITE CHANGE
The Politics of Labor Regulation
in Latin America

MATTHEW E. CARNES

STANFORD UNIVERSITY PRESS

Stanford, California

Printed and bound by CPI Group (UK) Ltd, Croydon, CR0 4YY

Library of Congress Cataloging-in-Publication Data

Carnes, Matthew E., author.
  Continuity despite change : the politics of labor regulation in Latin America / Matthew E. Carnes.
      pages   cm. — (Social science history)
  Includes bibliographical references and index.
  ISBN 978-0-8047-8943-1 (cloth : alk. paper)
    1. Labor laws and legislation—Latin America.   2. Labor policy—Latin America.   I. Title.   II. Series: Social science history.
KG432.C37   2014
344.801—dc23   2014010074

  ISBN 978-0-8047-9242-4 (electronic)

Typeset at Stanford University Press in 10/14.5 Bembo

For my parents—Lois and Ed Carnes

CONTENTS

TABLES AND FIGURES

Tables

Figures

ACKNOWLEDGMENTS

This book was born out of my experience in 1999 and 2000 working with displaced workers and their families in Honduras after Hurricane Mitch hit their country. Their dignity, and their search for stable employment in an economy that was left in total disarray, raised the questions that have driven me through my research and writing. I wanted to understand why workers experience such different fates in different settings and under different circumstances, and especially how the law and public policy shape divisions between workers in the economy. Even though my research would take me far afield, and this book would eventually feature case studies from the Andes and Southern Cone rather than Central America, the example and experience of those Honduran workers have continued to motivate and inspire me. In a sense, they were the first members of a vast community of people that have contributed to the book in direct and indirect ways, and to whom I find myself deeply grateful. In an admittedly too brief way, I wish to acknowledge that community here.

Stephen Haber has played a foundational role in my intellectual development for more than two decades, since I first set foot on the Stanford University campus as an undergraduate interested in Latin America. My appreciation for the keenness of his intellect and his commitment to his students has only grown over the years; it is one of my greatest desires to be able to emulate that commitment in my own life of scholarship. Isabela Mares shaped my thinking from early on, pushing me to consider the microfoundations of policy design and adoption. She has since become an inspiring colleague and friend, who continues to teach me and challenge me as we work on projects together. Mike Tomz and Alberto Diaz-Cayeros sharpened the empirical analysis in this book, both quantitative and qualitative, and forced me to think how the pieces of the puzzle fit together. In addition, I am grateful to David Laitin, Beatriz Magaloni, Alex Kuo, Jeremy Wallace, and Claire Adida for providing important comments on early drafts of this project.

In the Georgetown Department of Government, my academic home since 2009, I have been surrounded by a marvelous group of scholars and colleagues. George Shambaugh and Michael Bailey, as my department chairs over the past four years, have kept my committee service in check and given me the space and resources to concentrate on research and writing. Jim Vreeland has been a regular, and always constructive, interlocutor and reader of my work. I have benefited from productive and far-ranging conversations with Desha Girod, Dan Hopkins, Marc Busch, Raj Desai, Eric Voeten, David Edelstein, Abe Newman, John Bailey, Eusebio Mujal-Leon, R. Kent Weaver, Nita Rudra, Arturo Valenzuela, Harley Balzer, Jeff Anderson, Tom Banchoff, Marc Howard, Charles King, and Tony Arend. Further, Chester Gillis, the dean of Georgetown College, and Carol Lancaster, the dean of the Walsh School of Foreign Service, have encouraged me in my development as a teaching scholar in the Georgetown mold.

I am particularly grateful for the support of the Mortara Center for International Studies at Georgetown, and its director, Kate McNamara, who generously hosted a very productive workshop discussion of the book manuscript in the spring of 2011. At that event, M. Victoria Murillo, Robert Kaufman, Jennifer Pribble, Stephen Kaplan, Emmanuel Teitelbaum, Isabella Alcañiz, Jim Vreeland, Harley Balzer, and Jeff Anderson provided invaluable comments.

My students at Georgetown have been an inspiration for this book. I often had them in mind as I wrote and rewrote the manuscript, seeking to make it accessible to them and to a broader audience, and to answer some of the questions they asked when I would describe the project in my classes. In addition, several of my students directly contributed to the book as research assistants: Rachel Braun, Nora Hajjar, Joseph Incalcaterra, Elisa Jacome, Kathryn Martin, Michael Meaney, and Melinda Reyes. Morgan Zeiss was instrumental in the formatting and final preparation of the manuscript.

The project has benefited from two research leaves, each of which was a privileged time of quiet for research and writing. At the Kellogg Institute for International Studies at Notre Dame University in spring 2009, I had the opportunity to discuss my work with Robert Fishman; Timothy Scully, C.S.C.; J. Samuel Valenzuela; and the late Guillermo O'Donnell: each provided important ideas and insights drawn from long experience of Latin America. The Hoover Institution at Stanford University provided an intellectual home for me during the final phases of writing in 2011 and 2012, and I was fortunate to benefit from the good advice and support of Steve Haber, once again, and from Armando Razo.

During my initial research and subsequent development of the project, I benefited from conversations with a host of scholars and policy-makers in Latin America, including Ricardo Solari, René Cortázar, José Piñera, William Thayer, Yerko Lubitec Godoy, Pedro Irureta Uriarte, Marcela Peticara, Andrés Tapia, Javier Couso, and Rossana Castiglioni in Chile; Javier Neves Mujica, Martín Tanaka, Luis Negreiros Criado, Manuel Casalino Grieve, Elías Grijalva Alvarado, Alberto Felipe de la Hoz Salmon, Felipe Portocarrero, Rubén Espinoza, and Francisco Verdera in Peru; and Sebastián Etchemendy, Rubén Lo Vuolo, Noemí Giosa Zuazú, Enrico Soza, Alfredo di Pasce, Guillermina Tiramonti, Marta Novick, David Trajtemberg, Martín Campos, Mario Morant, Anibal Toreta, Victor de Gennnaro, Julio Godio, Hugo Mancuso, and Adriana Marshall in Argentina. At academic conferences, William Smith, Miriam Golden, Ed Leamer, David Rueda, Nolan McCarty, Lane Kenworthy, and José Alemán all provided insightful comments on elements of the theory and empirical analysis. In the last two years, I received extremely useful feedback on the project from five anonymous reviewers at *Latin American Politics and Society* and Stanford University Press. Further, at the press, Norris Pope was instrumental in shepherding me through the review process, and Stacy Wagner, John Feneron, Eric Brandt, Friederike Sundaram, and Martin Hanft saw me through the final rounds of manuscript preparation and editing. Two friends, Roy Elis and Ashley Jester, each read substantial portions of the final manuscript, helping me clarify the argument and tighten the prose.

My Jesuit family has provided me with both a spiritual and intellectual home over the last decade of academic work. While completing my doctorate, I had the pleasure of living in the Santa Clara University Jesuit Community. I received constant encouragement from Paul Locatelli, S.J.; Sonny Manuel, S.J.; Jim Reites, S.J.; Michael Zampelli, S.J.; Robert St. Clair, S.J.; Al Naucke, S.J.; Mario Prietto, S.J.; Luis Calero, S.J.; Paul Fitzgerald, S.J.; Mick McCarthy, S.J.; and Jack Treacy, S.J. In a particular way, Paul Mariani, S.J., and Jerry McKevitt, S.J., modeled for me the scholar's craft of envisioning and completing a book manuscript.

Jesuits in Latin America have opened their homes—and their list of contacts in government and academia—during my periods of research in the region. The community of the Colegio del Salvador in Buenos Aires has been a second home to me while writing and rewriting. Fernando Montes, S.J., of the Universidad Alberto Hurtado in Chile and Jeffrey Klaiber, S.J., of the Pontificia Universidad Católica de Perú each provided me with remarkable hospitality and access to their institutions' academic resources. My long-time mentors—Ricardo Falla, S.J., in Guatemala, and Juan Hernández Pico, S.J., in El Salvador—each followed the project from afar with interest and encouragement. Finally, Rodrigo Zarazaga, S.J., has gone above and beyond at every turn of this project; he discussed its early ideas, read drafts of the chapters, and then reread the full manuscript on more than one occasion. His sharp mind and deep knowledge of Latin America have greatly improved the book.

For the past five years, I have been blessed to live in the Georgetown Jesuit Community. The rectors of the community, Joseph Lingan, S.J., and John Langan, S.J., have shown me excellent *cura personalis* as a young professor, and the minister, Gene Nolan, S.J., facilitated my move to Washington and immediately made me feel at home. I have been humbled to serve alongside the good priests and scholars of the community, and I count them as dear friends: Brian Conley, S.J.; Patrick Rogers, S.J.; Phil Boroughs, S.J.; Kevin O'Brien, S.J.; Jim Duffy, S.J.; Chris Steck, S.J.; Otto Hentz, S.J.; Peter Rozic, S.J.; Francois Kabore, S.J.; Ryan Maher, S.J.; Steve Spahn, S.J.; and Mark Henninger, S.J. In a particular way, David Collins, S.J., and John O'Malley, S.J., have served as intellectual inspirations, and have lent me a compassionate ear when the travails of the academic life wore heavy. Howard Gray, S.J., has been a guide, both spiritual and personal, and a good friend.

Most of all, I find myself grateful for the support and encouragement of my family—my brother Jim, and especially my parents, Lois and Ed. They somehow had the guts to trust their son when he wanted to go to Latin America as a high school student, and they accompanied me time and again to the airport as I embarked on yet another journey to yet another country they had never visited. Through the years, they fostered my intellectual development and my passion and engagement with Latin America, especially as these matured into this project, and they kindly did it all without asking too many questions (especially not, "Is it done yet?"). It is a testament to their patience and their prayers that this project has come to completion as a book they can hold in their hands. I am proud to dedicate it to them.

ABBREVIATIONS

APRA   Alianza Popular Revolucionaria Americana (American Popular Revolutionary Alliance, Peru)

CGE   Confederación General Económica (General Economic Confederation, Argentina)

CGT   Confederación General de Trabajadores (General Confederation of Workers, Argentina)

CGTP   Confederación General de Trabajadores del Perú (General Confederation of Peruvian Workers, Peru)

CMSE   Compañía Minera San Esteban (San Esteban Mining Company)

CTA   Central de los Trabajadores Argentinos (Argentine Workers Central, Argentina)

CTCh   Confederación de Trabajadores de Chile (Confederation of Chilean Workers, Chile)

CTP   Confederación de Trabajadores del Perú (Confederation of Peruvian Workers, Peru)

CTS   Compensación por Tiempo de Servicios (Compensation for Time of Service, Peru)

CUT   Central Unitaria de Trabajadores de Chile (United Workers Central of Chile, Chile)

DNT   Dirección Nacional de Trabajo (National Department of Labor, Argentina)

FIM   Frente Independiente Moralizador (Independent Moralizing Front, Peru)

FDI   Foreign direct investment

FOCh   Federación Obrera de Chile (Workers Federation of Chile, Chile)

GOU   Grupo de Oficiales Unidos (Group of United Officers, Argentina)

ILO   International Labor Organization

OECD   Organization for Economic Coordination and Development

PJ   Partido Justicialista (Justicialist Party, Argentina)
PL   Partido Laborista (Labor Party, Argentina)
STP   Secretaría de Trabajo y Previsión (Secretariat of Labor and Prevision,
        Argentina)
UCR   Unión Cívica Radical (Radical Civic Union, Argentina)
UCRP   Unión Cívica Radical del Pueblo (Radical Civic Union of the
        People, Argentina)

Introduction: Continuity Despite Change

Early on a winter morning of 2005, a crowd of warmly dressed retirees gathered on a street corner in downtown Santiago, Chile. A murmur of happy chatter went up as a series of luxury buses arrived, bearing the names of scenic destinations outside the city—the thermal baths at Jahuel and Cauquenes, and the coastal cities of Valparaíso and Viña del Mar, among others. The pensioners boarded for relaxing day trips that had been heavily discounted and subsidized by their pension fund, the Caja de Compensación Los Andes. Behind them, other retirees entered the gleaming new headquarters of the Caja and looked forward to receiving benefits as varied as health care, income support, public lectures and discounted books, and access to athletic and vacation facilities.

On the same morning, hundreds of doctors in Lima, Peru, took to the streets outside the Ministry of Labor under much less auspicious conditions. They carried signs demanding the restoration of their wages, which had been severely cut under a series of governments, and they shouted slogans about their increasingly vulnerable jobs. Formerly they had been assured near lifetime job security, and seniority had allowed them to select choice placements in the capital's hospitals and clinics. Indeed, for a period in the late 1960s, Peru had guaranteed job protections to all workers, not just to doctors and health care professionals.

How did these workers end up in such radically different circumstances? One group kept their long-standing status and benefits, while another saw theirs eroded. This book argues that the answer lies in labor laws. In Latin America, labor laws function to divide, rather than unite, workers. They are not neutral rules of the game that apply equally to all workers in the economy, or that apply

1

in the same way across countries. Rather, their stipulations regarding hiring and firing, working conditions, and the functioning of labor unions make workers' lives highly unequal. They stratify workers and shape their long-term career paths, guaranteeing some individuals secure employment (and even retirement), while relegating others to serial short-term occupation and instability. Still other workers are cast outside the world of "legal" employment altogether, in unregistered jobs "off the books" in the informal sector.

Labor Laws in Latin America

This is a book about labor laws in Latin America. It studies legislation governing the employment and collective organization of workers in the region—a set of laws that has been the subject of intense political mobilization and contestation over the last century. It argues that these laws are more than simply the outcome of legislative processes. They function as institutional markers of economic and political status within societies (Collier and Collier 1979, 2002), and by their design can divide workers into winners like the pensioners in Chile or losers like the doctors in Peru. Indeed, this book shows that the seemingly arcane measures governing hiring, firing, and organizing have a massive impact on social stratification, economic development, social policy, and political competition and change. To understand outcomes as diverse as economic inequality (Marshall 2002; Groisman and Marshall 2005; Birdsall et al. 2011), informal employment (Almeida and Carnero 2007; Levy 2008), and even the "rise of the left" in Latin America in the 2000s (Levitsky and Roberts 2011; Edwards 2012; Huber and Stephens 2012), one must understand the politics of labor laws.

By international standards, Latin America's laws stand out as highly protective (or "rigid," as the literature often refers to limitations on the hiring and firing of workers). The legal framework in the region approximates the "conservative" European model of economic relations (Esping-Andersen 1990), in which employment was classically assumed to be long-term with a single firm, wage demands were moderated, and the government could play an important role—either de jure or de facto—in negotiations between firms and their employees. For much of the twentieth century, this highly regulated environment made these negotiations predictable and cemented labor's role in the workplace and the "political arena" (Collier and Collier 2002).

Since the 1980s these laws have come under fire and been subject to repeated calls for reform. Debt crises and economic stagnation in that decade produced the demise of the then-dominant import-substitution industrialization (ISI) economic model. Country after country undertook rapid rounds of trade liberalization, opened their financial markets, and privatized their state-owned enterprises and pension programs. The momentum of reform was expected to place protective labor laws on the chopping block, too. The restrictive labor system that had characterized the region for the previous three-quarters of a century was expected to be "flexibilized"—permitting the more rapid hiring and firing of workers and undermining labor union strength (Edwards and Lustig 1997; Cook 2007).

Surprisingly, the restructuring of labor regulations never happened, or at least not in the way expected. Most reforms consisted of additions to labor codes, rather than their dismantling (Murillo 2005; Murillo and Schrank 2005). And the few labor-weakening provisions that were passed proved to be short-lived; they were quickly opposed and revoked. Indeed, the overall trend among labor codes in Latin America between the 1980s and the present has been toward greater protectiveness of labor and enhanced union organizing rights, rather than less. Only Peru and Colombia bucked this trend by undertaking significant, lasting labor law liberalization.

In short, the status of labor laws in Latin America can be summarized by two stylized facts. First, they are highly rigid by international standards, but show significant variation across countries and economic sectors. Second, they did not undergo liberalization at the same pace, or at the same depth, as other segments of the economy (Lora 1997; Murillo 2005; Murillo and Schrank 2005).

Toward a Long-Term Theory of Labor Regulation

This book offers a microfoundational theory to explain both long-term differences in labor laws in Latin America as well to address punctual reform initiatives. It takes a perspective on labor codes that can only now be applied. Only by taking a long view, roughly a century after the adoption of the first labor laws in the region, and half a century or more since the period of labor's political "incorporation," can we see clearly the institutional stability that has prevailed in the region. In spite of alternation between authoritarian and democratic governments, and even through the major economic restructuring that followed the demise of import-substitution industrialization policies, labor codes in nearly every country have changed only slightly. And the few significant modifications that were introduced have been prone to reversal, with each country ultimately displaying a long-term equilibrium set of policies. Continuity, even amid massive political and economic change, prevails.

Yet stability does not imply uniformity. While Latin American labor codes do share similarities vis-à-vis other regions, they also display significant heterogeneity among themselves. It is this lasting heterogeneity that this book examines, and doing so requires significant theoretical innovation. Existing work has provided considerable insight into the political factors driving specific moments of labor law development and reform. It is excellent at explaining why a *specific* party or government leader acted to develop (or diminish) the rigidity of labor regulation at a *specific* point in time, or why *specific* unions or labor leaders pursued the mobilization strategies that they did (Collier and Collier 1979; Murillo 2001, 2005; Murillo and Schrank 2005; Cook 2007; Anner 2008, 2011; Blofield 2011, 2012). But it struggles to explain why a particular labor law configuration would *persist* over a long stretch of time, even through the administrations of vastly different presidents and parties, and it cannot explain why efforts at significant reform have been so unsuccessful.

This book offers a theory that gives special attention to structural economic factors, emphasizing how resource endowments shape the range of possible labor law regimes that a country can implement. Political action—which can seem unconstrained in some classic accounts of the region (Payne 1965; Collier and Collier 1979, 2002)—is significantly limited by the economic foundation on which it builds. And this is especially true in the field of labor regulation. While governments can impose short-term policy measures that are out of step with underlying economic structures, these policies will be costly to sustain and vulnerable to opposition by a range of actors. For this reason, labor codes prove remarkably dependent—over the long term—on the structure of employment and production of the economy.

Of these structural factors, the distribution of skills among workers is crucial. Skills have long been studied in political science accounts of advanced economies, where they are accorded a central role in the design of both economic and political institutions. They are one of the chief factors distinguishing various "varieties of capitalism" from each other (Hall and Soskice 2001; Thelen 2004). But skills have received less treatment in political science analyses of the developing world. This book examines skills within the context of the "hierarchical market economies" of Latin America (Schneider 2009), where low skill levels have been common. Yet, even at these relatively lower skill levels, significant differences exist across countries. And more important, differences in the *distribution* of skills—geographically and across industries—create very different contexts for labor relations, and make productive bottlenecks and the potential of economic "hold up" more or less likely. Where there is greater heterogeneity of skills among workers, and a significant portion of workers have developed advanced skills, demands for more extensive and protective labor regulation may be more likely to develop.

However, while the structure of production conditions labor law possibilities, it does not enact legislation. Indeed, the passage of labor law—whether through action by the legislature or executive decree—requires political action. To understand labor law outcomes then, it is necessary to examine political factors. Of central importance in this process is the organizational capacity of labor. Strong leadership, solidarity across firms and sectors of the economy, and linkages to political parties have been critical resources for labor as it seeks to achieve friendly legislation—and as it has sustained and defended that legislation against reform (Murillo 2001, 2005; Collier and Collier 2002; Cook 2007). In those countries in which workers have been unionized in larger numbers, and have collaborated across firms and industries in confederations, they have had greater economic and political impact. Size and strength have often allowed them to develop lasting ties to political parties that can then serve as partners (albeit not always reliable ones) in enacting labor legislation. Where workers have not enjoyed this kind of organization or relationship to political parties, their impact has been more muted on labor law development.

The Effects of Labor Laws: Institutional Markers of Status and Inequality

Labor laws are more than simply neutral legislative outputs designed to solve technical problems regarding workplace relations. Rather, they are indicators of the balance of political and economic forces within a country. Differing labor law provisions highlight and reinforce status differentials in society, especially among workers. This has been particularly true in Latin America—as illustrated in dramatic fashion by the benefits provided to Chilean Caja Los Andes members and the vulnerability of the Peruvian doctors. Laws function as an observable snapshot of existing political forces at each moment in time.

Examining labor laws in this way has a storied tradition in political science and in the study of Latin America. An earlier generation of research noted that labor law "is a highly visible and concrete policy statement around which political battles are fought, won, and lost, and around which political support is attracted, granted, and withheld. Especially for the years in which labor law is promulgated or modified, law thus provides a valuable point of reference for analyzing the larger political context" (Collier and Collier 1979: 971). Both of these points are crucial. First, laws are a political outcome that can be observed over time and across industries and countries, making them well suited for comparative analysis. They are focal points for political contestation, and they touch on real-world concerns of individuals, businesses, and government leaders. Workers take to the streets to achieve or protect benefits, and employers invest significant resources in ensuring that labor regulation fits their production needs. Governments—and those seeking political office—see labor laws as opportunities to win the lasting support of voters, activists, and campaign contributors.

Second, examining labor laws can help us understand larger political processes. As actors participate in political contestation over labor laws, they reveal many of their preferences that might otherwise be unobservable. They form worker or employer organizations, labor unions, and coalitions to act on their behalf. Governments or political parties can use labor laws as "inducements and constraints" to rally support or quell dissent (Collier and Collier 1979). Labor laws can function as political tools, and their formulation and reform (and implicitly their retention) signal the relative resources and interests of those who contest them.

In the broadest sense, labor laws lay bare inequalities among workers. In developing countries, labor laws often do not unite workers but divide them. Many laws are designed to apply only to workers in a particularly industry. For example, in Latin America white-collar workers have received significantly better treatment under the law than their blue-collar counterparts, and critical, skilled professions often have the most generous provisions. Rural labor, domestic work, and, in particular, work performed by women have been left unregulated or governed by starkly unprotective legislation (Brass 1999; Caraway 2007; Blofield 2011, 2012).

And the stratifying effect of labor laws is starkest where the power of the state is weakest. Indeed, Latin American labor laws—like legal frameworks in many developing countries—often lack enforcement. States have in many cases lacked the resources, and in some cases the political will, to monitor labor law compliance and to pursue and punish infractions. Thus labor laws must be seen as selective rights—both in their explicit design and in their implicit application. Legislation only meaningfully affects the lives of workers in the "formal" sector—those whose jobs are registered with the government and who pay taxes and make social security contributions. Without registration, enforcement of labor laws is greatly hampered, since the employment of these workers is predicated on evading the stipulations of the legal code. Labor legislation can even have perverse effects (Levy 2008). Stronger labor laws can create incentives for employers to hire workers "off the books," without registration and without coverage under social security schemes.

The trend toward informal employment in Latin America has become even more pronounced in recent decades. Since competitive pressures from globalization have not been met by reform in labor law, an increasing number of firms have chosen to hire "off the books," or workers have been shunted into self-employment. This leaves employment relations vulnerable, threatens revenue for social security programs, and leaves workers without coverage against economic and social risks. Recently, countries in the region have begun to introduce new modalities of employment regulation, with reduced or graduated protections, in order to transition workers from informal to formal status; these measures receive significant attention in this book. Likewise, they have introduced innovative social policy measures, aimed at reaching citizens who had previously been left out of the formal-employment-based social security programs (Carnes and Mares 2013, 2014; De la O 2013).

Finally, labor laws have enormous political implications. In the middle of the twentieth century, labor laws were introduced in many countries as a means of co-opting the rising industrial class. Indeed, organized labor became a major political force in nearly every Latin American country, gaining institutional linkages to leftist political parties or to the state through the laws that were established (Collier and Collier 2002). The large numbers of workers who were flocking to cities to work in factories were attractive to politicians as a source of electoral support and political mobilization. This model held throughout the 1960s and 1970s (when not interrupted by military coups), and is often credited with the surge of leftist governments in power in that period.

However, what labor laws can give they can also take away. New competitive pressures from globalization in the 1980s and 1990s, as well as deindustrialization, threatened to debilitate labor. The dislocation of workers from the unionized workforce sapped labor of much of its strength. Latin American politics shifted to the right or center-right, as parties that had formerly drawn their base of support from the working class seemed to shift their strategy to cater more broadly to the poor (Levitsky 2003), and under the influence of the "Washington Consensus" they adopted more business-friendly legislation (Cook 2007; Anner 2008).

But workers who remained unionized proved remarkably adept at mobilizing to protect existing labor codes. Indeed, they used the institutional strengths afforded them under the law to resist the dismantling of labor laws, and in some cases to overturn reforms that had the potential to hurt them. Labor codes, in fact, arguably became the foundation for a revitalized "rise of the left" in the region. Although reduced in numbers, unionized workers remained a powerful force, and in several countries they were critical to bringing a new generation of presidents with leftist leanings to power.

In short, labor laws have shown themselves to be crucially important markers of economic and political status, and they have a profound impact on outcomes as diverse as economic development and the functioning of democracy. They vary significantly across countries and economic sectors in Latin America, and they play a critical role in several of the most important issues of the moment. Their stability over time—even through the pressures of the 1980s and 1990s— helps us understand the growing informality and increased importance of the left that have followed.

Labor Laws as an Object of Study

Labor laws have several features that make them particularly amenable to analysis by political scientists. First, like all laws, they are political outcomes, the result of a decision-making process by political actors and sanctioned by the state. They represent the culmination of a political process, giving concrete form and practice to otherwise unobservable relationships within the economy and polity. This is as true under democracy, where decision-making is carried out largely transparently, through votes in the legislature or executive decree, as it is under autocracy, where the deliberative process is opaque. Under both regimes, laws can be taken as indicators of the relative balance of power of different political actors.

As noted above, examining labor laws in this way has an important history in political science (Poblete-Troncoso 1928a, 1928b; Oficina Internacional del Trabajo 1928; Poblete-Troncoso and Burnett 1960; Payne 1965; Córdova 1972, 1986, 1993; Wiarda 1978; Valenzuela 1979; Collier and Collier 1979; Bronstein

1990, 1995; Murillo 2005; Murillo and Schrank 2005; Murillo et al. 2011). Even when law does not "reflect the full reality of state intervention in labor organizations or labor relations," and may not always be applied, or applied in an even way, the labor code still "provides a useful source of data" at a "crucial phase in the policy process" (Collier and Collier 1979: 971). In this sense, labor law is a powerful measuring stick or thermometer for the politics of labor relations.

Second, labor laws are publicly observable. By definition, they are widely publicized and available for scrutiny. Even if the decision-making process that produces them is in some cases opaque, laws are public (generally promulgated in legal gazettes). They aim to be complete and to avoid ambiguity; they contain precise provisions and make fine distinctions that can have significant impact. These stipulations can be analyzed in detail, revealing measures that benefit some actors and hurt others. And the analyst can see the same data as a worker or employer or government official (even if each of those actors might evaluate that data differently).

This does not imply that labor laws are uniformly known or understood or respected by all citizens, or that they are consistently enforced by the state. In fact, labor laws may be ignored or unenforced for a variety of reasons. Citizens may not have sufficient time or literacy to seek out and study legal publications, and states may lack the financial and logistical resources to effectively monitor behavior in the labor market. In addition, the provisions of labor codes may impose costs—such as payroll taxes or contributions to social security—on employers and workers, and thus encourage evasion and extralegal employment. Similarly, labor laws may entail indirect costs for employers by mandating days or hours of rest for workers or by restricting a firm's ability to hire and fire as it wishes. Indeed, recent work shows that both compliance and enforcement vary considerably across Latin America, and even within countries. Some countries "turn a blind eye" to violations of their own labor laws in the face of globalization-driven competition, while others increase enforcement in the face of greater foreign direct investment (FDI) (Ronconi 2012). Where enforcement is higher, compliance with labor laws is higher (Piore and Schrank 2008; Schrank 2009; Ronconi 2010); unemployment is higher, too, but formal sector employment also rises, and income inequality falls (Almeida and Carneiro 2007). For this reason, labor laws must be analyzed both for their stated provisions and their distortionary effects; they have an impact as much in their evasion as in their observance.

Third, labor laws provide information not just about the balance of political power but also about economic relations. They stand precisely at the intersection of politics and economics. For governments, they are central features of national development plans, and they may be seen as tools for encouraging preferred growth strategies. For investors, they are indicators of one of the main costs of doing business. And for workers, they convey the promise of better or worse working conditions and a trajectory for job tenure, advancement, and stability (or conversely, vulnerability and turnover, depending on the provisions of the law). Few indicators tell as much as labor law about the structure of production in the economy and the development goals of a nation and its government.

Fourth, in recent years the field of economics has helped clarify many of the impacts of labor laws on economic outcomes. Analysts and interested parties have a sense of what is at stake in different labor law configurations. In Latin America, most attention has been given to the effects of labor regulation on unemployment, the transition of workers between jobs, and economic growth (Edwards and Lustig 1997; Lora 1997; Guasch 1999; Heckman and Pagés 2000, 2004; Lora and Pagés 2002). For example, "flexibilizing" labor regulations—such as temporary contracts and other new "modalities," which were widely adopted in the 1990s and receive significant analysis below—have a positive (although somewhat small) effect on formal levels of employment and the transition time between jobs (Heckman and Pagés 2000, 2004). Stricter job security regulations reduce turnover by driving high-turnover firms into the informal sector (Kugler 2000). And the workers most negatively affected by job security provisions are the young (Pagés and Montenegro 1999).

Fifth, labor laws have a number of similarities with social welfare policy, a policy area that has received extensive treatment by political scientists in recent years (Huber and Stephens 2001, 2012; Kaufman and Segura-Ubiergo 2001; Madrid 2003; Mares 2001, 2003, 2005; Segura-Ubiergo 2007; Haggard and Kaufman 2008; Rudra 2008; Brooks 2009; Pribble 2013). Labor laws and social welfare policy are both state-sanctioned means to help economic actors face economic risks. With labor laws, workers are ensured of a certain standard of treatment in the workplace, as well as specific stipulations about how they will be hired, under what conditions they can be fired, and the rights they have to leaves, vacations, severance pay, and other benefits. Employers are protected against being undercut on labor costs by competing firms, and they also may be able to lock-in workers and ensure against the poaching of better-skilled workers by rivals. As will be seen below, many of the theoretical insights of the literature explaining social welfare policy can be brought to bear fruitfully on the study of labor laws.

But labor laws are not just similar to social welfare policy; they are also integrally wrapped up with such policy. In Latin America, as in much of the developing world, social policy has been employment-based. Registration of one's employment with the state—and the capacity of the state to require and monitor such registration—has traditionally been a prerequisite for participation in social welfare programs. As a result, until very recently, only formal sector workers were included in social protection schemes; citizens whose employment was not registered, and who were not paying (or did not have a family member paying) into social security were excluded from social protection. In some cases, this perversely has left the poorest citizens out of social programs (Rudra 2008), while in others it has created incentives for workers to remain "informal" and eligible for non-work-related social policy (Levy 2008). Thus labor laws are the doorway to employment-based social security.

Of course, labor laws differ from social welfare policy in important ways. In and of themselves, they do not require tax collection, expenditures, and infrastructure development by the state in the same way that social policy programs do. In fact, they may involve only minimal activity by the state, as monitor and enforcer—unlike social policy, which, in developing and middle-income countries, has generally required an extensive government administrative apparatus. Indeed, although formal (legal) employment is the gateway to social welfare programs, these other programs have been liberalized more quickly and more extensively than have labor laws (Lora 1997). In the 1980s and 1990s, many workers saw their pension programs privatized or diminished, but a similar decline did not happen in labor law provisions.

Finally, labor laws—especially reforms to labor laws—have recently become an object of study in their own right by political scientists and economists. This work has been motivated by the competitive pressures brought on by globalization. As debt crises and increased trade flows forced fundamental changes in national economies, rigid labor laws were also called into question. Debates raged over how best to achieve "competitiveness," with businesses calling for greater flexibility in hiring and firing costs and for reductions in payroll and social security contributions (Zapata 1998). Traditional labor unions resisted change, while displaced and unemployed workers flowed increasingly into self-employment and the informal sector. Governments sought to face these new challenges by introducing a host of reform measures. But somewhat surprisingly, a "race to the bottom" in labor standards does not seem to have occurred. In fact, increased trade has actually increased the protectiveness of labor laws in the developing world. As companies from the rich world outsource production to developing and middle-income countries, they seem to bring their home countries' labor standards with them (Greenhill et al. 2009; Mosley and Uno 2007). And work focused on Latin America has identified several key variables to explain the reform trajectories undertaken in that region, including the role played by labor-based parties, division in labor union leadership (Murillo 2005; Murillo and Schrank 2005), democratic and authoritarian modes of reform, and the legacies of past policies and political histories (Cook 2007).

Contribution

This book thus stands in a long tradition, building on the early calls to study labor law, learning from the theoretical insights of studies of social policy, and following on the recent flowering of work on labor law reforms. But its scope is more comprehensive than that of previous work, driven by the perspective of history, which has allowed analysts to note the surprising continuity (amid diversity) of labor laws, despite changes in political climate and the international market. It takes a long-term view of labor laws and focuses on comprehensive labor law design, rather than piecemeal reforms. Its contribution is threefold.

First, it develops a novel theory to explain differences among labor codes in Latin America. This theory takes economic structural constraints as foundational and shows how these constraints—especially worker skills—interact with the political choices of governments, parties, and political leaders in the formation of labor law. It describes four hypothetical labor law equilibria and illustrates how various countries from the region fit into this typology. Further, the role of labor unions—their size, leadership, and organizational concerns—is brought front and center. More than passive actors accepting dictates from opportunistic parties, they present distinct demands in different circumstances, and exhibit differing forms of solidarity through time. Thus the theory here nuances earlier accounts that saw leaders or parties as relatively unconstrained in their policy proposals, able to manipulate labor laws without consideration of the underlying labor market structure, institutions, and unions. It also counters overly simplistic accounts that would see labor law as a simple reflection of demands from workers or the international system.

Second, the book focuses attention on a previously neglected period in history—the "preincorporation" period of the late 1800s and early 1900s—which it argues has had a lasting impact on the region. It suggests that the labor market institutions developed in this period, especially those designed to deal with labor shortages, were critical in establishing the expectations that would govern later employment relations and labor laws in Latin America. The need to attract workers with appropriate skills, and to ensure the uninterrupted production of key industries, led employers, and later the state, to agree to individual and collective agreements of various types regarding the treatment of workers and their organizations (Carnes 2014). These then served as a template for the later writing of labor laws, and continued to structure debates during the rest of the century. In this way, the book provides evidence that the later political "incorporation" of labor in the first half of the twentieth century (Collier and Collier 1979) did not emerge from a vacuum, but had deeper roots than is often acknowledged. Moreover, the same factors that shaped those early, preincorporation labor relations—the skill distribution in the economy and the organizational capacity of labor—were decisive both in the incorporation period and in the subsequent development and reform of labor laws throughout Latin America.

Finally, the book takes a more comprehensive perspective, both cross-nationally and cross-temporally, than previous work on labor in the region. Its theoretical claims are tested for all eighteen of the major economies in Latin America during the reform period of the 1980s through the 2000s, and its case study analysis spans the time from nineteenth-century preincorporation to the 2000s. In this way it develops a unified theoretical perspective on labor law development and reform, based on the interaction of skill distributions, worker organization, and opportunities for political action provided by political parties and leaders. While previous theoretical work has developed in response to particular cases, and been tested on only subsets of the countries from the region, this book takes a regionwide, long-term stance. It thus shows that the creation of labor law, on the one hand, and the formulation of labor law reforms, on the other, are constrained by the same factors, and thus should not be treated as wholly dissimilar processes.

Overview of the Book

This book addresses three interrelated puzzles about labor laws in Latin America. First, and most centrally, why do labor laws differ across countries?

Second, what accounts for long-run stability in labor codes in Latin America? And third, how do economic and political institutions evolve?

Chapter 1 develops a theory to explain variation in labor regulation, as well as address the questions of institutional stability and reform. The answer developed here is sensitive to the history of Latin America, and especially to the pattern of its labor laws, but it is constructed to be generalizable beyond the region. It begins by conceptualizing the theoretical range of possible labor codes in developing countries, describing four possible labor law regimes, and grounds these in a microfoundational account of business and labor preferences and strategies. It emphasizes structural factors—most notably the skill distribution in the economy—to account for cross-national differences. Where larger proportions of the population possess greater skills, workers are able to exert greater power, both individually and collectively, and present a credible threat to employers. In contrast, where fewer workers possess acquired skills, their ability to make demands on the basis of economic status is much more limited. But these skill-driven structural factors do not tell the entire story. In the short run, worker organization and ties to political parties—factors that have a long history in the literature—shape the introduction of new labor legislation and the likelihood of reform. Thus skill-distributions are the key to understanding long-term labor law configurations, while the political-organizational capacity of labor explains the short- and medium-term introduction and reform (or resistance to reform) of specific labor law measures.

Chapter 2 briefly describes the empirical strategy employed in the remainder of the book, explaining how quantitative and qualitative data are marshaled to test and illustrate the theory. Chapter 3 employs a quantitative cross-national dataset of individual and collective labor regulations in Latin America to test the main expectations of the theory developed in Chapter 1. It codes twenty-three different components of each nation's labor laws at three points in time—the 1980s, 1990s, and 2000s. This provides several new perspectives on labor laws in Latin America. First, it allows a comprehensive view of labor law design, revealing how different combinations of measures distinguish each of the cases. Second, it provides a finer-grained perspective on the reforms that were introduced and undertaken in the 1980s and 1990s, and shows how many were later overturned, or how offsetting changes in labor laws "compensated" workers or unions in moments of liberalization. Finally, a series of regression analyses provide substantial support for the theory developed in Chapter 1. Skill distributions and the organizational capacity of labor prove to be strongly correlated with laws regulating individual and collective labor legislation.

The three subsequent chapters trace out the historical process by which these variables have shaped labor law development in three representative countries. This process-tracing allows more precise analysis of the particular labor laws in play in each country, and permits a longer-term view than could be carried out with the quantitative dataset. The structural factors, including relative resource endowments of capital and labor, can be examined much more closely. For this reason, each chapter begins with a consideration of the institutional origins of labor codes, beginning in the late nineteenth and early twentieth centuries. It is in this early, preincorporation period that the exogenous influence of skill distributions and worker characteristics on labor laws can be most clearly detected. The remainder of each chapter examines critical moments of labor law development and reform, with special attention on the periods of (1) political "incorporation" in the middle of the century, and (2) economic liberalization in the late twentieth century. In a sense, then, the analysis is bracketed by two crucial tests of the theory: at the time of labor code formulation, when the main differences among countries were codified, and at the time of reform, when continuity prevailed over change, despite massive pressures.

The three countries examined comprise strikingly divergent labor law trajectories. Chile has displayed a combination of relatively strong protections of individual workers, but weaker guarantees of labor's collective rights—a "professional" labor code in the parlance of this book. Peru was historically one of the least labor friendly countries in its legislation, although it was marked by the highly politicized introduction of some short-lived protective measures. I refer to it as an "encompassing" labor law regime. In recent decades, it stands out among Latin American countries for the depth of the reforms it has implemented. Finally, Argentina has some of the most protective legislation in the region, and it has been extremely resistant to change. This book refers to its laws as a "corporatist" labor code.

Chapter 4 thus examines how Chile developed, and sustained, its surprising combination of protective labor codes governing individual workers, on the one hand, and debilitating laws governing collective action by workers, on the other. It looks to the early labor market institutions in the country, in which a select group of critical industries were the early trend-setters in the design of labor legislation. However, competition among unions fragmented the worker voice.

The result was a labor code focused on protecting the rights of individual workers, but which hindered the development of lasting ties across economic sectors for collective action. When the country undertook reform under the Pinochet regime, initial repressive measures did not signal the end of Chile's labor market institutions. In fact, in 1979 most provisions of the earlier labor code were reinstated, albeit with more restricted coverage. Subsequent democratic governments have only marginally changed the labor code.

Chapter 5 explains how Peru developed a labor code that afforded very few protections of any kind, and how this code was manipulated—in very brief, politically charged moments—to produce surprisingly protective outcomes. It shows that the country's fluid labor market in the late nineteenth century did not produce the same kinds of demands for individual labor protections as were observed in Chile, and complicated the development of worker organization and solidarity. Later, military governments imposed highly protective laws, but these were both short-lived and restricted in coverage. When reform came in the 1990s, it was under democracy, not autocracy like Chile, but the maintenance of the long-term legal framework was the same: the Fujimori government essentially restored the very narrow labor laws that had been Peru's long-run equilibrium.

Finally, Chapter 6 describes how Argentina developed its remarkably supportive labor regulation regime, which is among the strongest—on all measures—in Latin America. It traces the roots of the legal system to patterns of labor recruitment and production in the late 1880s that fostered a relatively skilled and organized labor movement. Later, Perón drew these workers into his coalition, offering them extensive protections for their employment and collective labor relations. These laws served as the template for subsequent decades, and bound workers into a tight relationship with the Peronist party, until the reformist Menem came to power in the 1990s. He successfully carried out the greatest liberalization of labor laws in the nation's history, but the result was short-lived. He was forced to withdraw the measures while still in office, and over the subsequent Kirchner governments, Argentina's "corporatist" labor institutions returned to prominence (albeit with diminished coverage of the workforce).

The Conclusion summarizes the main contributions of the book. First, it highlights the analytical insight gained from examining labor codes as "regimes"—comprehensive bodies of legislation that govern workers as individuals and as collective bodies. This perspective permits the recognition of patterns across time—most notably, remarkable continuity across the last century—that were previously observed only in particular cases or during the reform period. Second, it describes the implications of the book's findings for labor law development and reform in the future, as well as for the links between labor laws and social policy. Finally, it notes the important work that remains, especially on the margins of the labor code. Indeed, a significant concern throughout this book is the way that laws invite evasion and informal employment; the conclusion considers the need to better understand extralegal employment, even as efforts are made to bring it under the legal framework.

Chapter 1

Explaining Enduring Labor Codes in Developing Countries: Skill Distributions and the Organizational Capacity of Labor

Over the last century in Latin America, workers have been crucial political actors. Their incorporation into political movements, parties, and the state has allowed governments to rise, or condemned them to fail (Collier and Collier 2002). Organized labor has mobilized massive numbers of voters at critical moments during elections, and it has taken to the streets in protest at reforms. This is as true over the last century as it is today, even if it takes a new form in recent decades (Etchemendy and Collier 2007).

The institutional foundations of labor's strength in Latin American are the region's labor codes. Latin America's labor laws are among the most protective and rigid in the world, restricting the ability of employers to fire workers and providing extensive employee benefits and organizing rights for unions (Heritage Foundation 2009). These laws give workers rights in both the economic and political spheres, and serve as a gateway to participation in state-organized social security programs. And against all expectations, they have remained this way even during the era of globalization and restructuring for economic competitiveness (Murillo 2005; Murillo et al. 2011). But legal provisions governing labor are also highly uneven in the region, with considerable variation across countries and economic sectors. What explains variation in labor law provisions, both those regarding the individual hiring and firing of workers and the collective action of organized workers? And why have Latin America's labor codes been the hardest economic policy area to reform?

Too often, past analyses have treated these as separate questions. They have developed explanations of initial labor law development and differentiation (Col-

19

lier and Collier 2002 is a masterpiece in this regard) or of the process of reform and resistance (Murillo 2005; Murillo and Schrank 2005; and Cook 2007 are outstanding examples). This work provided significant insights into labor's incorporation into the state or political parties, and into the role of parties and competition and historical legacies in shaping reform trajectories. But rarely have these two literatures been able to dialogue with each other. Indeed, the Latin America of the reform period was posited to be fundamentally different from that of the incorporation period.

With the perspective of history, this book argues that the answers to the questions of difference and stability in labor codes are interrelated. Looking at Latin America now, after the dust has settled from the flurry of reformist measures and economic liberalization of the 1980s and 1990s, what stands out is continuity over the long term. Thousands of changes in specific measures within labor codes have not fundamentally altered legal systems that first came into force sixty, seventy, and eighty years ago. This is a perspective that has only become possible in recent years, with the advantage of the long span of history. And it is a perspective that can only be gleaned by looking at labor codes in a new way—as coherent bodies of regulations, and not simply as piecemeal measures. It is in these comprehensive labor codes that we can see the striking continuity over the last century. In other words, by looking at the forest that is the legal environment governing labor, rather than the trees of specific laws, we can appreciate how much continuity has reigned in the region, even despite change.

This chapter develops a microfoundational theory to explain variation in labor law outcomes across Latin America, and by extension, across all developing countries. Its basic premise is that country-level differences in labor codes, and the stability of those labor codes through time, can be explained by a common set of factors. First, higher *skill levels* in the workforce are posited to be tied, over the long term, to more protective and more generous laws governing individual labor relations. Second, greater *organizational capacity* among workers is hypothesized to permit more effective political action such that, over the short to medium run, laws governing collective labor relations will be more developed and provide greater rights and freedoms to labor unions. Together, these two hypotheses allow us to explain long-term variation in the labor codes of different countries. Short-term deviations from the predicted equilibria are possible, but they are likely to be much more fragile and short lived, emerging only when nondemocratic governments or labor-allied parties are able to temporarily impose such measures on the system.

Several steps are required to make this argument. First, the chapter develops a typology of "labor law regimes" that takes into account multiple elements of each country's legal code. These regimes allow us to see how specific laws interact, especially those governing the individual contracting of workers, on the one hand, and the collective activity of worker organizations in unions, on the other. The result is an objective, measurable understanding of labor codes that permits comparison over time and across countries.

Next, the chapter lays out the theoretical framework for understanding the initial origins and historical development of the labor law regimes. Because these legal regimes tend to be lasting and stable, it focuses first on long-term *economic* constraints of labor policy. It argues that over the medium to long term, labor relations are constrained by existing economic conditions, in particular the resource base of labor and capital and national development programs. Labor laws must take into account the economy's underlying economic conditions—most important, the skill distribution among workers and the skill needs of employers—or face constant pressure for change. For this reason, the theory developed below treats skill profiles as a critical constraint on labor law development over long periods of time.

The theory further argues that *political* factors play a role primarily in the short to medium run and in specific, focused reforms. Politics provides the mechanisms for interest articulation that result in labor legislation. Among these mechanisms, I focus most attention on labor's role in the political process, which I call the "organizational capacity of labor." This concept captures the extent to which labor is united as a political and economic actor, has effective leadership and substantial resources, and functional ties to political parties and leaders. It is complemented by other political factors, including the institutional framework of the regime in power, government partisanship, legacies of previous governments and labor regulations, and pressures from international financial institutions and private investors.

The theory concludes by mapping the relationship between these economic and political factors, on the one hand, and resulting long-term labor law configurations, on the other. This provides a framework for the empirical work that follows in subsequent chapters, which consists of both quantitative cross-national testing in Chapter 3 and historical case studies in Chapters 4 through 6. The final section of the chapter discusses how the theory developed here relates to previous work and outstanding questions about labor law in Latin America.

A Preview of the Argument

For ease of understanding, Figure 1.1 depicts the key elements of the theory developed in this chapter in schematic fashion, prior to their full development in later sections. Begin on the right-hand side, which describes the dependent variable: the labor law configuration in country i at time t. Note that the outcome is a single configuration, or "regime," that contains interrelated individual and collective measures. The emphasis is on explaining not just particular labor law measures (although these will be given significant consideration), but the labor code as a whole.

The left-hand side of the diagram displays the causal factors that are hypothesized to determine labor law configurations. First, the theory developed in this chapter gives special attention to the way that economic resource endowments shape labor relations and labor law. Among these factors, it hones in on the distribution of the skills in the economy—across workers, geography, and industries—as a medium- to long-run constraint on labor law configurations. The subscript i refers to the country-level skill distribution; the lack of a time subscript indicates that the skill distribution is taken as fixed in the medium to long term (since worker training and education sufficient to alter the skill distribution in the economy take significant time). Skills determine the demands that workers make regarding workplace treatment and rights, as well as the relative responsiveness of employers and governments who need worker support. I argue below that it is this slow-changing skill endowment that makes labor law configurations so lasting and resilient. Empirical evidence in Chapter 3 will show that countries throughout Latin America have only marginally changed their relative skill profiles over recent decades, and that labor codes have remained similarly stable over that same period.

Second, political factors shape Latin American labor codes. I concentrate most attention on what I term "the organizational capacity of labor." This concept captures the political institutions and processes that shape interest articulation and determine regulation, allowing workers to effectively demand different kinds of labor rights and benefits. The subscripts i and t indicate that, at the country level, labor's organizational capacity may display short- to medium-term fluctuations. Union strength, leadership, and political ties can all change through time, even from leader to leader or government to government. As a result, they can have dramatic effects on the labor code in the short run. On multiple occa-

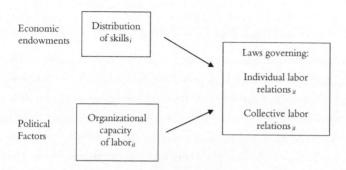

*The distribution of skills and the political-organizational
capacity of labor shape resulting labor-law regimes.*

Figure 1.1. An Overview of the Argument

sions, labor law reforms have been used throughout the region to court votes or
stave off worker unrest, or to attract investment or reassure creditors.

As Figure 1.1 shows, both skills and labor organization have an impact on the
entire labor code. Nevertheless, I will argue that each is more closely associated
with one portion of the labor code. The distribution of skills plays a dominant
role in determining the medium-term range of possible individual labor regulations, while the organizational capacity of labor is most closely associated with
ongoing regulation governing collective labor relations.

In addition to labor's organizational capacity, a number of additional political factors highlighted in earlier work on Latin American labor also play a role
in the final shape of labor regulation. These include the governing regime type
(authoritarian or democratic, for example) (Haggard and Kaufman 2008; Mares
and Carnes 2009), government partisanship (Murillo 2005; Murillo and Schrank
2005; Murillo et al. 2011; Huber and Stephens 2012), legacies of past governments and existing policies and organizations (Cook 2007; Etchemendy and
Collier 2007; Etchemendy 2011; Caraway 2012), and the international system
(Ronconi 2012). They are not depicted in Figure 1.1, as they can be understood
as exerting their influence through, or in interaction with, the organizational
capacity of labor.

With this schematic overview of the book's argument in mind, we can enter
into the details of the theory.

1.1. Conceptualizing Labor Law Configurations

This study takes national-level labor regulation as its dependent variable. It focuses on the set of written legal provisions that govern labor relations within a national economy. In Latin America, these laws are generally the product of the legislature. The executive, however, has also played a very active role in formulating labor regulation, and in many countries has used decree powers to make significant changes to the laws governing workplace treatment, hiring, and firing. And in some countries, most notably Uruguay, the judicial branch also plays an important role in setting standards in labor relations through its interpretation of the constitution and other laws. Thus the labor laws examined in this study are those statutes written, publicly promulgated, and published in the domestic *Código Laboral*, regardless of the branch of government in which they originated. I use the terms "laws" and "regulation" interchangeably, for ease of presentation, to indicate this written body of state-sanctioned regulatory policy.

It is crucial to distinguish the labor laws examined in this book from other important labor market and political outcomes. Labor regulation, as understood here, is restricted to the written laws "on the books." In Latin America, compliance with labor law is known to be far from universal, and to vary across countries and policy areas, but the dimensions and explanations for evasion are still poorly understood. Important work has recently begun examining labor law enforcement (Mosley and Uno 2007; Almeida and Carneiro 2007; Anner 2008; Ronconi 2010, 2012). Based on studies of a small set of cases and limited temporal scope, this literature suggests that compliance is enhanced when governments undertake stronger enforcement efforts, and that more democratic and more left-leaning governments are more likely to seek to enforce their labor laws (Ronconi 2010, 2012), and that compliance increases and violations of labor law decrease as foreign investment increases (Mosley and Uno 2007; Greenhill et al. 2009; Ronconi 2012). Nevertheless, much work remains to be done to understand the political and economic determinants of enforcement and compliance. This book incorporates insight from these nascent studies wherever possible, but it must leave a fuller study of the politics of enforcement and compliance to future work.

Labor laws have an outsize impact beyond the workplace in Latin America, both economically and politically. First, they set the terms for participation in the region's employment-based social security programs. Legal employment constitutes the point of entry to a host of state-regulated benefits, including pensions and health care. Workers who are employed "off the books" do not enter into these social programs. Likewise, labor laws confer political rights—to organize and meet, to collect dues, to strike—that allow workers to more easily make their voice heard, especially through alliances with political parties. Indeed, labor laws can set up two tiers of citizenship—one for formally registered workers, who are "insiders" to the state's social security measures and to certain political parties, and one for informal-sector workers, who are "outsiders" in the worlds of welfare and electoral politics (Rueda 2005). Throughout this study, I seek to keep distinct the direct effects of labor laws in labor relations, on the one hand, and their indirect effects on economic and political incorporation, on the other. The focus here is on the former. But their impact on the latter cannot be denied, and will form an important part of the story told in the case histories presented in Chapters 4 through 6.

In addition, labor regulation is distinct from the economic policies or priorities of the sitting government. Leaders have a variety of mechanisms that they may employ to affect the labor market, ranging from subsidies to employers and control of monetary policy and exchange rates, on the one hand, to training programs or unemployment benefits for workers, on the other. The use of these policy tools is, of course, related to the labor law environment. But labor law is among the least wieldy mechanisms in the state's arsenal for implementing policy; it often requires significant time to pass, and as will be seen below, it is among the slowest policies to change. Similarly, this study does not examine voluntary norms adopted by industries or groups of employers. While significant new initiatives have been taken by particular firms and industries in recent years, they constitute a fundamentally different object of study. And they are likely to be driven by a very different economic and political process than domestic laws that have passed through the state's policy-making process.

In sum, this study examines written labor laws, whether passed by the legislature, executive, or judicial branches, that apply broadly throughout the national economy. In some cases, it also considers laws written to apply only to particular industries, especially in the early years of labor law development. This emphasis on written law allows for analytic clarity and precise comparison across countries and over time. And it permits careful tracing of the causal process that produces particular labor law configurations.

The Labor-law Policy Space

The comprehensive focus of this book requires carefully defining the labor-law policy space. Surprisingly, this has not been done in previous studies. Most comparative work has focused on examining a limited set of laws across a small number of cases, and thus it has considered particular laws detached from the overall labor code.[1] Comprehensive analyses of labor codes as wholes—the combinations of labor laws that exist in a given country—are lacking. This fails to appreciate the ways that laws interact with one another. The legal environment has an impact on economic activity and political competition precisely through the combination of measures that exist. And workers, firms, and politicians are acutely aware of how specific measures can be traded off one for another. Greater job stability might be ensured, but with less expectation for regular wage increases because of diminished collective bargaining regulation. Or unions might be given a greater capacity to raise funds, but be limited in their ability to use those funds to underwrite strike activity. And individuals may be willing to accept longer hours or less overtime pay if they believe that stronger union rights will allow them to renegotiate such benefits in a future bargaining round. Understanding how legal measures fit together, and not just their individual stipulations, is crucial to understanding the politics of labor regulation.

In this section, I delineate the policy space in which labor law functions. After arraying legal measures across two dimensions, I develop a "conceptual typology" (Collier et al. 2012) of labor law regimes—consisting of different combinations of labor law provisions. This typology is a first step in understanding the variation that exists across labor codes. The subsequent section will develop a political theory of labor code variation.

Legal scholars distinguish two principal types of labor laws based on the area of labor relations that they regulate (Botero et al. 2004; Murillo 2005). I use these two types to construct the labor law policy space. First, provisions that cover the hiring, treatment, expectations, and firing of workers are called "individual" laws. These provisions cover the presumed duration of employment, working conditions, rest and leave policy, firing procedures and severance pay, and so forth. And second, "collective" labor laws govern the collective action of worker organizations. They set the rules of the game for the organization and registration of labor unions, the administration of resources and the selection of leaders within unions, and the permitted activity of worker organizations in strikes and protests. They also set standards for collective bargaining and dialogue between workers, their firms, and the state.

In principle, these two kinds of labor regulation are independent of each other. No particular combination is preordained or a priori superior to others. For example, stipulating mandated severance payments does not require also regulating the length of vacation or the maximum number of hours a worker can be employed in a given week (even if workers and business *do* consider how such measures are related). Similarly, establishing rules for the payment of union dues need not also force the state to govern how union elections are run or how collective bargaining is carried out. And most importantly, laws governing individual and collective labor relations may be passed independently of one another. A country could have extensive regulation of collective regulations but lack oversight of individual relations, or could heavily intervene in individual labor relations but leave the collective activity of workers unlegislated. The particular combination that exists in a given country will be the product of economic and political institutions and contestation in that nation. Individual workers, firms, and politicians form their preferences over each piece of legislation while considering other pieces of legislation, conditional on their own place in the economy and political sphere.

Figure 1.2 arrays possible labor law configurations along two dimensions. The vertical axis describes provisions governing individual labor relations, while the horizontal axis describes measures that regulate collective labor relations. The origin represents a country without regulation of any kind; moving up the vertical axis or rightward along the horizontal axis represents increasingly stringent labor regulation, which brings added rights or benefits to labor.[2] The resulting two-dimensional space describes the range of possible labor laws.[3] Countries that are higher up have stronger individual provisions, while those that are further right have stronger collective provisions. Any combination of laws can be located within this space.

A Typology of Labor Law Regimes

In Figure 1.2, four ideal-type labor law regimes are presented. The first, closest to the origin in quadrant I, might be termed an "unregulated market." It has no, or minimal, labor law provisions. Employers and workers are free to negotiate, on a case-by-case basis, the terms of each worker's employment. No legal provision is made for collective organizations of workers. The laws of supply and

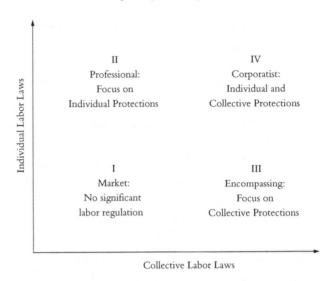

Combinations of individual and collective labor laws result in four possible labor law regimes.

Figure 1.2. The Policy Space and a Typology of Labor Law Configurations

demand are expected to operate untrammeled in such a market. The state exercises little to no role, although it might engage in some enforcement measures if the criminal code or civil order is violated (perhaps through violence associated with labor mobilizing or workplace mistreatment).

A second labor law regime is described by moving up the vertical axis to quadrant II. In this regime, individual labor relations are significantly regulated but collective labor relations are not. Workers in such an economy are guaranteed stable jobs, and must be well compensated with severance pay when (under carefully defined circumstances) they must be laid off. They may be entitled to significant vacation and liberal leaves, and their regular workday and workweek are governed by strict provisions regarding overtime and remuneration. But the collective action of workers is not similarly regulated. I call this outcome a "professional" labor law regime, because workers are legally protected free agents, whose modal employment is presumed to be of medium to long duration. And any collective action by workers does not involve the regulation or sanction of the state.[4] As will be seen in Chapters 2 and 3, Chile and Uruguay are examples of countries that inhabit this professional quadrant.

A third outcome can be found in quadrant III, moving to the right of the market labor law regime. In this regime, collective labor relations are highly regulated, with significant regulation governing the activity of labor unions or other worker organizations and federations. Membership and registration requirements for labor unions are stipulated by law, as are organizations' access to and use of their funds, and rules for collective bargaining and strikes. There may be additional provisions that govern interunion relations, establishing, at the extreme, central coordination by a single, dominant federation or confederation, or, at the other extreme, making interunion coordination difficult. But in this regime, little or no provision is made for governing individual labor relations. This does not mean that workers are mistreated, but that worker rights and status are secured (or ensured) through collective action and firm-level agreements, and not through legislation on worker treatment and individual contracts. I call this outcome "encompassing," because the legislation facilitates collective worker activity and provides for legally empowered worker organizations in the economic realm (and subsequently may shape labor's status and behavior in the political realm). Chapters 2 and 3 will show that Peru has often had a labor code that places it in this quadrant.

Finally, a fourth outcome involves significant regulation of both individual and collective labor relations. Job tenure is ensured through extensive legislation on hiring and firing (and prohibitively high severance pay provisions), and workers are ensured of state regulation of working conditions, leave, and overtime policies. Likewise, activity by organized groups of workers is sanctioned and regulated by the state, with predictable procedures for registration, administration, and collective negotiation or strike activity. I call this outcome "corporatist" because it bases labor market relations on legally organized bodies of rights-endowed workers. It is ripe for centralized intervention by the state, since unions are amply provided for in the labor code. The analysis in Chapters 2 and 3 will indicate that Argentina and Mexico are examples of countries that display this corporatist labor law configuration.

Three important caveats about this typology must be made. First, the four ideal types do not have an a priori rank ordering. It should not be assumed that the corporatist quadrant IV would necessarily be the preference of workers (or business). Rather, each regime represents a distinct configuration of laws governing individual and collective labor measures, and all might accomplish important goals of the state or appeal to business or labor. The market regime, as expected by classical economics, facilitates the free and rapid contracting and firing of labor, as needed for minute-to-minute production needs, but may discourage permanence and job-specific skill acquisition. The professional regime invests individual workers with rights and privileges that ensure them of job stability and encourage their commitment to a productive career in a single firm or industry, but may limit mobility and productive turnover. In the encompassing regime, unions and labor confederations represent workers and serve as interlocutors with the state and employers, and this may facilitate the carrying out of national economic goals or plans. But it also may diminish the importance of individual worker initiative. Finally, the corporatist model provides extensive regulation for both individual and collective relations, establishing a "high floor" for labor relations, ensuring the status of individual workers and giving unions recognition and status in collective bargaining. But it also may segment workers according to their industry of employment, producing inequality among workers. Further, it may constrain the ability of businesses to adapt to changing conditions by endowing worker organizations with virtual veto power over necessary economic restructuring. It is the most rigid of the labor law configurations.

Second, the typology here presents ideal types in order to describe the theoretical range of possible labor law regimes, but countries may have legal codes that locate them at intermediate positions on the two dimensions. The individual and collective dimensions are conceptualized as continuous variables, so legal codes could take any value on them. There are no bright-line distinctions between them. This will be especially important in the empirical analysis in the next chapter, because it allows for more precise specification of the labor law configuration within each country. The four regimes are meant to help highlight some of the complementarities and tensions inherent in differing labor law configurations. As will be seen below, a country need not be an extreme case of a regime to reflect some of the characteristics that have been noted thus far.

Finally, the labels—market, professional, encompassing, and corporatist—are used with particular caution. They are not meant to prejudice the theory-building in the next section of this chapter, or suggest the causes or goals of each labor law configuration. They do not imply (or rule out) an ideological underpinning to each regime, nor are they meant to convey all that these terms have come to connote in popular or specialized literatures. Rather, in this delineation of the policy space, they are intended to be understood as a neutral shorthand. But they also provide additional texture to a classificatory framework that could seem overly schematic, and they resonate with the history of Latin America. The next section develops a theory of the economic and political origins of these differing labor law outcomes.

1.2. Foundations of Labor Law: Resources and Economic Structure

The theory presented here begins with the labor market. It might seem obvious to begin discussion of labor laws with the labor market, and the underlying structure of the economy. But many accounts of Latin American labor policy have not done this. Instead, they have emphasized politics over economics, or have afforded politicians tremendous latitude in the design of labor market policies. Even recent work, which is motivated by the economic pressures of debt crises and globalization that have sparked the need for labor market reform, has concentrated most attention on the political determinants of the resulting reform.

This political focus has not been misguided. In fact, this politics–driven work has produced a host of centrally important insights, most especially showing how under certain circumstances politics can trump economics in labor market policies (Payne 1965), resulting in labor practices that seemingly defy economic needs. Politicians can use labor policy as "inducements and constraints" to woo the support of workers (Collier and Collier 1979), and then to structure state and party institutions for long-standing labor alliances (Collier and Collier 2002). Political parties have established important linkages to labor unions, and the dynamics of these ties have been especially important in recent years under globalization in shaping (and in some cases, limiting) changes to labor laws across countries (Valenzuela 1979; Burgess 2004; Murillo and Schrank 2005; Magaloni 2006). In addition, political "legacies" of previous governments and past policies constrain later policy choices in powerful ways (Cook 2007; Etchemendy and Collier 2007; Caraway 2012). The deepest of these legacies are the initial legal institutions initially brought in by colonizing powers (Botero et al. 2004).

But this politics–first approach may have also overlooked the significant extent to which politicians are constrained by economics, especially over the long run. In fact, by concentrating on seemingly path–departing interventions by the state or politicians in labor market outcomes, previous analyses may have given undue emphasis to exceptional moments of political change. These moments can be deceptive for two reasons. First, the outcomes they produce may be very short-lived. Indeed, Latin America is a region that has been plagued by a swinging pendulum of political change (often tied to swings between democracy and nondemocracy), and labor policy has been no exception.[5] Some of the most far reaching changes in labor law have been overturned after just a few years.

Second, and perhaps more important, successful policy-making may be driven not just by getting the politics right but also by getting the economics right. Labor policies that last and that achieve consensus (or at least do not undergo reversal) do so because their provisions are consonant with the prevailing economic order. It is hard to imagine them enduring over the long term if they were not. Studies that concentrate on the political process may thus obscure the extent to which lasting policies reflect the underlying economic structure of the society. And focusing on moments of political debate may mislead, because policies that are most in harmony with economic conditions may also prove to be uncontroversial. An academic focus on the fray may miss the importance of the silence.

The most basic features of an economy are its endowments of capital and labor. These set the parameters for the development of a nation's productive capacity, and shape the preferences of workers and employers regarding state intervention and regulation (Solow 1956). This was true in the earliest years of labor law formulation in Latin America, and has continued to be true throughout its history. This book traces the origins of the labor law in the region to the end of the nineteenth and start of the twentieth century—significantly earlier than other accounts of labor's political "incorporation" in the early to mid-twentieth century—when two shifts happened in production. First, the cities became loci of increasingly sophisticated industrial and craft production, accompanied by the growth of financial services and administration that were needed to make this production efficient (Haber 1989). An increasingly educated and skilled workforce was needed to serve in these critical new functions in the economy. Second, mines and intensive plantation agriculture drew large numbers of workers to isolated geographic areas and offered opportunities and incentives for organizing collectively. Based on these new modes of employment, workers would articulate their first demands for the regulation of labor relations by the state. And the mechanisms present in that early round of labor regulation—built on worker skills and organization—have continued to be critical in subsequent labor law development. The next two sections take up these mechanisms in turn.

Skill Endowments as Medium- to Long-run Constraints
on Labor Law Development

Labor markets, and the workers in them, can be distinguished by their skill distributions. Skills, in this sense, can be conceived broadly to include attributes as diverse as intelligence, physical strength, aptitude for specific or complex tasks applicable to particular industries, and even the willingness to relocate or live in particular geographic areas. In most cases in the developing world, these skills represent a cost borne by the worker to devote time, money, and attention to learning particular functions or developing strengths or to relocation. They may also represent an investment by employers in training their workers with the skills needed for their particular productive processes. In either case, these costs play a role in determining the preferences of workers for their lifetime employment trajectory and for the terms of their employment (Estevez-Abe et al. 2001; Iversen 2005; Mares 2001, 2003). Likewise, employers seek to retain workers with scarce skills specific to their production processes, and to prevent poaching of skilled workers by their competitors. For this reason, the skill distribution plays a critical role in shaping the labor regulation undertaken by the state.

Skill distributions are entrenched in local economic institutions, and as a result tend to be very slow to change. Skills are typically acquired from another skilled individual, either through apprenticeship or training or in schools. Consequently, existing skill equilibria constrain the path of subsequent skill development. Ambitious individuals who wish to acquire skills, but who live in low-skill environments, may find it very difficult to do so or may have to pay high costs to pursue skill acquisition elsewhere. Further, firms tend to make investments with local skill endowments in mind (Acemoglu 1998); their production, at least in Latin America, has more often replicated local (low) skill endowments over time rather than transformed them (Schneider 2009). Proactive governments may seek to rapidly increase the skill profile of their workforce by promoting skills and education, but these efforts face an uphill battle. On the one hand, a base of qualified teachers must be created, and on the other, workers with increased skills may not find firms ready to hire them for suitable jobs. Thus changing skill distributions is a task of decades, if not generations.

In Latin America, the first labor laws began to emerge in the late nineteenth and early twentieth centuries, during a time of significant economic change. Prior to that period, labor relations had been largely unregulated. Employment depended only on the mutual agreement of employer and employee in "spot markets," and tended to be short term. This was particularly well suited to enterprises that employed unskilled workers, who made up the vast majority of workers in the largely agricultural economies. Since these workers were easily interchangeable, they could not make demands without fearing loss of employment opportunities. And employers had little reason to make concessions to such workers.

However, the advent of manufacturing and the concentration of workers in cities and mines began to transform labor relations. Factory production and mining required a labor force that would be more stable and that could be trained in specific tasks that were essential to the productive process, as well as a transportation network to get goods to market and export. At this point, the skills that workers brought to the workplace became salient. Workers with specialized, nonhomogenous skills—often brought from Europe, or from geographically distant areas within the country—had greater bargaining power vis-à-vis their employers. In Latin American countries, the first (nonmilitary) workers to successfully organize and make demands for better working conditions were craft workers, including printers, who had emigrated from Europe and brought training from that environment. Likewise, workers who had acquired technical skills in vital industries and relocated for their work, such as railroad workers, miners, and even meatpackers (who were vital in Argentina's beef-export industry), were the first to demand services from their employers such as infirmaries, dining rooms, and kindergartens (Lobato 1998).

Labor laws were introduced, at least in part, to deal with the growing threat of potential disruptions caused by the rapidly shifting labor market, and to channel skilled workers into productive positions in newly vital industries. Both workers and employers saw the state as an ally in achieving their goals: workers in these sectors sought to ensure regular employment and better working conditions, while employers sought to prevent labor unrest and limit workers' demands. The first labor laws that were written addressed both of these demands in key industries. They guaranteed (and limited) hours of work, minimal hygiene, and workplace safety. And they also provided state sanctions and support to break strikes that threatened production. Over time, these same demands were made by other skilled or semiskilled industries, and labor regulation became more expansive, beyond the initial set of key emerging industries. The subsequent chapters of this book show how closely labor law development followed the trajectory of skill differentiation.

The converse is also true. Where skill levels remained low and undifferentiated throughout the economy, the demands and labor law results were likewise lessened. Without specialized skill profiles, and in contexts of labor surplus, the threat of disruption of production was greatly diminished. Trouble-making workers could easily be fired and replaced. Workers anticipated this reaction from their employers, so they often moderated their demands for job stability or saw defections from their ranks. In such environments, both workers and employers sought legislation that would promote easy and frequent turnover of workers. The workers preferred this outcome because it improved their chances of being hired if they found themselves out of work (which had a higher probability in fluid, homogenous labor markets). And employers wanted the freedom to meet production needs precisely, jettisoning workers who were not needed and hiring others as the possibility of sales rose.

Generalizing, then: In highly bifurcated skill distributions, conflicting demands of high- and low-skill workers become especially apparent. At the extremes, high-skill workers demand restrictive hiring and firing measures (to protect their investment in specific skills), while low-skill workers seek to weaken or overcome such legislation. Indeed, the lowest-skill workers face the risk (and high probability) of employment "off the books," without formal contracts or laws. These informal, unskilled workers do not have the same preferences for labor regulation as their formal, skilled counterparts. They see labor regulations as a barrier to entry to their employment in the formal sector. Both they and their employers recognize that complying with labor codes raises the contracting cost of hiring them (by including severance pay provisions or paid leave, for example), and they thus resist the adoption of such measures. In fact, anecdotal evidence suggests that some of these workers will even choose to forgo being contracted formally (and gaining the protections of labor laws) in return for increased wages in the near term.

In sum, relative skill levels serve as a foundation for, and constraint on, labor law demands and outcomes. In contexts where higher skill levels are widespread, laws governing individual contracting will favor job stability and provide significant protections to skilled workers. Alternatively, where low-skilled labor predominates, labor law will be less extensive and will favor high employment by encouraging job rotation during periods of unemployment. Since skill distributions change only slowly, labor laws are likely to be highly stable over time. In cases where politicians impose labor law outcomes that are not consistent with the underlying skill distribution, pressure from both workers and employers is expected to spark reform. Where skills exceed labor law design, high-skill workers will threaten production with strikes and other forms of "hold-up"; and where labor laws exceed skills, excluded low-skill workers will push for change or accept jobs outside the formal sector that do not entail legal protections. In other words, out-of-equilibrium outcomes will not last long, because they create incentives for defection, exit, or rewriting of laws. Over the medium to long term, skills condition the feasible set of labor law measures.

1.3. Mechanisms of Labor Law Development: Collective Action and Political Influence

While the distribution of skills provides an underlying rationale for demands for regulation of labor relations, it does not explain precisely how and when legislation will be proposed, passed, or reformed. Indeed, as long as demands come primarily from isolated individual workers or firms, it may be easier for interested parties to create private solutions (in the form of contracts), rather than public ones (in the form of laws). It is the collective action of workers and employers—in formal or informal associations or unions—that introduces a political dynamic to the labor market. Laws are attractive vehicles precisely because they organize labor relations at the industry or economy level, affecting more than individuals or single firms with their stipulations.

The political function of labor legislation has been extensively studied and well documented, as noted above. One strand in these accounts stresses that labor law essentially serves political parties and leaders, as they seek to build coalitions of supporters and compete in elections. Laws can be "inducements and constraints," alternately attracting votes of workers who benefit or limiting their capacity to challenge the regime by constraining rights to strike, use union funds, and organize independently (Collier and Collier 1979, 2002). Other accounts emphasize the demands made by organized workers or by employers. At the center of all these accounts is the collective organization and action of labor. Workers become interesting in politics when they present a united front, and can deliver large numbers of votes or supporters.

Labor's "Organizational Capacity" as a Short- to Medium-run Determinant of Labor Laws

I label the collective ability of workers and worker organizations to influence political outcomes the "organizational capacity" of labor. It is independent of skill levels, deriving simply from the size and cohesiveness of unions or other worker collectives. Greater numbers mean that labor can threaten greater disruption of the economy, "holding up" key industries, and can promise greater political support, mobilizing workers in the streets and at the polls. Below I detail three factors—organizational, economic, and political—that make up this organizational capacity.

First, coordination among workers is facilitated by formal organizations to represent their interests. At the local level, workers in the same firm may note particular needs or risks they face, and thus have incentives to demand employers make private provision for them. These bodies of workers generally take the form of craft guilds or labor unions at the firm or industry level. They may also be articulated into larger industrial federations or national confederations of union representatives from various industries. In the nations with the most developed labor legislation in Latin America, worker organization began early with craft guilds, and then expanded to take on an articulated, multitiered structure of sector-specific federations and national labor confederations. These higher-level bodies are more effective in achieving labor-friendly labor legislation to the extent that they control greater resources (more members and greater funding) and to the extent that their leadership is united. Indeed, divisions in labor union leadership during the reform period in Latin America have resulted in less labor friendly outcomes (Murillo 2001).

Economically, coordination on labor regulation is more likely to occur when structural economic conditions promote worker solidarity and cooperation. High employment and job stability are conducive to worker organization. In addition, restrictive trade policy, by protecting workers in particular industries, may facilitate worker coordination. The import-substituting policies in Latin America between the 1930s and 1970s not only served to protect workers but also effectively made them "insiders" to that development model (Haggard and Kaufman 2008). They could enjoy stable jobs, with ready opportunities for union organizing, as long as those trade protections and government subsidies persisted (Haber et al. 2008). Further, there were significant incentives for cross-sector union solidarity, and this gave the movement additional strength in negotiating with its principal employer and interlocutor—the state. Conversely, unemployment or export price volatility can undermine worker coordination, as workers are in increasingly precarious positions that preclude their collaboration. The period of market reforms in the 1980s and 1990s, with its reduction in trade protections, rapid set of privatizations, and increased unemployment, saw significant declines in unionization rates. Labor's coordinating ability diminished dramatically under these circumstances.

Politically, coordination can happen when labor possesses institutionalized means of communication and interest representation; in democratic settings, this happens primarily through political parties. In many countries, labor has allied itself closely with a particular labor party or government. In these cases, labor laws are expected to reflect the electoral success of the labor party or leader. This hypothesis is consistent with "power resources" theories of the welfare state and social policy, which see left-oriented parties as more closely aligned with the interests of industrial workers, and hence more likely to confer the benefits of social welfare spending upon them (Esping-Andersen 1990; Huber and Stephens 2001). Murillo (2005) and Murillo and Schrank (2005) extend this logic to the period of labor law reforms. They argue that reforms to collective labor law were easier to pass, and generated more political support from labor union supporters, than were reforms to individual codes; union leaders, in particular, saw their status protected, and firms did not see as great a threat to competitiveness in collective laws as they did in reforms to individual protections and job stability measures for workers.

Political interests in labor law are primarily short term. Politicians are necessarily myopic—interested first and foremost in the next election, or the threat of the next strike—so they are unlikely to take a long-term interest in labor law development. In fact, labor law may offer the greatest marginal gains (in votes) when it offers change that is radical, drawing in previously left-out workers. Parties, in contrast, may have an interest in cultivating longer-term ties to labor, as they seek to build lasting coalitions across multiple elections. They seek to do this through incremental, regular concessions to labor in the short-run, which will not unnecessarily raise resistance from employers. Thus closer bonds between labor and political parties are likely to produce regular concessions in labor regulations. And associated parties are likely to champion organized workers and unions when flexibilizing reforms are proposed.

As will be seen in the empirical chapters that follow, the introduction of the first labor laws in Latin America was a response, at least in part, to the growing organization and size of the labor movement in the late 1800s and early 1900s. Regulation was a way to deal with the "social question" of massive labor relocation and growing organization, concentrated living and working conditions, and the influx of new workers through international migration. These workers could cause significant disruption of the economy if they walked out or went on strike. And they constituted a significant electoral prize, one that could be brought into the state or particular parties through the introduction of legislation that met their demands and channeled their activity (Carnes 2014).

Among legal measures, the most important for binding workers to parties were those that guaranteed status and rights for unions and federations—or to use the terminology above, collective labor regulation. This legislation further cemented workers into their unions, and provided means of coordination and control through federations and confederations. In many cases, it outlawed, or limited the political rights of, rival unions. In other words, dominant unions could use labor law as a barrier to entry against challengers, and parties could use legislation to reward their principal partners. Ultimately, this produced alliances in which labor provided votes, stable production, and wage restraint; the state provided laws guaranteeing job stability, union organizing rights, and continued political influence for the unions in the government (Collier and Collier 2002).

This is not to suggest that unions do not have an interest in individual labor regulation. They seek to represent the interests of their members, which include greater rights and protections in the workplace. And indirectly, this serves to strengthen worker organizations. Better protected and regulated workers make the union stronger, such that politically active workers cannot be dismissed as easily, and can serve as leaders and advocate with greater freedom.

In sum, the collective action of workers adds a political dimension to the development of labor laws. It strengthens the hand of workers beyond their individual-level skills, and it makes collective solutions—as found in laws—attractive to policy-makers and firms. The coherence and unity of the worker movement is critical in this process. As the unity and mobilizational capacity of workers increases, workers can demand that labor relations undergo increasing regulation. In particular, they can promote the interests of their union or association, seeking to provide it with greater resources, status, and voice—the set of policies that govern "collective" labor relations. Thus, as the organizational capacity of labor organizations increases, the regulation governing collective labor relations is expected to undergo pressure for further development and protectiveness.

The Importance of Context: Institutions, History, and the International Environment

Labor laws do not emerge from a pristine state of nature, but instead are heavily colored by several contextual factors. The literature points to three such factors, often posited as alternative hypotheses: political institutions, political history, and the influence of the international economic and financial order. Although we will see that these factors are not sufficient to provide a full explanation for the intraregional variation and change over time observed in this study, each provides additional texture to the account developed here.

First, labor regulations build upon the existing legal and institutional framework in a country. Research has shown that French- and Spanish-based statutory labor codes (in Latin America and Africa) tend to be more protective and rigid in cross-national comparisons than are English-based common law labor regulations (in North America and the Antipodes) (La Porta et al. 1998; Botero et al. 2004). Thus the protectiveness of some features of the labor codes in Latin America may be attributable to a shared legacy of inherited institutions. Nevertheless, the common colonial legacy cannot explain the significant variation that countries across the region display, nor the ways they have changed through time.

In addition, political regime type shapes the ways that interests are aggregated and decisions reached regarding labor regulation. Autocratic regimes are, by definition, less immediately beholden to their populations, and are able to implement policies and reforms with greater freedom. This may lead them to be more volatile in their policy choices, and they may display a greater capacity to ignore the demands of workers. Democracies, in contrast, permit greater independent interest-group activity by their citizens, and present politicians with electoral competition that requires them to outbid one another to attract votes (Haggard and Kaufman 2008: 14; Alemán 2010). As a result, they might be expected to be more responsive to the demands of workers, and hence more likely to implement generous labor provisions and to limit retrenchment. And even within democracies, the legislative mechanism matters: executive decrees may differ from laws drafted by the legislature. Electoral competition and the possibility of legislative defeat constrain the executive from passing more radical legislation (Saiegh 2011). The analysis in this book shows that autocracies are indeed capable of enacting more rapid and extensive labor code changes, but surprisingly, they may do so not only to limit labor rights but also to increase them. Democracies, in contrast, are generally more incremental in their approach to labor legislation, but they may do so both to expand and contract the protectiveness of the law.

Countries are also constrained by their political history. Previous experiences and policies can loom large in current policy design, and countries often react against disruptive past experiments (Cook 2007). Thus countries that have experienced radical governments in the past may be wary of sweeping reform in the present, while countries with less radical pasts may be more likely to undertake far-reaching change. In addition, it may be that those that have strayed less from their skill-driven equilibria experience less need for reform in later periods, while those who have imposed equilibrium-departing labor laws are more prone to reform. Cook (2007) shows that states that experienced radical governments had the strongest flexibilizing reforms, in a reaction against the extremes of their socialist or strongly left-leaning experiments. States with legacies of state-corporatism engaged in trade-offs to preserve the delicate balance of forces that had been included in those regimes. And states that had emerged from revolutions were the weakest at enforcing their labor codes, so they had the least need to reform them.

In addition, countries are constrained by the international institutions and the market when designing and reforming their labor laws. Recent years have brought a number of competing pressures to bear on labor law provisions. On the one hand, the second half of the twentieth century saw the growing influence of the UN's International Labor Organization (ILO). Through its resolutions and international pressure, this body sought to promote the adoption of a minimum floor of labor standards throughout the world. Developing countries, aspiring to show their economic responsibility toward their citizens, saw the passage of ILO-promoted measures as a way to advertise their modernity (Meyer et al. 1997). Alternatively, in the face of heightened competition to attract capital and produce goods at lower costs for export, developing countries have faced pressures to cut back on costly labor regulations. This would reduce the regulatory burden on employers, minimizing labor costs and facilitating hiring and firing. International lenders also pressured for these sorts of "flexibilizing" reforms. Thus the international context placed competing pressures on labor law: toward a "race to the top" through international standards promoted by the ILO, and toward a "race to the bottom" caused by competition.

Existing work suggests that both outcomes have occurred. On the one hand, labor codes have been written more strictly in recent years, in line with the ILO's recommendations, but this has effectively shunted a significant part of the labor force in developing countries into the informal sector (Rudra 2008). Codes have not "raced to the bottom," but more and more workers have been consigned to the bottom. On the other hand, increased trade, brought on by globalization, has seen a diffusion of developed-world labor standards to the developing world. Increased trade with wealthier countries has brought improvement in both labor standards (Greenhill et al. 2009) and practices (Mosley and Uno 2007).

Thus each of these factors—institutional heritage, regime type, policy history, and international influences—can helpfully describe patterns common to the development of labor laws in the region, but none is sufficient in itself to explain both the cross-national and cross-temporal variation in labor codes observed in Latin America over the last century. For this reason, they are not included among the central explanatory variables in the theory that follows. Nevertheless, they will be considered throughout the empirical analysis later in the book, especially to show the leverage gained by using the theoretical insights developed in this chapter.

1.4. The Determinants of Labor Law Regimes

Now, with both the labor law policy space defined, and the causal theory specified, we can map the relationship between the causal story and its diverse outcomes. Figure 1.3 does precisely this. It should be recalled from Figure 1.2 that the entire space above and to the right of the origin represents increasing amounts of labor legislation. Movement up the vertical axis indicates higher levels of regulation on individual labor relations, while movement along the horizontal axis represents greater regulation of collective labor relations. Taken together, these two measures determine a country's labor law regime, which can be summarized by the four ideal types described above.

Figure 1.3 places the principal explanatory variables along the axes, indicating that the interaction of these two factors contributes to the development of distinct labor law regimes. Both factors contribute to increases in the regulatory environment. At the same time, the theory has highlighted direct effects that each of the causal factors may have on portions of the labor code. Skill levels are expected to be directly correlated with laws governing individual labor relations. Where workers have more highly developed (or distinguishable) skills, they become more difficult to substitute for one another. As a result, differentially skilled

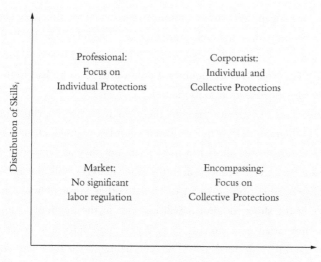

Combinations of skill levels and the political-organizational capacity of labor yield four labor law regimes or equilibria.

Figure 1.3. Predictions Regarding Labor Law Configurations

workers can demand better treatment—whether in terms of working conditions, job tenure, or other benefits—than workers in a homogenous economy. Similarly, employers in specialized industries have an interest in retaining such workers, so they may acquiesce to the "professional" labor law regime as a means of locking in skilled workers.

Likewise, the theory predicts a relationship between the political-organizational capacity of labor and the development of laws governing collective labor relations. Unions and worker organizations have a direct interest in securing laws that protect and extend their own rights as organized bodies—over the selection of union leadership, the use of union funds, and the freedom to undertake collective action (such as strikes). The "encompassing" regime gives unions this status, even if individual worker protections remain weak. And in countries where unions have built linkages to political parties or particular politicians, collective labor law becomes a means of locking in union status in subsequent rounds of the political cycle.

Taken together, these direct effects mean that, where the skill diversity in an economy is high, and when worker organizations are well developed and strong, the "corporatist" regime is likely to be observed. A skilled workforce, with significant worker organization by economic sector, is able to effectively negotiate both extensive individual and collective labor laws. Such laws are likely to be in the interest of employers, who wish to retain their skilled workers, and in the interest of politicians, who see significant political gains to be had from incorporating worker organizations into their electoral base.

It is important to reiterate that this theory is meant to explain long-term labor law configurations. It focuses on *lasting* labor law regimes. Deviations from these expectations in the short run may occur, but they are anticipated to be short-lived if they lack a foundation in the labor market's skill distribution and in the relative organizational capacity of labor. In other words, politics can trump economics in the short run, but it will lose out in the medium to long run. Indeed, authoritarian governments, as well as some democratic governments, can decree (and have decreed, as will be seen below) labor laws that have little relationship to the underlying economic configuration. But these have proven unsustainable, and reform has been fairly rapid. In particular, undifferentiated economies, with largely homogenous workers, find it difficult to sustain labor law outcomes in the upper half of the policy space. Similarly, unorganized or fragmented labor movements cannot maintain a legal regime in the right half of the policy space. Thus, by explaining labor law equilibria, the theory developed here also explains why reforms carried out by powerful political actors may be unsuccessful.

Feedback Effects and the Endogenous Nature of Labor Law Development

This book examines labor laws primarily as outcomes. The theory presented thus far treats labor laws as the product of political contestation, conditioned by resource endowments. More specifically, the distribution of skills in the economy establishes the foundation for labor code configurations, and the political-organizational capacity of labor shapes the translation of regulatory demands into law.

Nevertheless, labor law, once established, becomes an explanatory variable in its own right. Labor law changes the rules of the game, and this shapes the decisions and behavior of actors throughout the economy. Political scientists refer to this as a "feedback effect" (Pierson 1993). Labor laws are not the end of the story; they represent temporary markers of existing alignments, and they can change the skill distribution and organizational strength of labor, even as they themselves remain subject to reevaluation and change. Policies, and the coalitions

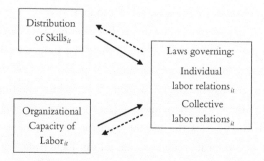

Once in place, labor laws provide new rights and resources
to some actors. This creates incentives for workers to adapt
their skill profiles to the legal regime, and for unions to
modify their strategies and recruitment practices. Over the
long run, this can reshape political competition and even
contribute to changes in resource endowments.

Figure 1.4. Labor Law Feedback Effects

they engender, can undermine existing institutional arrangements and lead to
"path departing" reforms (Brooks 2009; Thelen 2004).

Figure 1.4 presents this "feedback" process graphically. The solid arrows indicate that labor laws are the product of resource endowments and political
contestation. But the dashed arrows indicate how the laws come to reshape both
the political process and relative resource endowments. In the short to medium
term, labor laws can change political coalitions. For example, new laws governing collective action may facilitate union formation, or increase the resources
available to labor unions, and thus give labor a stronger voice and make it more
attractive for partnering with a political party or elected leader (Marshall 2005).
Alternatively, more rigid laws governing the hiring and firing of workers might
lead businesses to withdraw from the economy, or to form new employers' associations charged with changing the laws. And the particular production needs
of highly skilled industries might produce cross-class coalitions, in which both
employers and workers in a given industry support laws that encourage permanence in the same job. Thus these new coalitions may be the source of pressures
for reforms in the labor code. The "feedback" process in this way changes political coalitions at work in the country or industry, their demands, and perhaps the
next iteration of labor laws.

In addition, changes in labor laws can produce, over a long enough time horizon, changes in resource endowments. For example, laws that give status or rights to more highly skilled workers over others may induce workers throughout the economy to acquire additional skills. Or, perversely, laws that encourage turnover of workers may discourage workers from seeking additional education or vocational training. Indeed, Schneider (2009) argues that such a "low-skill trap" exists in Latin America; the current regulatory environment creates incentives for businesses to locate only low-skill jobs in Latin America, and creates a disincentive for workers to incur the costs of improved skills.

It remains an empirical question to measure how quickly, and how radically, skill endowments can be changed. The next chapter shows this is a slower process than might be imagined by policy-makers. Most countries have shown only incremental change in skill levels, even as governments have undertaken significant spending on improving schooling and vocational training. It may be that such change occurs only over generations, as skill levels undergo the slow process of change. And, as we will see, the result of this slow change has been a very slow change in labor laws, as well.

In fact, feedback effects have largely reinforced, rather than weakened or destabilized, the existing labor market skill equilibrium and its associated laws. Labor market institutions are "sticky," and the reason is, at least in part, economic. Once production facilities—whether factories, farms, mines, or workshops— have been set up, workers adjust their skill acquisition to fit those facilities. Laws may be written to fit those production conditions, and they thus regularize hiring workers of a certain skill level and with commensurate levels of benefits. Change would require departing from this equilibrium. In addition, firms may choose to seek efficiency within their existing capital resources, rather than making the costly investment to change technologies and find new workers (Acemoglu 1998). Thus the skill base of the economy is often replicated, rather than changed, as a result of the stickiness of the labor market equilibria. Indeed, if laws change pre-emptively, say by setting a new standard for employment that is above the prevailing equilibrium, firms may simply evade the new provisions, or choose not to hire workers, or even exit the market.

Labor market stickiness is also political. Labor laws invest certain workers— those in unions, and especially those in unions with ties to political parties— with the resources to resist change (Pierson 1993, 1994). These labor market "insiders" have the protected ability to mobilize to protest change, as well as the financial resources and ties to power, that make them a force to be reckoned with (Rueda 2005). In addition, governments may find it easier to preserve labor-friendly regulations for their supporters than to preserve other policies. Social welfare policies are costly, but labor laws impose little cost on governments; it is the private sector that must bear most of the cost of compliance. Thus labor codes largely reinforce the labor market equilibria that give birth to them.

1.5. Summary and Conclusion

In short, the theory developed in this chapter produces a set of testable hypotheses about the variation in labor laws. First, where skill levels are higher, laws governing individual labor relations will, over the long term, be more developed and more "rigid" or generous to labor. Second, where the political-organizational capacity of labor is greater, over the short to medium term, laws governing collective labor relations will be more developed and provide greater rights and freedoms to labor. These two hypotheses allow us to explain the long-term variation in labor law regimes in different countries. And third, short-term deviations from the above equilibria are likely to be fragile and short-lived, driven by the political manipulation of authoritarian or semiauthoritarian regimes or political parties whose electoral needs make them ripe for regulatory capture (Stigler 1971).

The theory developed in this book represents a significant advance over previous approaches for several reasons. First, it can explain both the origins of labor law regimes and their persistence through time. The skill profile of a nation, because it changes only slowly, acts as a structural factor limiting the kinds of labor laws that can be sustained. Environments with higher proportions of their workers in the skilled and semi-skilled sectors present a greater demand for job security and organizational rights; any deviations from these outcomes will provoke constant pressures toward reform. Indeed, as will be seen in Chapters 4 through 6, in Argentina—a relatively high-skilled country—the 1990s reforms that jeopardized job security met with strong labor opposition and were overturned after only a few short years; in contrast, in Peru—a relatively low-skilled country—the military-imposed job stability measures from 1970 could not be sustained once authoritarian rule was removed.

Second, this theory can effectively speak to the evolution of labor regulations under both authoritarian and democratic regimes. Since both types of regimes

have incentives to construct coalitions that will support them in the medium
to long run, they will need to be responsive to the demands that come from
labor when it presents significant hold-up power over the economy and when it
has a developed organizational capacity and membership. Authoritarian governments have greater ability to deviate from the skill and organization predictions,
given their freedom from the need to regularly stand for re-election. Democratic
governments, on the other hand, are more prone to the inter- and intraparty
competition that make labor a perennial concern.

Third, this theory dialogues well with earlier work on Latin American corporatist institutional development. It creates a framework for understanding how
labor and particular parties or governments become bound together in lasting
relationships, and provides a political mechanism for changes in that relationship through time. Too often, the existing literature bifurcates into older conceptual work on corporatism and newer studies of policy design and impacts.
This theory bridges that divide, linking labor laws and labor market policy in a
comprehensive understanding of corporatist politics.

Fourth, the theory developed in this chapter is general enough that it should
be applicable to other regions of the world. The key independent variables—
skill levels, organizational capacity, and political competition between parties
or other rival actors—are testable across the globe. Thus the theory does not
rely on a Latin American "exceptionalism" or arguments about colonial institutions or culture, but instead explicitly models variables that can be measured
across regions and time periods. Indeed, this theory better links studies of labor
regulation and labor policy in developed nations with that of Latin America
and the developing world. The skill level argument builds on recent work on
Organization for Economic Coordination and Development (OECD) nations
(Thelen 2004) and applies it for the first time to the Latin American cases. And
the organizational capacity argument has a long history in the study of labor
relations. Bringing these insights together helps explain the surprising variation
and ongoing stability observed in Latin American labor laws in the last century.

Chapter 2

Using Multiple Methods to Understand Labor Law Development in Latin America

The remainder of this book tests the theoretical framework developed in Chapter 1 with data drawn from Latin America. It employs a mixed-methods approach, in order to capitalize on the different kinds of data available, both quantitative and qualitative. The first test consists of a cross-national quantitative analysis, employing a newly coded dataset on labor laws across Latin America. This permits a rigorous test of the theory using a standardized scale of labor law provisions across the region's major economies, formalized in econometric models whose underlying assumptions are made fully explicit. But this analysis is limited by data availability to the period from the 1980s to the 2000s, and at best only can detect correlations between explanatory variables and the labor law outcomes. The second test is a series of historical narratives of three crucial cases—Chile, Peru, and Argentina. These countries represent three of the four hypothesized outcomes from the theory (the fourth—an unrestrained market without labor laws—no longer exists in any Latin American country). The qualitative historical narratives allow me to marshal a much broader body of evidence, and do not require the simplifying of complex phenomena into numerical values or reliance on proxy variables. They allow the historical story to be told, and shed light on the process and mechanisms by which labor laws took shape.

In this brief chapter, I describe the two-pronged empirical strategy employed in the following chapters. I first describe the quantitative approach, highlighting the method employed in converting labor laws into numerical values, as well as noting the strengths and limitations of such an approach. Then I lay out the qualitative approach, providing a rationale for the selection of cases based on their divergent values on the dependent and independent variables. In particular, I compare the evolution of worker skills and organizational capacity across the three cases, and lay out the theory's predictions for each country.

2.1. A Quantitative Comparative Analysis

Labor laws do not have an accepted, standardized measure. The UN's International Labor Organization regularly collects data on labor law provisions across countries but has not developed a methodology or measure for comparing these provisions. This complicates making meaningful comparisons among countries, and often leads researchers to limit their analysis to the examination of particular laws or specific instances of labor law reform. This has been fruitful (Murillo et al. 2011; Murillo 2005; Murillo and Schrank 2005; and Cook 2007 are particularly notable) but may fail to capture dynamics that apply to the labor code as a whole, in which individual and collective measures may interact in the ways highlighted in Chapter 1. In recent years, surveys such as the World Bank's *Doing Business* have begun to develop quantified scores to describe labor regulations across countries, and economists (Botero et al. 2004; Chor and Freeman 2005) have assembled datasets on cross-national labor regulation. But both of these measures lack temporal scope; the former covers only the period from 2004 forward, and the latter consists of a single observation (from approximately 2000) on a limited set of countries.

To give a better sense of cross-national and cross-temporal variation in labor law provisions in Latin America, I construct a numerical scoring for labor code measures in each of the eighteen major Latin American countries. Drawing on information gathered by the International Labor Organization (Vega Ruiz 2005), and on the labor codes of each country, I examine legal measures at three points in time—prior to the reforms in the 1980s, after the first major wave of reforms in the 1990s, and in the postreform period of the 2000s (through 2005). I code twenty-three different features of these legal codes for each of the eighteen countries in each period. I follow the definitions developed in Chapter 1, examining laws according to whether they govern individual or collective labor relations.

Individual Labor Laws

Individual labor laws govern the hiring, firing, and workplace treatment of individual workers. I compile thirteen such individual measures, which address general employment contracting conditions, limits on the workday and work week and overtime hours, entitlements to days of rest and vacation, maternity leave, and dismissal requirements and mandated severance pay packages (full descriptions of the measures can be found in Table 2.A at the end of this chapter). In addition, I give particular attention to laws guaranteeing stability of employment; in Latin America, stability has been a central feature of the legislation governing individual labor relations, and "indefinite" employment has been the presumptive norm for most jobs. However, in recent years, most countries have introduced new "modalities" of employment, including "fixed-term" provisions that are not presumed to be indefinite. In the dataset assembled here, I include five provisions of these fixed-term contracts, including the number of conditions under which they may be applied and the length of time for which a worker can be employed as "temporary."

In order to illustrate how these provisions vary across countries and over time, Table 2.1 details several salient individual labor law measures.[1] All figures are for a worker with three years' seniority, and reforms in the codes are indicated in boldface type. The first two columns in Table 2.1 deal with the modalities for fixed-term employment that exist in the labor code. Expanded in the 1980s and 1990s, fixed-term contracts broke with the traditional presumption that labor contracts were indefinite; many countries, including Peru and Chile, had enshrined the assumed permanence of the labor relationship in their constitutions. Yet, in the reform period, Peru in particular stands out for codifying fifteen different kinds of temporary contracts during the labor reform of Alberto Fujimori in 1991. These were undertaken to combat high unemployment by making hiring requirements, including severance payments and contributions to social security, less onerous by eliminating them during the trial or introductory period. Other nations, including Venezuela and Brazil, expanded temporary contracts in the 1990s, and Paraguay and Nicaragua have done so in the 2000s. In addition to introducing new modalities for fixed-term contracts, three nations extended their duration during the reform period, as seen in the second column of Table 2.1. Probation was extended from three to six months in Peru under Fujimori, while it was set at three months in Argentina under Menem and one month in Nicaragua.

The third column in Table 2.1 examines the maximum number of hours of work per week (above which an overtime premium must be paid). In Latin America, these traditionally were set at either forty-four or forty-eight hours per week, implying a six-day work week, which in some cases entailed only a

Table 2.1. Comparison of Selected Terms of Individual Labor Contract Laws in 18 Latin American Countries, 1980s–2000s

Country	Decade	Modalities of Fixed-Term Contracts	Maximum Trial Period under Fixed-Term Contracts	Maximum Hours of Work per Week	Maximum Overtime Hours of Work per Week	Premium for Overtime Work (Daytime Hours)	Mandated Annual Vacation Days	Mandated Maternity Leave
Argentina	1980s	4	0	48	na	1.50	14	8
	1990s	6	3	48	7	1.50	14	8
	2000s	6	3	48	7	1.50	14	8
Bolivia	1980s	4	3	48	12	2.00	6	8
	1990s	4	3	48	12	2.00	6	8
	2000s	4	3	48	12	2.00	6	8
Brazil	1980s	3	3	48	12	1.20	30	12
	1990s	4	3	48	12	1.20	30	12
	2000s	4	3	48	12	1.20	30	12
Chile	1980s	1	0	48	12	1.50	15	18
	1990s	1	0	48	12	1.50	15	18
	2000s	1	0	45	12	1.50	15	18
Colombia	1980s	3	2	48	12	1.25	15	8
	1990s	3	2	48	12	1.25	15	12
	2000s	3	2	48	12	1.25	15	12
Costa Rica	1980s	2	0	48	12	1.50	12	18
	1990s	2	0	48	12	1.50	12	18
	2000s	2	0	48	12	1.50	12	18
Dominican Republic	1980s	2	0	48	24	1.30	12	10
	1990s	2	0	44	24	1.30	12	12
	2000s	2	0	44	24	1.30	12	12
Ecuador	1980s	5	3	44	12	1.50	15	8
	1990s	5	3	40	12	1.50	15	12
	2000s	5	3	40	12	1.50	15	12
El Salvador	1980s	2	1	44	na	2.00	15	na
	1990s	2	1	44	na	2.00	15	na
	2000s	2	1	44	na	2.00	15	na
Guatemala	1980s	2	2	48	24	1.50	10	8
	1990s	2	2	48	24	1.50	15	8
	2000s	2	2	48	24	1.50	15	8
Honduras	1980s	2	2	44	24	1.25	15	10
	1990s	2	2	44	24	1.25	15	10
	2000s	2	2	44	24	1.25	15	10
Mexico	1980s	3	0	na	9	2.00	10	12
	1990s	3	0	na	9	2.00	10	12
	2000s	3	0	na	9	2.00	10	12
Nicaragua	1980s	2	0	48	na	2.00	15	12
	1990s	2	1	48	9	2.00	15	12
	2000s	3	1	48	9	2.00	15	12
Panama	1980s	2	3	48	9	1.25	30	14
	1990s	2	3	48	9	1.25	30	14
	2000s	2	3	48	9	1.25	30	14
Paraguay	1980s	3	2	48	9	1.50	12	12
	1990s	3	2	48	9	1.50	12	12
	2000s	6	2	48	9	1.50	12	12
Peru	1980s	3	3	48	42	1.00	30	8
	1990s	12	6	48	na	1.25	30	8
	2000s	12	6	48	na	1.35	30	8
Uruguay	1980s	2	3	48	8	2.00	20	12
	1990s	2	3	48	8	2.00	20	12
	2000s	2	3	48	8	2.00	20	12
Venezuela	1980s	2	0	48	12	1.25	15	12
	1990s	4	0	44	10	1.50	17	18
	2000s	4	0	44	10	1.50	17	18

half day of work on Saturday. A number of the labor codes explicitly call for at least one full day of rest, and some specify that Sunday should be the preferred day for this rest. However, during the reform period, several countries made this day of rest more flexible, and in four cases the maximum number of hours was decreased. Ecuador embraced the shortest mandated work week at forty hours, while Venezuela and the Dominican Republic scaled down to forty-four hours per week and Chile adopted a 45-hour work week.

The fourth and fifth columns of Table 2.1 show that there is significant variation between countries in both the maximum number of overtime hours that are permitted in a given week and the premium paid for overtime work. Some nations, such as El Salvador and Peru, do not place a limit on the maximum number of overtime hours, while others allow as many as twenty-four hours per week (Dominican Republic, Guatemala, Honduras), and still others restrict overtime to only seven (Argentina), eight (Uruguay), or nine hours (Mexico, Nicaragua, Panama, Paraguay). The mandated wage premium on overtime hours ranges from as low as 20 percent in Brazil to as high as 100 percent in Bolivia, El Salvador, Mexico, Nicaragua, and Uruguay. During the reform period, few changes were made to these overtime premiums, with only Peru and Venezuela changing their codes to make them more generous.

Finally, the sixth and seventh columns in Table 2.1 examine variation in laws governing vacation and maternity leave. Vacation varies from six days per year in Bolivia to thirty days per year in Brazil, Panama, and Peru. Most countries mandate roughly two weeks of vacation time (twelve to fifteen days). Maternity leave has been the target of consistent pressure from international organizations promoting maternal health, and the International Labor Organization (ILO) has since 1952 called for twelve weeks of license; in 2000 it revised this figure upward to fourteen weeks' leave in its Convention 183. As a result, during the period under study, Latin American nations converged on a twelve-week maternity leave, although a number of countries continue to offer only eight weeks (Argentina, Bolivia, and Guatemala) or other shorter periods. Only Chile, Costa Rica, and Panama met the fourteen-week standard throughout the period, and Venezuela revised its laws to include an eighteen-week leave in 1990s.

Collective Labor Measures

Collective labor laws govern unionization and collective action by unions. I include six measures of collective labor laws, including provisions for collective dismissals, the government recognition of labor unions, the legitimate parties in collective bargaining agreements, and the level at which collective bargaining takes place and the coverage of collective bargaining agreements. Much like the laws governing individual employment relations, these collective measures vary considerably across countries and across time.[2]

First, I analyze whether collective dismissals are permitted. In Latin America, such collective dismissals tend to be highly regulated, with several countries limiting collective dismissals to exceptional cases (such as when there is danger of the failure of the firm). By the 2000s, however, an increasing number of countries had liberalized the ability of firms to shed workers, allowing them to do so to increase competitiveness. Next, I include a measure of the parties that must be notified if firms wish to pursue collective dismissals. Some countries require that both the Ministry of Labor and the relevant unions must be given prior notice—increasing the number of veto players in the process—while others allow firms to make collective dismissals at will. Most countries made few changes to this requirement, with the exception of Argentina, Peru, and Venezuela, all of which made it more restrictive.

Another crucial feature of collective labor law is the legal recognition of, and privileges granted to, labor unions. While some countries, largely in Central America, allow unions to organize without government intervention, most countries provide for government sanctioning of unions, and some award privileged legal status to particular unions. This creates dominant, and in many cases, monopoly unions with disproportionate bargaining powers. I include measures of the required number of workers to form a union, and the relative level of government support for collaboration among unions and labor federations or confederations in the dataset. The former measure—required number of workers—represents a trade-off between union freedom, on the one hand, and the possibility of fragmentation and competition of unions, on the other. The latter measure creates opportunities for collective action across unions or economic sectors, and may provide mechanisms by which labor or the state silences dissident voices.

Finally, collective bargaining has traditionally been one of the most important activities of unions in Latin America, shaping opportunities for wage increases, improved workplace treatment, and other benefits. The dataset includes two measures of collective bargaining regulations: the level of collective bargaining and the coverage of collective bargaining outcomes. The first of these captures whether negotiation takes place at the firm or industry level (or is unregulated), while the second describes the extent to which collective bargaining outcomes apply to workers in the firm or industry beyond those who are members of the union. I code more highly cases that allow bargaining at the industry or sector level rather than limiting it to the firm level, and that automatically apply the outcomes of collective bargaining to all workers in the affected firm or industry. Over the period, three of the cases—Peru, Argentina, and Chile—made changes to their laws to permit or favor industry-level bargaining, while other countries did not modify their earlier provisions. Peru also more clearly regulated coverage of collective bargains, limiting them to the unions involved, while Nicaragua and El Salvador extended coverage of bargaining outcomes to all workers in the affected firm or industry.

Labor Law Indexes

The dataset consists of values for each of the twenty-three variables, normalized to run from zero to one, with higher values indicating labor regulations that are more restrictive (to employers) or more protective (to unionized, formal sector, workers). I then sum these scores to produce three summary indexes as dependent variables for analysis in Chapter 3. The first of these is an index for individual contracting terms. Uruguay, Argentina, Mexico, and Costa Rica stand out as the leaders on individual regulations, while Bolivia, Colombia, and Peru are the weakest in the region. Second, I sum the measures of collective regulations to produce an index of collective labor relations law. Argentina and Mexico are the strongest on this index, and Uruguay, Ecuador, and Chile are the weakest.[3]

I construct a third measure of the cumulative labor code by summing the individual and collective indexes. This provides a single summary measure for comparing labor codes across countries, and captures the ways that individual and collective labor laws might interact within a country's overall labor code. By this measure, Argentina and Mexico have the most extensive labor codes, while Bolivia, Guatemala, El Salvador, Peru, and Colombia have the least protective.

Finally, as will be seen in Chapter 3, the individual and collective labor indexes can be used to place country labor codes into the two-dimensional policy space described in Chapter 1. The underlying hypothesis is that combinations of individual and collective laws form labor law "regimes" that might not be captured if we limited analysis to summed values of the indexes.

The Advantages and Disadvantages of Quantifying Labor Laws

Systematically coding labor laws in this way has several advantages. First, it permits comparison of labor codes across a common set of metrics. Laws, by their nature, are highly complex and use a language that can vary across national contexts. This dataset translates complex qualitative data into tractable quantitative measures. Second, it permits critical analysis of the labor code, allowing us to detect patterns in the data that might be otherwise overlooked. Third, the coding method is transparent, so that it can be replicated (or questioned or enhanced) by other scholars. And fourth, the coding is sensitive to the diverse forms that labor law can take in countries across Latin America. The ILO publication from which it draws includes not only laws and decrees but also jurisprudence. This is particularly important in assessing the case of Uruguay, where court rulings have played an important role in shaping the regulation of labor.

Most important, the quantitative scoring of each country's labor laws makes possible a series of econometric tests of each of the hypotheses developed above. Arguments linking skill levels to individual labor laws, and the organizational capacity of labor to collective labor laws, can be tested together and independently. Likewise, these arguments can be tested against the other principal theoretical claims in the literature regarding the effects of partisanship, trade, economic growth, and foreign direct investment. For the first time, a systematic "horse race" of competing theories can be carried out across Latin American cases. To foreshadow the results in Chapter 3, I find that skill levels (proxied by the average years of schooling of the workforce) and organizational capacity (proxied by union density figures) are significantly associated with greater cumulative labor codes, as well as the individual and collective components of the labor laws, and that they also are strongly related to the labor law regimes described in Chapter 1. These findings provide initial confirmation for the theory.

However, using this quantitative dataset, and an econometric approach, comes at a cost: the data are drawn from an ILO collection that includes only three observations for each country—one for each decade of the 1980s, 1990s, and 2000s. It does not capture the year-to-year changes in labor provisions, and the piecemeal, incremental process of labor law change. Collier and Collier (1979) suggest that the political dynamics around labor law are most visible (and give evidence of the salience of laws) when those laws change. Examining the labor codes through snapshots might miss the crucial moments, or "critical junctures," during which political factors make labor laws change.

This concern is particularly important in a case like that of Argentina, in which (as we will see below) liberalizing reforms undertaken in 1991 were largely reversed just a few years later in 1997 (Cook 2007: 74–80; Murillo 2005). The single observation in the dataset for Argentina in the 1990s captures only the latter outcome. But that single observation bears a striking continuity with the 1980s and 2000s observations. In fact, one of the most important findings of this book is that labor codes in the 2000s remain surprisingly consistent—across the region—with their precursors in the 1980s.[4] With regard to the Argentine case, for example, the dataset prompts the question of why Argentina preserved (and even increased) its highly protective labor code. The Menem reform can thus be seen as a temporary departure from a deeper political and economic equilibrium that produces (and preserves) labor-friendly legislation.

Another concern about this quantitative, econometric approach is its limited explanatory capacity. At best, statistical modeling can detect correlations between variables—such as the skill levels and organizational capacity of labor, on the one hand, and labor code measures, on the other. It remains silent on the question of causality, and leaves open to question the mechanisms through which skills and organization have their effect on the formulation of laws and regulation. In addition, it requires simplification at several points: in the coding of variables, which limits analysis to concepts that can be measured and evaluated quantitatively; in the relationships tested, which must be assumed to be unidirectional and exogenous; and in the number of complicating covariates that can be included in the models. As a result, in spite of their rigor and transparency, statistical findings can seem stark and even oversimplified. For this reason, I complement them with qualitative case studies, constructed as "analytic narratives."

2.2. Analytic Narratives: Chile, Peru, and Argentina

The second prong of my empirical strategy seeks to put flesh on (and test) the relationships that are detected in the econometric tests, by constructing "analytic narratives" of particular historical cases (Bates et al. 1998). This is particularly important because statistical testing can only show correlations between variables, and cannot establish causation or the direction that causal arrows run. In this case, there is the possibility that the explanatory variables (skill levels and organizational capacity) are shaped by the dependent variable (labor laws); as noted in Chapter 1, the labor law environment may have "feedback effects" and encourage workers to acquire certain sets of skills or to form unions and take collective action in particular ways. To deal with these concerns about endogeneity and the direction of causation, I test my theory with historical analyses of the development of labor codes in Chile, Peru, and Argentina. Historical case studies allow me to examine the period of initial labor law formulation, a time in which causation could only have run in one direction—because labor laws did not yet exist. Consequently, skill levels and union organizational capacity can be taken in this early period as truly exogenous explanatory variables, and I can trace out the role they played in the design and evolution of the laws that were adopted.

Analytic narratives are a particularly apt method for further testing the theory developed in Chapter 1. First, they explicitly seek to model with historical evidence the relationships and strategic interactions that gave rise to labor laws (Levi 2003). The theory "provides categories and a framework"—workers of varying skill levels and organizational capacity, in particular economic and political contexts—"in terms of which conjecture about the causal mechanism is formulated" (Arias 2011). In particular, it focuses on "key actors, their goals, and their preferences" (Levi 2003). Second, analytic narratives allow me to emphasize the institutional context in which historical labor law developments occurred (Levi 2003; Bates et al. 1998). Indeed, we will see that early shortages of labor—especially skilled labor—and early experience of union organization and activity, gave rise to labor market institutions that structured later political competition and eventual labor law development. In other words, an analytic narrative approach helps focus attention on the mechanisms by which structural economic factors and political competition shaped the legal environment for labor.

I construct analytic narratives for three country cases, representing the professional, encompassing, and corporatist regimes suggested by the model. As will be seen more clearly in Chapter 3, the choice of cases is given by the data. Chile's labor laws place it firmly in the "professional" regime; Peru's legal environment associate it with the "encompassing" regime (following the reforms of the 1990s under Fujimori); and Argentina's labor regulations place it in the "corporatist" configuration.[5] The data shows that no Latin American case remains sufficiently unregulated to qualify as an example of the "market" outcome. Figure 2.1 highlights these differing labor law regimes across the cases. By surveying the evolution of each country's skill distribution and the history of its labor movement, as well as the party-union linkages and other factors, the developmental path of each labor law outcome can be detected.

The analytic narratives consist of careful historical process-tracing (George

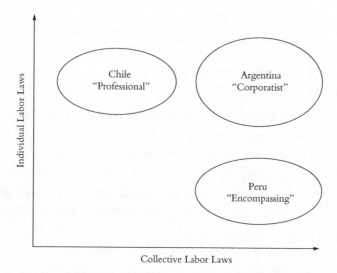

Case selection corresponds to variation on the dependent variable;
each of the three existing labor laws regimes is represented.

Figure 2.1. Case Selection for Analytic Narratives

and Bennett 2005) examining within-case variation and change through time. They focus on two key historical moments. First, they examine the early development of labor laws, focusing in particular on the first measures introduced. Examining the origins of the labor codes frees us from concerns about endogeneity, since causality can only run in one direction; any reciprocal effect of labor laws can only begin after they have been introduced. Second, they trace out the development of labor codes through time, examining how changes in the relative skill endowment and labor's organizational capacity gave rise to strategic action focused on changing (or resisting change in) labor laws.

In this sense, the analytic cases carry out explanatory work that the econometric analysis cannot. The econometric analysis is limited by the unavailability of data prior to recent decades. Many economic variables simply were not measured, or not measured in a comparable fashion across cases, until the latter decades of the twentieth century. Yet even when good time-series data does not exist, punctual observations for specific countries may be available. Historical analysis can make the most of these occasional observations, and leverage them with other extant data, to uncover the causal processes within cases. Process-tracing thus serves as an additional plausibility test for the findings in the econometric analysis. It seeks to uncover the factors, debates, and decisions that the models suggest drove legal developments.

Skill Distributions and Organizational Capacity in Comparative Perspective

The analytic narratives, by definition, devote their attention to within-case variation across subnational geography and time. Before entering into them, it is helpful to briefly compare the three cases on the two independent variables highlighted by the theory in Chapter 1—skill distributions and labor's latent capacity for organization. For ease of presentation, I divide the comparison into two broad periods, corresponding to the first and second halves of the twentieth century. I rely on data drawn from the Montevideo-Oxford Latin American Economic History Database, as well as some additional observations from Engerman, Sokoloff, and Mariscal 2012. In no way should this brief introduction itself be considered a test of the theory. It is merely intended to set the cases in comparative context, and lay the groundwork for the historical cases that follow in Chapters 4 through 6.

Direct measures of skill levels are not available on a consistent basis for the late nineteenth century or early twentieth century across Latin America. However, as education began to become a developmental priority during that time period, governments made an effort to track enrollment, and these figures can provide some sense of the share of the population that was receiving at least a primary education.[6] Figure 2.2 displays primary school enrollment as a share of total population in Argentina, Chile, and Peru in the first half of the twentieth century. At the turn of the century, Argentina was significantly ahead of both Chile and Peru in enrollment, educating nearly double the share of its population as did Peru. Indeed, Argentina had become the regional leader in education and skills for two reasons. First, like Chile, it had attracted immigrants from Europe, most of whom tended to be higher skilled than the native-born population. Because of its size and proximity to Europe, it saw a greater influx than did Chile of these immigrants. They valued education, and sought to pass it on to their children. Likewise, President Domingo Sarmiento famously toured the world studying educational practices in the 1840s; he subsequently made educational spending a priority, using the federal government to intervene and improve educational performance throughout the territory.

In terms of literacy, Argentina led the pack early. In 1869, literacy in Buenos

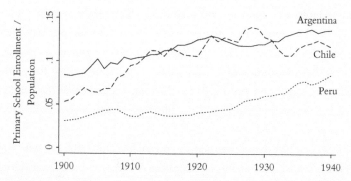

In the period of initial labor law development, the three countries had markedly different levels of primary school enrollment. Argentina was the clear leader at the turn of the twentieth century, with Chile lagging a generation behind. Peru did not catch up until the second half of the century.

Figure 2.2. Primary School Enrollment in Argentina, Chile, and Peru, 1900–40. *Source:* Author's calculations from Montevideo-Oxford Latin American Economic History Database.

Aires stood at 23.8 percent; by 1895, this figure had risen to 45.6 percent. In contrast, literacy in Santiago, Chile, was only 13.3 percent in 1854 and 25.7 percent in 1875 (Engerman, Sokoloff, and Mariscal 2012: 135). By 1914, Argentine literacy had topped 60 percent (138). Literacy in Chile was only 40 percent in 1907. Regional variation was great, though, and Santiago had a literacy rate of 50.6 percent. It was only in the 1920s that Chile began to catch up with Argentina, achieving 66 percent literacy in 1925 (while Argentina enjoyed 73 percent literacy). Peru lagged far behind in 1925, with only 32 percent of its population literate (144–46). Nevertheless, urban centers such as Lima saw its literacy climb above 50 percent.

In terms of the theory developed in Chapter 1, high skill endowments are associated with greater worker interest in, and ability to achieve, labor regulations. In particular, where worker skill profiles are higher, we expect more extensive individual labor regulations, protecting workers against dismissal and offering better workplace treatment or benefits. Based on this data on schooling and literacy, Argentina is expected to be the early leader in individual labor law development, followed by Chile given its subsequent increase in educational levels and skill profile. Peru, with its limited literacy and slow advance in school enrollment, would be expected to be much less likely to develop individual labor

regulation. However, regional concentrations of better skills in each country—
especially in the capitals and urban centers—would provide opportunities for
the development of labor codes targeting better-skilled workers. Indeed, as will
be seen in the case studies, early labor codes were often written for particular
industries, or made distinctions between the skilled white-collar *empleados* (who
received significant protection) and unskilled blue-collar *obreros* (who received
less protection).

In the second half of the twentieth century, Chile closed the gap with Argentina, and the two stood out among educational leaders in the region (Uruguay,
Costa Rica, and Cuba also performed very well). Figure 2.3 depicts primary
school enrollment in the 1940–2000 period. Peru catches up in enrollment in
the 1950s, but the effects would not be felt until that generation finished its
schooling and moved into the workforce in the 1960s and 1970s. During this
period, many unschooled adults went back to school as well. Unfortunately for
Peru and its workers, though, by the 1970s secondary and higher education were
becoming the key markers of better skills. In the 1980s, the average Peruvian
worker had six years of schooling; the average Chilean had nearly seven years,
and the average Argentine had more than seven years (Barro and Lee 2000).
While the skill differential had closed by this period, the econometric analysis in
Chapter 3 shows that it still had a significant effect on labor code evolution. In
addition, the design of labor codes had largely been locked in by the earlier skill
distribution, making fundamental change of the Peruvian system, toward greater
coverage and generosity, all but impossible.

The theory in Chapter 1 also posits that labor codes are driven by the organizational capacity of labor. In Chapter 3, I use data on unionization of the
workforce as a measure of the latent capacity of labor to act in a coordinated
fashion, but this data is not available for earlier periods. For this reason, here I
use data on the share of employment in manufacturing. The movement of the
labor force from rural agriculture to the cities provided an early opportunity for
organization into unions, so this measure captures the concentration of workers
that made collective action more likely. Admittedly, it does not include mining,
which also brought workers together geographically, with shared interests, and
proved to be another seedbed for unionization. Nevertheless, it provides at least
a first approximation of the relative capacity for organization across the cases.

As can be seen in Figure 2.4 Argentina was the far and away early leader in the
share of its workforce in the manufacturing industry. Even in 1900, a fifth of its

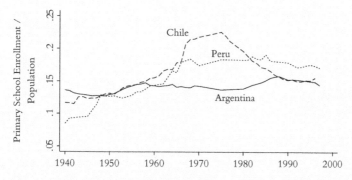

In the second half of the twentieth century, the skill differential between countries closed significantly. Nevertheless, the design of earlier labor codes continued to constrain subsequent labor law development.

Figure 2.3. Primary School Enrollment in Argentina, Chile, and Peru, 1940–2000. *Source:* Author's calculations from Montevideo-Oxford Latin American Economic History Database.

employment came from manufacturing. Chile had about one-sixth of its workforce in manufacturing. And Peru saw nearly all of its workers in agriculture or mineral extraction; manufacturing was extremely underdeveloped in the early decades of the twentieth century. All of these figures remained largely constant until World War II.

This distribution of the relative employment shares suggests—based on the theory—that Argentina would be the most likely to develop extensive labor regulation. The country's greater manufacturing workforce, and the collective action potential of the workers concentrated in factories and cities, made them more capable of making demands of the state. It also made them a focal point for ambitious politicians seeking to win supporters. Chile and Peru both lagged behind on manufacturing employment during this period, so we would expect their labor regulation to be less developed than that of Argentina. Indeed, even as late as 1950, Peru had only a nascent manufacturing sector. Spread widely across the country's rugged geography, and across economic sectors as diverse as agriculture, mining, and personal services, workers found it hard to organize or make common cause.

In addition, Argentina saw three massive waves of immigration from Europe in the latter half of the nineteenth and early twentieth centuries. These workers brought not only greater education, but also an experience of worker organiza-

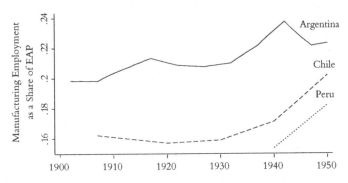

Manufacturing employment gives a rough approximation of labor's latent potential for organization. Argentina had a significantly greater share of its population employed in manufacturing than either Chile or Peru in the first half of the twentieth century.

Figure 2.4. Employment Shares in Manufacturing, Argentina, Chile, and Peru, 1900–50. *Source:* Author's calculations from Montevideo-Oxford Latin American Economic History Database.

tion and union activity, from their home countries. They were quick to organize mutual aid societies in their new home, and to form unions, and to link those unions together in federations. They became a powerful, well-articulated political force by the late 1930s and early 1940s. Chile also experienced significant European immigration, but in smaller numbers, and this was concentrated in the central coast and Santiago. These workers formed mutual aid societies and unions, but their geographic concentration, small numbers, and different economic sectors of employment led to disagreement on goals, hampering collaboration across unions. The movement grew rapidly but remained fragmented during the first half of the twentieth century. Finally, immigration to Peru included many Chinese workers, who did not enjoy citizenship rights, and with whom native-born Peruvians were less willing to coordinate action.

In short, through 1950, Argentina had characteristics—both in terms of its larger manufacturing workforce and its immigrant population—that gave its labor force a greater opportunity to successfully organize, and that made it most apt to develop labor regulations. Peru stood as the least likely to achieve significant labor regulation in this regard. In the postwar period, this pattern did not change substantially. As can be seen in Figure 2.5, the three countries maintained their relative ordering in terms of manufacturing employment.

However, the figure also shows the regionwide process of *deindustrializa-*

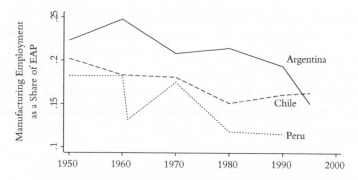

Deindustrialization in the second half of the twentieth century shrank the pool of organized workers but did not change the relative ordering of the countries under examination.

Figure 2.5. Employment Shares in Manufacturing, Argentina, Chile, and Peru, 1950–95. *Source:* Author's calculations from Montevideo-Oxford Latin American Economic History Database.

tion, a decline in manufacturing employment. The process began in the 1960s but became even more pronounced once Latin American economies started to dismantle their protected, import-substituting industries, and open their borders to greater trade. Argentina had the farthest to fall, and it showed the most rapid decline in industrial employment. By the 1990s, privatizations of state-run companies and the competitive restructuring of private firms had dramatically shrunk the core of the unionized workforce. Many commentators expected that this would undermine Argentina's labor movement, and would lead to a rewriting of its protective labor laws. And in fact, the government of Carlos Menem undertook just such reforms. But they proved unsustainable. The movement retained its presence in key sectors of the economy, and was able to demand the removal of reforms that threatened its members. Workers in Peru were not able to prevent similar reforms in their country. Much as in the period of labor law origins, the relative organizational strength of labor was important in this period of labor law reform.

In sum, the qualitative analysis in Chapters 4 through 6 examines three cases that allow us to study the major mechanisms of the theory at work. They vary on the dependent variable, with Argentina representing a corporatist labor law regime, Chile representing a professional regime, and Peru an encompassing regime. They also show important variation on the theory's key explanatory variables, with Argentina displaying relatively high values on measures of education and labor's organizational capacity, Peru exhibiting relatively low achievements on both measures, and Chile mixing relatively high skills with lower worker organization. The case studies permit a finer-grained approach to each of these measures within each national context, and allow for more careful process-tracing (with more precise measurement of variables) from skill distributions and organizational capacity to labor law outcomes.

2.3. Conclusion

This chapter has provided an overview of the empirical strategy employed in the remainder of the book: a two-pronged approach that makes use of both quantitative, econometric hypothesis-testing as well as qualitative process-tracing in the form of analytic narratives. While not a test unto itself, it has provided the rationale for the tests that follow. This "mixed-methods" approach allows us to understand the complex process of labor policy formation through diverse optics, and to maximize our confidence that we have detected the causal mechanisms at work. In addition, this chapter has introduced the coding process employed in the quantitative analysis. It has described the particular labor law measures included in the dataset, as well as described the strengths and weaknesses of the econometric approach. Finally, the chapter has sought to justify the selection of cases, and provide some comparative leverage on them, prior to the case studies.

Appendix Table 2.A.   Labor Regulation in Latin America—
Variables in the Labor Law Dataset

Variable	Decscription
Individual Labor Contracts	
Presumption of Indefinite Contract	Equals one if labor contracts are presumed to be indefinite unless expressly stipulated otherwise in the labor contract. Equals 0.5 if temporary contracts become permanent after a given lapse of time, or if indefinite contracts can be adjusted to temporary status. Equals zero if contracts are not presumed to be indefinite or if the nation has no law or regulations regarding the length of indefinite contracts.
Modalities of Fixed-Term Contracts	Measures the number of modalities under which workers can be contracted for temporary purposes. Normalized from 0 to 1, with higher values indicating less modalities (more protection/permanence in work relationships). The highest number in the sample is 12 and the lowest is 2.

Variable	Deｃscription
Minimum Duration of Fixed-Term Contracts	Measures the minimum duration of fixed-term contracts. The variable is normalized from 0 to 1, with higher values indicating a lower minimum duration of fixed-term contracts (higher protection). If there is no legally mandated minimum, then the variable equals zero. The highest observation in the sample is 12 and the lowest is 0 months.
Maximum Duration of Fixed-Term Contracts	Measures the maximum cumulative duration of fixed-term contracts. Where fixed-term contracts can be renewed, includes the maximum number of renewals. The variable is normalized from 0 to 1, with higher values indicating a lower allowed duration of fixed-term contracts (higher protection). If there is no legally mandated ceiling or fixed term contracts can be renewed without limit, then the variable equals zero. The highest observation in the sample is 60 days and the lowest is 0.
Maximum Duration of Trial Period	Measures the maximum duration of trial periods for contracts. The variable is normalized from 0 to 1, with higher values indicating shorter trial periods (more worker protection). If there is no legally mandated trial period, then the variable equals zero. The highest observation in the sample is 6 months and the lowest is 0 months.
INDEX: Use of Fixed-Term Contracting	Measures the protection to workers through limits set on contract lengths. Computed both as the sum of the normalized values of the preceding variables and as an average of the preceding Fixed-Term contracting variables.

Contract Law Provisions

Maximum Number of Hours per Day	Measures the maximum duration of the regular workday, in hours (excluding overtime). Coded "na" when no law exists. The variable is then normalized from 0 to 1, taking on higher values for lower maximum hours (more protection). The lowest value in the sample is 8 and the highest is 12.
Maximum Number of Hours per Week	Measures the maximum duration of the regular workweek, in hours (excluding overtime). The highest observation in the sample is 48 and the lowest is 40. The variable is normalized from 0 to 1, with higher values (more protection) for shorter work weeks.
Days of Mandated Rest per Week	Measures the number of rest days provided by law. The variable is normalized from 0 to 1. The highest value in the sample is 2 days and the lowest is 1.
Maximum Hours of Overtime (Weekly)	Measures the maximum number of overtime hours that can be worked in a week. If there is no weekly restriction on hours, then I code this variable as "na." The variable is normalized from 0 to 1, with higher values corresponding to less hours permitted of overtime (more protection). "na" is coded as zero. The lowest value in the sample is 8 hours and the highest is 42 hours.
Maximum Hours of Overtime (Yearly)	Measures the maximum number of overtime hours that can be worked in a year. Some countries determine this figure on the basis of the allowed weekly hours of overtime, while others mandate a set total figure that cannot be exceeded even if the cumulative effect of weekly overtime would seem to permit it. I first code a raw figure of total overtime hours per year, and then normalize this figure with a variable that takes values from 0 to 1, with higher values indicating less overtime hours permitted. If there is no weekly restriction on hours, then I code this variable as "na." The maximum value in the sample is 320 and the minimum is 100.

Variable	Decscription
Government Oversight of Overtime	A dummy variable that indicates whether government authorization is needed before overtime hours are permitted. Equals one if administrative authorization is required, 0 if it is not, and "na" if there is no legislation.
Worker Consent to Overtime	A dummy variable that indicates whether worker consent is required for overtime work. Equals one if worker consent required, 0 if it is not, and "na" if the country has no regulation to this effect.
Premium for Overtime Work	This variable measures the ratio of the overtime wage over the normal wage. The overtime premium is often two-tiered in Latin America, with differential rates based on day or nighttime hours worked. If the overtime structure has only one tier, I code overtime night hours as "na." Each variable is normalized from 0 to 1, with higher values representing a larger overtime premium (more protection). For daytime hours, the minimum value in the sample is 1 and the maximum is 2 times the normal wage; for nighttime hours, the minimum is 1.5 and the maximum is 3 times the normal wage.
Deferred Remuneration	This variable measures the number of additional wage payments paid out on an annual basis, expressed as the number of additional months' wages included in these payments. Traditionally, many countries refer to these payments as "aguinaldos." The variable is normalized from 0 to 1, with higher values representing higher deferred remuneration payments. The minimum observation in the sample is 0 and the maximum is 2.
Annual Days of Vacation	This variable measures the number of days of vacation permitted annually for a worker with three years of seniority. The variable is normalized from 0 to 1, with higher values representing a greater number of days of vacation. The minimum observation in the sample is 6 (Bolivia) and the maximum 30 days (Brazil, Peru).
Duration of Maternity Leave	Measures the length of mandated minimum maternity leave, expressed in number of weeks. The variable is then normalized from 0 to 1, with higher values representing longer durations for maternity leaves. The minimum observation in the sample is 8 weeks and the maximum is 18 weeks.
Notice Period for Dismissal	Measures the length of time in which notice must be given for unjustified dismissal (i.e., at the employer's discretion and not due to worker misconduct). Expressed in number of days. Assumes the dismissed worker has three years of seniority. The variable is normalized from 0 to 1, with higher values representing longer required notification periods. The minimum observation in the sample is 15, although several nations do not specify a required a notice period and are thus coded as 0, and the maximum observation is 60 days.
Dismissal Indemnization	Measures the one-time payment to workers dismissed for reasons other than misconduct. Expressed in number of months. Often, these payments are calculated as a mandated number of days' or weeks' wages for each year or portion of a year served. I have calculated all of these values presupposing a worker with three years of seniority. The variable is normalized from 0 to 1, with higher values representing larger severance payments. The minimum observation in the sample is 1 and the maximum is 12 months.
INDEX: Contracting Terms	Measures the protection to workers through regulation of contracting, overtime, severance pay, etc. Computed both as the sum of the normalized values of the preceding variables and as an average of the preceding contracting terms variables.

Variable	Decscription
INDEX: Individual Labor Rights Law	Measures the protection to workers from both legislation governing fixed-term contracts and general contract provisions. Computed as the sum of the two indexes above: Fixed-term contracts and Contracting terms.

Collective Relations

Collective Dismissal Authorization	This variable indicates whether prior authorization must be sought from government or unions. It takes on the following values: zero if no parties must be informed or give authorization prior to collective dismissals, 1 if workers or unions must be informed, 2 if the Ministry of Labor must be informed, and 3 if both the Ministry of Labor and unions must be informed. It is then normalized from zero to one, with higher values representing more cumbersome procedures for collective dismissals.
Government Recognition of Labor Unions	This variable indicates whether labor unions may organize independently or require authorization and recognition from the government. It takes on the following values: zero if there is no regulation, one if labor unions can organize without government approval, and two if government recognition confers legal personhood and the ability to negotiate on behalf of labor. It is then normalized from zero to one, with higher values indicating greater legal status of unions through government regulation and recognition.
Parties in Collective Bargaining	This variable indicates the number and balance of parties that are recognized by law to participate in collective bargaining. The variable takes on a value of zero if both firms and workers have one representative union or employer organization each in bargaining, a value of one if business is represented by multiple firms or organizations and workers by only one union or federation, a value of two if business is represented by only one firm or association and labor is represented by multiple unions or federations, and a value of three if both business and labor are represented by multiple bodies or organizations.
Level of Collective Bargaining	This variable indicates the level at which collective bargaining agreements take place. It takes on a value of zero if there is no governmental regulation regarding negotiation level, one if bargaining and agreements are limited to the firm level, and two if bargaining and agreements can happen at the level of economic activity/industry. The variable is then normalized from zero to one, with higher values representing negotiations at the industry level, which are generally viewed as conferring great bargaining power on unions.
Coverage of Collective Agreements	This variable indicates who is covered by collective bargaining agreements. It takes on the value of zero if there is no clear governmental regulation or individual agreements have priority over collective ones, one if union members are the only beneficiaries of collective agreements, and two if collective bargaining agreements automatically extend to all workers in a firm or economic activity. The variable is then normalized from zero to one, with higher values representing greater coverage of collective agreements, giving labor a larger population interested in collective negotiation outcomes.
INDEX: Collective Relations Law	Measures the protection of collective labor relations. Computed both as the sum of the normalized values of the preceding variables and as an average of the preceding collective variables.

Cumulative Labor Code

INDEX: Cumulative Labor Protection	Computed as the sum of the indexes for Individual Employment Law and Collective Relations Law (above).

Chapter 3

Latin American Labor Laws in Comparative Perspective

Latin American labor laws have proven more protective, and more resistant to change, than expected under globalization. But labor laws in the region are also remarkably diverse in their provisions, with some countries according workers and worker organizations rights that approximate those of European welfare states, and other countries more closely resembling the liberal economies of North America. What explains this remarkable and lasting diversity?

Existing accounts help explain patterns that distinguish Latin American labor laws from those of other regions, but do not address the causes of intraregional variation (Botero et al. 2004). And a growing body of literature helps us understand the politics of reform and resistance to reform, but not the underlying differences across cases (Madrid 2003; Murillo 2005; Murillo and Schrank 2005; Cook 2007; Kaplan 2008). To date, the extremely important work on the mid-twentieth century political incorporation of labor has not been extended to the era of globalization (Collier and Collier 2002, 1979). The burgeoning literature on the political determinants of social policy and other welfare state measures has not been equaled in, or adequately tested with regard to, national labor regulations (Mesa-Lago 1978, 1994; Murillo 2001; Madrid 2003; Müller 2003; Castiglioni 2005; Segura-Ubiergo 2007; Rudra 2008; Haggard and Kaufman 2008; Brooks 2009).

This chapter tests the theory developed in Chapter 1 to explain differences in labor laws in Latin America. That theory emphasizes structural factors—most notably the skill distribution in the economy—to account for cross-national differences. But these skill-driven structural factors do not tell the entire story. In the short run, worker organization and ties to political parties—factors that have a long history in the literature—shape the introduction of new labor legislation and the likelihood of reform. Thus skill distributions are the key to understanding long-term labor law configurations, while the political-organizational capacity of labor explains the short- and medium-term changes and developments in particular labor law measures.

The chapter begins by presenting the results of a systematic quantitative analysis of national labor codes in Latin America. To do so, it develops a dataset that permits econometric testing across the full set of cases in the region, and that provides strong evidence for the impact of skill distributions and the organizational capacity of labor in explaining cross-national labor code variation. It focuses on the period from the 1980s to the 2000s. This temporal frame is chosen for two reasons. The first is pragmatic: comparable, cross-national data of good quality is lacking before the 1980s. While some countries have reliable time series on some of the indicators of interest over this period, many do not; and even when data is available, the definitions and methodologies used in collection are different enough that meaningful comparison is rendered impossible.

More important, the analysis in this chapter concentrates on the 1980s–2000s period because this is the critical timeframe in which reform was expected to take place. The pressures for change in the late 1980s and early 1990s were enormous. Debt crises had led international financial institutions and businesses to call for liberalizing nearly every aspect of Latin American economies. Financial markets were being liberalized and high trade barriers dismantled. And the first indications were that labor laws might be rapidly flexibilized, too. Indeed, the early actions of the Fujimori government in Peru and the Menem government in Argentina seemed the harbinger of things to come. Both enacted a series of decrees that weakened job stability measures and that permitted hiring workers on a "temporary" basis, with less than full benefits. But, as will be seen below, in Argentina many of these initial measures were overturned within the first few years after their introduction, and similar measures did not spread to other countries. The result is that the 2000s labor codes look surprisingly like the 1980s labor codes. For this reason, the 1980s–2000s period constitutes an ideal laboratory for testing the theory developed above; it includes observations from the period prior to globalization, through the years of greatest reform pressure, and into the postreform equilibria of the 2000s.

The chapter proceeds as follows. Section 3.1 presents evidence on the cross-national variation in labor codes within Latin America, and highlights the continuity that labor laws today exhibit with their predecessors in the 1980s. Section 3.2 briefly reviews the theory developed earlier to explain both long-term continuity and difference, and short-term change, in labor laws. The third section presents a series of econometric tests that confirms the link between skill levels, political-organizational capacity, and labor laws. Section 3.4 further disaggregates labor law provisions to show how particular combinations of skills and organizational capacity result in distinct labor law outcomes. The final section concludes by summarizing the major findings and suggesting their implications for labor law design and reform today.

3.1. Variation in Latin American Labor Codes

Research into Latin American labor codes has highlighted two stylized facts. First, the region's labor laws tend to be quite protective by international standards. For example, nine of the major Latin American countries have provisions for hiring and firing that are on a par with, or more rigid than, those of France and Sweden; even the most liberal labor codes, in Uruguay and Chile, are only slightly more permissive than that of Belgium, and remain far from the flexibility of the United States, Canada, or Singapore (Heritage Foundation 2009). Second, Latin American labor codes did not undergo liberalization at the same rate as other economic regulations during the 1980s and 1990s; in fact, in many cases, labor laws were made more rigid during that period (Cook 2007; Murillo and Schrank 2005; Madrid 2003; Kaplan 2008; see Anner 2008 for a contrary interpretation).

To better understand these trends, Figure 3.1 presents standardized labor law scores for each country in the 1980s and in the 2000s.[1] Of the eighteen major Latin American economies, only two show a decline in their overall labor law protectiveness over this period: Peru and Colombia. The remaining countries either show no change or an increase in the rigidity of their laws.

Figure 3.2 compares the labor scores for each country in the 1980s and 2000s, and the striking continuity becomes even more apparent. The figure plots the cumulative labor code score from the 1980s, on the horizontal axis, against the cumulative labor score for the 2000s, on the vertical axis. Eight countries line up on the 45-degree line, showing no cumulative change in their labor codes, while eight are above the line, showing an increase in the protectiveness of their labor laws. Only two countries—Peru and Colombia—display a cumulative reduction in the protectiveness of their labor regulation.

In spite of these broad similarities, however, the diversity of labor law provisions

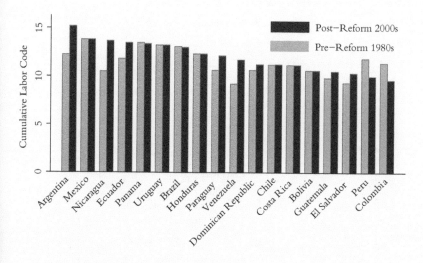

The trend in labor laws has been to maintain, or increase, labor regulation.

Figure 3.1. Cross-National Variation, with a High Degree of Stability, in Labor Codes, 1980s–2000s

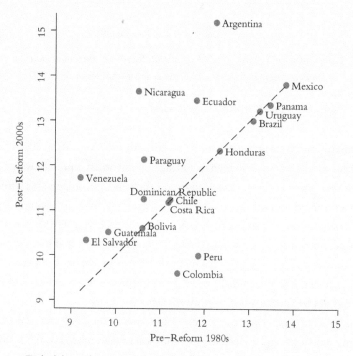

Eight labor codes were unchanged; eight increased; only two decreased.

Figure 3.2. Stability of Pre- and Post-Reform Labor Codes, 1980s–2000s

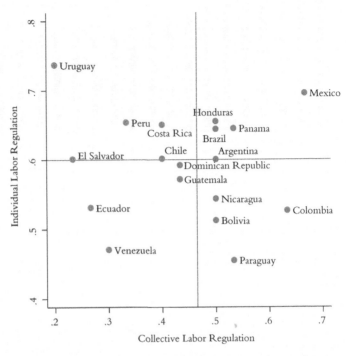

Latin American countries showed significant diversity in their combinations of laws governing individual and collective labor relations in the 1980s.

Figure 3.3. Pre-Reform Labor Codes, by Country

in Latin America is surprisingly large (Cox Edwards 1997;Vega Ruiz 2005). Some countries set severance pay so high that firing senior workers is prohibitively costly, while others provide various mechanisms for the rapid, uncompensated turnover of workers.Vacations in the region vary from a generous thirty guaranteed days of paid leave per year to a meager week. Some countries have laws that foster collective action by unions, providing certain unions with privileged status or access to funds, while other countries fragment the power of unions and curtail their political power. And intriguingly, more generous provisions in one area of labor law need not be accompanied by similar largesse in others.[2]

Figure 3.3 disaggregates the region's labor laws in the 1980s into two components: individual and collective provisions. Labor laws related to the hiring or firing of individual workers, or to individual job benefits, are measured along the vertical axis; labor laws governing the collective activity of unions and worker organizations are depicted along the horizontal axis. Higher scores indicate

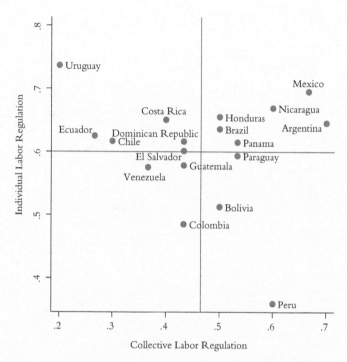

By the 1990s, the region showed increasing levels of regulation, but Peru decreased on individual regulation and Colombia decreased its collective regulation.

Figure 3.4. 1990s Reform Labor Codes, by Country

more protective laws (these are often referred to by businesses and economists as "rigid"). Cross-hairs, set at the median for each dimension, separate the figure into four quadrants. The figure is striking for the diversity of labor law combinations it presents. Countries such as Venezuela and Ecuador in the 1980s had very flexible labor codes—on both collective and individual measures—while others, most notably Mexico, had highly protective provisions on both counts. In contrast, Peru and Uruguay combined rigid individual provisions with weak guarantees of collective activity by workers; and Paraguay, Bolivia, Colombia, and Nicaragua protected the collective capacity of unions but were relatively weak on individuals' labor rights.

Figure 3.4 shows several kinds of realignments in the 1990s. The cross-hairs are maintained at their prereform levels, in order to facilitate observation of the changes through time. First, as noted above, the countries that were weakest on both measures each improve on at least one indicator, meaning that the unregu-

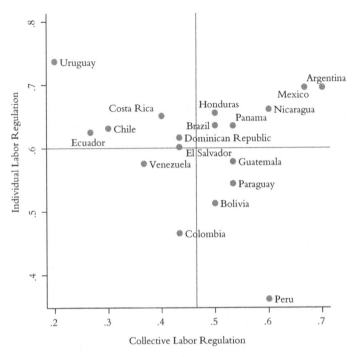

The 2000s showed little change from the 1990s. Labor law regimes are diverse but tend to be stable. Nearly all countries stay in the same quadrant throughout the 1980s–2000s period.

Figure 3.5. Post-Reform Labor Codes, by Country

lated, lower-left-hand portion of the figure is now nearly empty. Uruguay continues to stand out in the upper-left-hand section, but it is joined by Chile and Ecuador—the former because it weakened protections on collective activity and the latter because it improved individual worker protections. Peru, which under Fujimori implemented one of the most radical restructurings of individual employment policy in the region, moves to the bottom-right-hand quadrant. Colombia falls on both the collective and individual measures, while Bolivia remains unchanged. Finally, in the upper-right quadrant of Figure 3.4, Argentina moves past Mexico as the most highly protective labor regime in the region. Nicaragua also sees a significant increase in both its individual and collective labor regulations.

Figure 3.5, which again maintains the cross-hairs at the preform level, shows that only minor changes in the labor policy regimes occurred in the region in the 2000s. Strikingly, no globalization-driven convergence has taken place

(Drezner 2001; Kaplan 2013). Even with the regulation introduced in the 1990s, most countries remain in the same quadrant of the figure that they inhabited in the 1980s. What explains this pattern of persistent difference? A suitable answer must take into account both short-term factors that can explain the increased regulation of the 1990s and also the overall stability of national labor law regimes over the long term. The following section develops a theory of political opportunities and structural constraints to explain this phenomenon.

3.2. A Theory of Labor Laws

Labor laws are the product of economic and political dynamics. But the process by which this occurs remains contested in the existing literature. One strand of theorizing emphasizes the top-down policy-making process, in which aspiring or ruling elites use labor laws as "inducements and constraints" to control or win the support of the industrial working class (Collier and Collier 1979, 2002). In another formulation, the bottom-up political action of the working class, motivated by ideology, worker solidarity, or inspired leadership, produces demands and mobilization for particular legal protections (Godio 2006; Torres 2004; Valenzuela 1979). Political parties on the left and populist presidents have been hypothesized to be the critical political link between supply and demand of labor legislation (Murillo 2001; Collier and Collier 2002; Burgess 2004). The legacies of previous governments and their policies are also seen as crucial in the kinds of reforms undertaken by subsequent governments (Cook 2007). And a final strand of analysis brings economic interests to the fore, considering the interests and actions of businesses and employers (Schneider 2009; Thorp and Bertram 1978).

However, while this rich body of work has constructed compelling accounts of punctual labor law reforms (and resistance to reforms) in particular countries, it struggles to describe the larger picture of labor regulation across Latin American cases. And alternative accounts that are more explicitly cross-national treat local political and economic factors as epiphenomenal to labor law configurations; they collapse all Latin American cases into a single labor law regime because of their shared origin in French civil law (Botero et al. 2004). The theory developed below seeks to remedy these shortcomings by accounting for both long-term variation across countries, grounded in national structures of production, and shorter-term reform measures, explained by the political-organizational capacity of labor actors.

Economic Structure: Differing Skill Distributions

The structure of production of an economy—which is dictated by resource endowments of capital and labor—makes certain types of labor relations more or less likely. Given by nature, geography, and early settlement patterns, resource endowments form the foundation for later economic exploitation and development, and their effect tends to be extremely long lasting.[3]

Among resource endowments, skill distributions are particularly important to a country's production function, and they are critical to understanding long-term labor law equilibria. Skill levels have direct effects on worker productivity and worker suitability for diverse tasks. Governments have incentives to take skill levels into account when formulating economic policy and legislation. Indeed, recent work has shown that worker skill levels and patterns of capital formation and investment go hand in hand, as labor, business, and government coordinate around the perceived resource constraints of each country. In Latin America, a "low skill trap" has been credited with contributing to the distinct type of "hierarchical market capitalism" that predominates in the region (Schneider 2009; Schneider and Soskice 2011).

The *distribution* of skill levels in the economy is crucial to the dynamics of the labor market and the institutions that govern them. Where the workforce is largely homogenous and unskilled, workers can be easily substituted for one another. Individual workers have little capacity to make demands that will affect the overall labor force. In fact, when a few skilled workers find themselves in a largely unskilled society, they have an incentive to forgo broad mobilizing and instead seek to negotiate private benefits. These benefits may include special contract provisions or special sectoral legislation that applies only to them or the industries in which they work. The majority in the unskilled workforce, on the other hand, will have little economic reason to undertake collective action (since employers will retaliate and defection will be rewarded). Employers will be able to bid down wages and contract provisions. And governments that intervene to impose politically motivated legislation will find those policies have distortionary effects, and eventually they will be met with pressure for reform.

As the workforce becomes more heterogeneous, and especially as skilled workers become the majority, workers become less interchangeable. Both employers and workers have incentives to seek legislation that will facilitate worker stability. Investments in skill-acquisition (firm-level training for employers, or schooling or apprenticeships for workers) makes both parties seek to limit disruptions or displacement in individual labor relations. And when higher-skilled workers constitute a significant portion of the workforce, legislating broad measures to guarantee job security and benefits is simplified. Similarly, skilled workers' shared interests (even across industries) may make it easier for them to coordinate to strike and "hold up" not just a firm or an industry but the entire economy. Thus where *mean worker skill levels* are higher, in equilibrium the labor legislation is likely to favor protective, or rigid, individual labor contracts.

Skill distributions thus present a crucial foundation for long-term labor market equilibria. Labor legislation that reflects this equilibrium is likely to be longlasting, while legislation that deviates from it is likely to face mounting economic pressure for change.

Political-Organizational Capacity of Labor

While the distribution of skills provides an underlying economic rationale for labor law equilibria, it does not explain how and when such legislation will be proposed or reformed. Worker interests are likely to have little force until they are coordinated, and brought into the "political arena" in which policy is formulated. Political action is required. I call the capacity for political action the *organizational capacity of labor*. It consists of several factors, including many factors drawn from earlier studies of labor law formulation and reform cited above, such as unity or solidarity, a shared ideology, leadership, mechanisms for interest representation and expression, and economic resources to undertake costly action. As the workforce becomes larger and more heterogeneous, these means of organization become increasingly important. Workers' unions and confederations may serve many of these functions of coordination and organization among the labor force.

In order to influence legislation, organized labor requires linkages to political power. These linkages may arise as direct consequences of the size and organization of the movement, as workers coordinate to take to the streets in strikes and manifestations or take to the ballot box to support a preferred candidate. But they may also be fostered through ties to political parties; indeed, in Latin America, parties have sought to build lasting linkages to particular labor unions or federations. Alternatively, some populist leaders have concentrated on building worker-led coalitions to support their rule. To the extent that labor has such institutionalized ties to power through parties or direct ties to populist executives, it may be more effective in securing protective legislation.

In particular, organized labor focuses on achieving protection of its own status as a collective body. Labor leaders seek regulations that allow them to remain in privileged positions, and unions themselves seek greater economic resources and independence. Employers may be willing to concede such regulation if it comes with regularized structures for collective bargaining and wage moderation. And sitting governments may embrace collective labor legislation as a way of cementing the political support of large groups of workers. Thus as organizational capacity grows, we expect both a greater capability for short-term action regarding labor law formulation and reform, and an increase in protective legislation regarding collective action.

Labor Law Regimes based on Skill Levels and Organizational Capacity

Based on the hypotheses generated above regarding the skill distribution within the economy and the organizational capacity of labor, labor regulation may be described by four broad "labor regulation regimes." These are summarized in Figure 3.6 below. The horizontal axis indicates the degree of organizational capacity of the labor movement, incorporating each of the factors described above. The vertical axis represents the distribution of skills in the economy, ranging from homogeneous, unskilled labor to a middle range of increasingly skilled labor to an economy of workers with high levels of specific skills.

The area closest to the origin in Figure 3.6 represents an economy with little or no skilled labor and no organized labor movement. It exhibits very little regulation that is protective of labor, either individually or collectively. This is an unbridled "free" market in the truest sense: regulation either does not exist, or it is designed to facilitate the movement of labor through simplified hiring and firing procedures.

As the skill level increases in the economy, workers are able to demand greater protection because their absence, resulting from strikes or exit, presents a higher "hold up" cost to the economy. As a result, employers may willingly grant more protective labor contracts, or they may form a coalition with skilled workers in favor of protective labor laws, as both have incentives to foster job stability. Workers seek assurance of higher wages or better returns on their investment in skills, and employers anticipate higher productivity from their skilled workers. I expect the result to be highly protective legislation governing individual

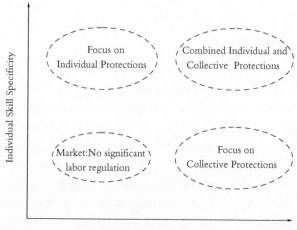

Organizational Capacity of Labor

Figure 3.6. Predictions Regarding Labor Law Configurations

contracts. Where skills are concentrated in a narrow segment of the workforce, this legislation may be selective, focused only on the key skilled sectors. The legislation may not make any provision regarding collective labor relations, since worker organization is low in this quadrant.

As the organizational capacity of workers increases—along the horizontal axis in Figure 3.6—workers can threaten coordinated action against the government or economy. At the extreme, economy-wide encompassing worker organizations internalize the costs of their own individual-level demands, and thus moderate their calls for increased wages and more protective job protections. Instead, they focus on collective rights, which confer potential power in later bargaining rounds. Thus in the lower-right-hand quadrant, we observe higher collective protections but we do not see a similar rise in individual protections.

Finally, the combination of widespread skill diffusion in the economy and a labor force with high collective action potential produces the upper-right-hand outcome in Figure 3.6, in which both individual worker contracts and collective relations are highly protected. Here, many workers have critical skills and unions are highly organized and united. Encompassing union confederations and professional organizations unite differentiated workers with a shared interest in job stability and continued organizational strength, and they are ripe targets for overtures from political parties or populist governments.

3.3. Testing the Determinants of Labor Code Provisions: Quantitative Analysis

The next two sections test the theory sketched above using data on labor codes for the 1980s through 2000s, as described in the previous chapter. The dependent variable is a continuous cumulative score for each country's labor laws: a snapshot that facilitates easy comparison across cases. In employing such a continuous measure of national labor codes, this analysis differs from earlier work that examines the determinants of discrete changes in particular labor law provisions using discrete-choice models (for example, Murillo, Ronconi, and Schrank 2011). Instead, it follows a modeling strategy similar to work in economics that examines aggregate labor code variation across a broad sample of international cases using regression models (Botero et al. 2004). In the following paragraphs I describe each of the variables included in the models.

Distribution of Worker Skill Levels

The distribution of worker skill levels in the economy was hypothesized to indicate the general structure of production in the economy, which functions as a critical constraint on demands for labor regulations from both workers and employers. I employ a measure of *years of schooling*—the average cumulative number of years of schooling for the population over fifteen years of age—as a proxy for the distribution of worker skills.[4] Average schooling figures indicate more than simply the mean educational attainment in an economy, as they are highly correlated with the distribution of skill complexity in the economy. Economic studies have shown that where average educational attainment is higher, there is also greater heterogeneity of worker skills (Bombardini et al. 2012). In other words, where general skill levels are higher, so too are skill profiles more differentiated in the economy.

Differentially skilled workers, the theory has argued, are likely to have greater capacity to "hold up" the economy, or to harm particular businesses should they go on strike or exit to other firms. In settings where production is highly differentiated, both workers and employers have a shared interest in establishing predictable labor relations that ensure worker stability. This is all the more true in settings in which firms invest in costly training for their workers in specific tasks that may not be portable to other firms or industries. Thus we expect to see the *years of schooling* measure correlated with the protectiveness of the labor code.[5] In addition, we expect skill levels to particularly affect provisions for hiring and firing of individual workers, since the investment in skill acquisition is an individual investment.

Political-Organizational Capacity

Political-organizational capacity, as outlined above, is a complex concept composed of labor solidarity, talented and united worker leadership, and connections to the political system through political parties. I operationalize this political-organizational capacity of labor with data on *union density*—the percentage of the nonagricultural workforce that belongs to labor unions.[6] This measure reflects realized capacities: it indicates how successful unions have been at attracting members. It implicitly reflects worker evaluations of the perceived strength of unions, the capabilities of their leadership, and their likelihood to obtain benefits in wages, workplace practices, or legislation. Admittedly, though, it obscures other important aspects of organizational capacity, such as the latent pool of "good" leaders in the labor movement, or the underlying solidarity of workers in the economy, or linkages between labor unions and particular political parties. Nevertheless, the realized capacities of labor organizations serve as a hard standard for measuring the relative strength and resources of the labor movement, and thus constitute a good proxy for the analysis that follows. I expect that greater political-organizational capacity will be correlated with more protective labor laws, and that this effect will be strongest for laws governing collective labor relations. Unions have an interest in protecting and preserving their own rights and benefits, so their strength will be marshaled to achieve more ample collective freedoms.

Alternative Hypotheses

Regime type may play an important role in the labor legislation of Latin American nations (Haggard and Kaufman 2008; Carnes and Mares 2007). The literature suggests that democratic regimes, because they must cater to a broad swath of the population in order to win election or remain in office, will be more redistributive than autocracies and target more legislation to the needs of the median voter (who in an unequal, democratic society, will have an income below the mean) (Meltzer and Richard 1981). Historically, however, most labor protections—including job security measures and pension plans, as well as rules for collective bargaining and union representation—were established under authoritarian governments. Given these contradictory theoretical predictions, I choose to remain agnostic in the analysis below about the effects of regime type on labor legislation.[7]

Partisanship may also shape labor legislation. The literature has frequently suggested that parties on the left of the political spectrum are more apt to pass legislation favorable to workers when in power (Murillo 2001; Calvo and Murillo 2004). Reasons for this behavior can be ideological or pragmatic, but in either case left parties are theorized to be more responsive to the calls of workers for more social spending, labor legislation, or policies protective of their interests.[8] Because the literature suggests that left party governance often has a cumulative effect, or subsequent governments may react against the partisan behavior of their predecessors, in the models below I include both the contemporaneous vote shares and the preceding decade lagged vote shares for parties on the left.

I also include a number of control variables in my statistical testing. First, *population* is taken to indicate the size of the available labor force, which Marx expected to function as an "industrial reserve army" of homogenous workers, all competing for scarce jobs, and "hold[ing] the pretensions [of the active labor force] in check" by demanding *less* protective labor legislation (Marx 1978: 422–27). Next, *economic development* and *growth* have long been argued to give rise to increased welfare state policies and may thus have an effect on labor laws; in previous studies, the evidence for this relationship is strong for the OECD countries, but weaker for the developing world (Wilensky 1975; Huber and Stephens 2001; Adsera and Boix 2002; Mares 2005). I thus include measures of GDP per capita and economic growth below.

International economic ties and competition may affect labor law configurations. *Trade* may lead governments with more open economies to enact social programs to compensate workers who may be threatened by external competition (Cameron 1978; Katzenstein 1985; Rodrik 1998). In my analysis, I include the literature's standard measure of trade—exports plus imports as a percentage of GDP. In addition, in the era of globalization, *foreign direct investment* (FDI) may play a role in diminishing violations of labor rights—either by bringing "best practices" regarding labor to newly installed factories, or by attracting the oversight of NGOs concerned about labor violations under FDI (Mosley and Uno 2007; Greenhill et al. 2009). I include measures of both FDI stocks and flows in my analysis below. The sources employed for all independent variables are described in Table 3.A at the end of the chapter.

OLS Results for National Labor Regulations

Given the relatively small number of available observations and concerns about serial correlation among the observations for each country, I employ ordinary least-squares (OLS) regression models with standard errors clustered by country. Table 3.1 reports the results for five models of the determinants of labor regulations in Latin America. Model 1 is bare bones, focusing on the two hypothesized determinants of labor regulation regimes. Union density, the proxy for organizational capacity, is statistically significant and positive, consistent with the theory's expectations. Likewise, years of schooling, the proxy for skill levels

Table 3.1. Determinants of Labor Regulation in 18 Latin American Countries, 1980s–2000s

(Dependent Variable: Cumulative Labor Regulation Score)

VARIABLES	(1) Base Model	(2) With Democracy	(3) With Partisanship	(4) Economic Controls	(5) Preferred Model
Union Density	0.0408**	0.0402**	0.0427	0.0481**	0.0516**
	(0.0162)	(0.0164)	(0.0292)	(0.0176)	(0.0198)
Years Schooling	0.417**	0.459**	0.390*	0.334	0.411**
	(0.156)	(0.183)	(0.188)	(0.262)	(0.149)
Population				0.250	
				(0.377)	
GDP per capita				0.141	
				(0.943)	
GDP growth				−0.0314	
				(0.0630)	
Trade				0.0228	
				(0.0167)	
FDI Stocks				0.0223	
				(0.0144)	
FDI Flows				−0.118	
				(0.0898)	
Left Vote			0.00550		
			(0.0192)		
Lagged Left Vote			−0.0309*		−0.0250***
			(0.0156)		(0.00710)
Democracy		−0.307			
		(0.446)			
Constant	8.763***	8.707***	9.440***	2.562	9.217***
	(0.893)	(0.891)	(1.481)	(5.787)	(0.973)
Observations	53	53	22	51	46
R-squared	0.287	0.296	0.386	0.370	0.352

Robust standard errors in parentheses.

*** p<0.01, ** p<0.05, * p<0.1.

and distributions, is statistically significant and positive. Substantively, the effect of years of schooling is quite large: an increase of one standard deviation from the mean (5.7 years to 7.2 years) would move a country up by 0.54, which is slightly less than the difference between Honduras and Brazil. The effect of union density, despite its seemingly small coefficient, is even larger. A one standard deviation increase from the mean of union density (16.7 percent to 27.9 percent) would move the labor score up by 0.61, which is about half the difference between Peru and Costa Rica.[9] Given that the cumulative labor score varies within the region from a score of 9.19 to a score of 15.19 (mean 11.83), these effects of increased schooling and union density imply a one-third standard deviation change in a country's cumulative score, or roughly 10 percent of the existing variation in the region.

Model 2 adds a dummy variable for democratic regimes to the first model. Consistent with the historical observation that social policies and labor regulations have been developed under nondemocracy, the coefficient for democracy is negative. However, the results are not large enough to justify crediting regime type with causal influence in either direction. Both union density and skill levels retain their positive coefficients and statistical significance in Model 2.

Model 3 considers the influence of left parties and the partisan makeup of governments. It employs two different variables. First, it includes a variable for the *contemporary* share of left party votes for the lower house in each country. This variable has a positive, but not statistically significant, effect. Any effect of the sitting government on the cumulative labor code is too weak to detect in this model. However, the *legacy* of partisan governments in the previous decade exerts pressure in the opposite direction. Having had more left-leaning governments in the decade prior to the labor law observation is associated with lower labor protection scores in the present. This may mean that past experiences of left-leaning government pushes subsequent governments to be more reactionary, consistent with one of the theories advanced by Cook (2007). The coefficient on union density narrowly fails to achieve statistical significance in this model, and the years of schooling variable only does so at the 10 percent level, but the values of the coefficients are largely consistent with the previous models.

Model 4 adds a battery of economic control variables. Neither population nor income per capita nor growth rates have significant effects. Likewise, trade, and FDI stocks and flows, do not have statistically significant effects. Admittedly, in Model 5, the coefficient on years of schooling does not attain statistical significance. Given the small number of observations and the large number of co-variates being estimated, as well as the likely correlation between the economic variables and the years of schooling measure (which is employed as a proxy for the country's production function), the reduced significance of years of school-ing is to be expected.

Model 5 presents a preferred model by dropping variables that have not reached statistical significance in previous models. In this model, both union density and skill distributions are associated with more rigid, protective labor codes, while a legacy of a more left leaning government is associated with more flexibilized labor codes. Thus at the aggregate level, labor codes are a function of both economic structural constraints and political mobilizations and reactions.

3.4. Disaggregating the Components of the Labor Code

The analysis thus far has focused on the cumulative labor code as a dependent variable. But Figures 3.3 through 3.5 above showed that the components of the labor code also vary significantly, and that individual and collective regulations can be combined in a variety of ways across Latin American cases. Further, earlier analyses have suggested that individual and collective regulations may undergo different reform processes, and indeed may be explained by different political and economic causal factors (Cook 2007; Murillo 2005; Murillo and Schrank 2005). Therefore, I disaggregate the cumulative labor regulation score into two separate dependent variables: an individual component and a collective component.

Simply estimating separate OLS equations for each of these dependent vari-ables is likely to produce inefficient parameter estimates since the equations will be linked by their disturbances. Therefore, I employ seemingly unrelated regression, a method that applies generalized least-squares regression to the system of equations to be estimated without the efficiency loss of OLS (Zell-ner 1962; Greene 2003). This procedure simultaneously estimates equations for each of the dependent variables of interest, allowing the researcher to observe the impact of hypothesized independent variables on each. Table 3.2 presents the results. Given the small size of the dataset, I only model the principal inde-pendent variables based on my theory and the earlier analyses of the cumula-tive labor codes; however, the inclusion of other controls does not substantively change the findings.

Table 3.2.   Determinants of Individual and Collective Labor Laws,
18 Latin American Countries, 1980s–2000s

VARIABLES	(6a) Indiv. Laws	(6b) Collective Laws	(7a) Indiv. Laws	(7b) Collective Laws	(8a) Indiv. Laws	(8b) Collective Laws
Union Density	0.0250	0.0158**	0.0250	0.0152**	0.0254	0.0169*
	(0.0157)	(0.00784)	(0.0157)	(0.00764)	(0.0224)	(0.00912)
Years Schooling	0.417***	0.000105	0.415***	0.0437	0.438*	−0.0448
	(0.117)	(0.0586)	(0.128)	(0.0623)	(0.234)	(0.0951)
Democracy			0.0141	−0.321*	0.0890	−0.144
			(0.381)	(0.185)	(0.637)	(0.259)
Left Vote					0.0344	−0.0282***
					(0.0213)	(0.00867)
Lagged Left Vote					−0.0378**	0.00640
					(0.0172)	(0.00700)
Constant	6.732***	2.031***	6.735***	1.972***	6.640***	2.822***
	(0.723)	(0.362)	(0.726)	(0.354)	(1.647)	(0.670)
Observations	53	53	53	53	22	22
R-squared	0.235	0.071	0.235	0.121	0.283	0.541

Seemingly Unrelated Regression Models. Standard errors in parentheses.
   *** $p<0.01$, ** $p<0.05$, * $p<0.1$.

Equation 6a examines the principal determinants of the individual labor regulation scores. Union density has a positive effect, as before, but it does not reach conventional levels of statistical significance. However, years of schooling has a positive, statistically significant relationship with individual labor regulation. Equation 6b conducts a similar analysis of the determinants of collective labor regulation scores. Here, union density has a positive, statistically significant effect, while the years of schooling variable loses significance. Taken together, these two models suggest that union density exerts its influence on the overall labor code by increasing the protectiveness of laws that govern the *collective action* of workers, while skill levels impact the overall labor code by increasing the laws that govern *individual employment* relations. This is consistent with the theory developed above.

   Equations 7a and 7b add a variable for democracy to the previous models, and the significant correlation between union density and collective laws, and years of schooling and individual laws, is unchanged. A negative effect of democracy (at the 10 percent level) appears on the collective labor laws; increased democracy is associated with less protective regulation of collective action, perhaps because under democracy such collective action is presumed to be the norm and thus to require less explicit legal protection.

   Models 9a and 9b further add left vote shares and lagged left vote shares to the estimations. This reduces the number of observations, and as a result the correlations between union density and collective laws, and years of schooling and individual laws, fall to the 10 percent level. Nevertheless, the consistent pattern of association between these variables is shown to be quite robust. In addition, left votes in the current period are correlated with reduced protections of collective relations, while left votes in previous periods are associated with reduced regulations on individual hiring and working conditions. The first suggests that left parties in power have a greater space in which to dismantle measures that protect the status of their organized supporters, perhaps because unions feel safer when the left party is in power (and the party in power may control other resources to compensate unions in the short term). The latter finding suggests that the legacy of left-party governance may have created pressures for competitive reforms, especially regarding individual worker contracting.

To sum up thus far, the evidence from the statistical testing of the cumulative labor codes and their components provides considerable support for the hypotheses developed above. The importance of the organizational capacity of labor and the skill level of workers in the economy come through particularly clearly, and each has a greater effect in the policy realm to which it is more closely related by the theory. Democracy has only a very limited effect on labor codes, in some specifications, while partisanship has divergent effects across individual and collective labor law outcomes.

The Determinants of Labor Law "Regimes"

The theory above suggested four hypothetical combinations of individual and collective labor laws, calling them labor regulation "regimes" or types. These are summarized graphically in Figure 3.7. The outcomes range from no regulation of either individual contracts or collective contracts (Quadrant I), to systems that protect individual contracts but not collective organizing rights (II), to those that protect collective rights without protecting individual labor relations (III), and finally to those that protect both individual and collective labor regulations (IV).

Thus far, the econometric testing has focused primarily on estimating the determinants of the additive total of labor protections, on the one hand, and its disaggregated components—individual and collective—on the other. However, these models have not yet tested the relationship between skills, labor organization, and the four possible labor law regimes suggested by the theory.

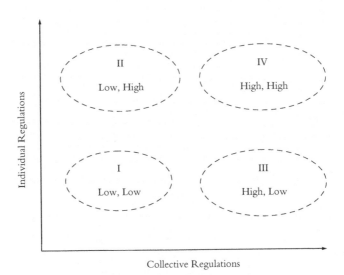

Figure 3.7. Testing for Labor Law "Regimes"

I employ a multinomial logit estimation to test for determinants of selection into one of the four hypothesized labor regulation regimes. Multinomial logit estimates the determinants of a categorical dependent variable that is nominal rather than ordinal. This modeling technique "can be thought of as simultaneously estimating binary logits for all possible comparisons among the outcome categories" (Long 1997: 149). I choose to set Quadrant I as the reference category because it involves no (or little) labor regulation; it therefore constitutes the theoretical "null" case of a labor market without government legal intervention. The models estimated with logit seek to explain departures from this comparison category of no regulation, implicitly answering the question, "Which factors are most important in explaining movement from no regulation to the legal regime described in each category?"

Given the small number of observations in this dataset, the findings in the multinomial logit estimation can only be taken as suggestive. In addition, the process being modeled may only imperfectly fit with logit's presumption of proportional substitution among categories, since states may more readily switch between some quadrants than others (Train 2003: 51–52). Thus I interpret my results in this section to constitute a robustness check on my earlier findings, and to give some intuition about the plausibility of the theoretical claims about the four possible labor law regimes detailed above.

Table 3.3. Determinants of Selection into Labor Regulation Regimes

	(9)	(10)
Quadrant II		
Years Schooling	0.676★★★	0.832★★
	(0.262)	(0.290)
Union Density	0.053	0.087
	(0.054)	(0.067)
Lagged Left Vote		−0.011
		(1.211)
Constant	−4.654★★★	−5.594★★
	(1.747)	(2.454)
Quadrant III		
Years Schooling	0.355	0.632★
	(0.286)	(0.349)
Union Density	0.069	0.176★★★
	(0.050)	(0.061)
Lagged Left Vote		−0.079★★
		(0.038)
Constant	−2.860★	−4.035★★
	(1.687)	(1.897)
Quadrant IV		
Years Schooling	0.373	0.548
	(0.366)	(0.341)
Union Density	0.110★★	0.243★★★
	(0.052)	(0.073)
Lagged Left Vote		−0.118★★★
		(0.037)
Constant	−3.627	−4.183★
	(2.576)	(2.183)
Observations	53	46
Wald χ^2	8.84	51.74
Prob > χ^2	0.18	0.00
Log-pseudolikelihood	−66.56	−47.91
Pseudo R-squared	0.09	0.25

Multinomial logit coefficients are reported with clustered standard errors (by country) in parentheses. Quadrant I is the comparison group. ★★★ $p<0.01$, ★★ $p<0.05$, ★ $p<0.1$.

Table 3.3 presents the results of two models estimated using multinomial logit. Given the demands I am making on this small dataset, I limit the independent variables in Model 9 to those highlighted by my theory and in Model 10 add the lagged left vote share, which has been consistently significant in previous analyses. I concentrate discussion of the findings on Model 10.

First, years of schooling, the proxy for skill levels, is statistically significant in both models comparing selection into Quadrant II rather than Quadrant I. This implies that skill levels play a role in movement along the vertical axis, as predicted by the theory. However, skill levels do not play a significant role in explaining selection into Quadrant IV, as the theory would have predicted. This may be the result of the problems of using multinomial logit on this small dataset, or may indicate that the effect of skill levels is weaker in settings with high levels of unionization.

Second, union density, the proxy for the political-organizational capacity of labor, is significant and positive (as expected) in the models comparing selection into Quadrants III and IV rather than Quadrant I. I take this as support for the hypothesis that organizational capacity works most directly to foment more protective collective regulations, which movement into Quadrants III and IV represents. In accounting for movement from the left to the right along the horizontal axis, union density is the best predictor in the models.

Finally, the lagged left vote plays a significant, negative role in the models for movement toward all three quadrants. This means that countries that had labor-friendly, left-leaning parties in power in the previous period are more likely to see their labor codes liberalized (reduced) in the present period.

Taken together, the findings regarding disaggregated labor code measures and labor law regimes provide an interesting perspective on the role of partisanship. First, the multinomial logit models suggest that, consistent with Cook (2007), the legacy of left-leaning parties in power makes countries ripe for liberal reforms; the lagged left-vote share is significantly correlated with labor law retrenchment in the present period. And second, when combined with the models of individual and collective provisions (especially 8a and 8b), left-leaning parties that are currently in power are more likely to introduce and carry out liberalizing reforms toward their own supporters. Interestingly, past governance by the left makes individual labor laws the target of reform, while current governance by the left makes collective laws the target of reform.

3.5. Conclusion

This chapter has tested several political and economic explanations of labor law variation, finding consistent support for the importance of structural economic factors (as observed in skill distributions, proxied by the average years of schooling) and the organizational capacity of labor (as proxied by union density figures) in the shape of the overall labor code. Further, each of these variables seems to exert an independent effect on portions of the labor code, with skill levels more closely related to individual protections and organizational capacity more closely tied to the collective labor laws. The level of democracy has no significant effect on the overall labor code, but may play a role in the shaping of collective labor relations. Partisanship seems to have an effect through its legacies, with a history of left-governments being associated with less protective labor laws. And current left-party strength is also associated with less permissive laws governing collective action.

Further, the multinomial logit analysis has suggested in a preliminary fashion that the four hypothesized labor regulation "regimes" are distinct analytic outcomes that correlate significantly with skill levels and union density. Thus these variables help us understand not simply total (additive) protections, or even elements of the labor code, but the *combinations* of elements that make the labor codes distinct across countries.

This chapter makes several significant contributions over earlier efforts at understanding labor regulation in Latin America. First, it highlights important variation across countries in the design of labor codes. By employing a quantitative dataset that describes the labor code as a whole, rather than concentrating only on reform measures, it turns attention to the heterogeneity of Latin American labor laws. To date, no other study of which I am aware has decomposed labor codes this thoroughly or suggested how components complement one another in labor law "regimes."

Second, it brings both long- and short-term political and economic factors into its explanation of variation in labor laws. Earlier cross-national work had collapsed Latin American cases into a homogenous set of colonial legal code–driven labor regimes, in which economic factors and political contestation over the last century were largely epiphenomenal. This chapter suggests that local economic conditions and political factors matter, and that these have meaningful impacts on the design of labor regulations across countries.

Intriguingly, though, this chapter has shown that labor codes are not explained by precisely the same political and economic processes as other social welfare policies. Some of the best correlates of social spending, such as trade openness, do not bear a statistically significant relationship to labor code protectiveness. This suggests that workers and employers—and governments—view labor legislation as a distinct policy realm, and it may account for why labor relations lag behind all other areas of the economy on the reform agenda. Long-term structural conditions, seen most clearly in worker skill distributions, function as a constraint on labor law design. And existing political-organizational capacity among workers and their ties to political parties shape the likelihood and design of reforms when they are considered.

Of course, the quantitative analysis carried out here can only detect aggregate patterns of labor law formulation and reform, and this analysis is further limited by its temporal scope because of data availability.[10] Additional work is needed to better specify and trace the political processes by which economic structural factors are translated into labor laws. Adequately testing these processes requires careful single-country and comparative case histories that examine competing demands of workers of different skill levels, employers in diverse industries, and governments of different partisan stripes. Such relationships should be examined not just in the reform period of recent decades, but in a particular way in the early years of labor law formulation. Indeed, examining the earliest labor laws allows the researcher to observe the exogenous impact of skill distributions and worker organizations on nascent labor codes. The following three chapters undertake exactly this kind of process-tracing.

Appendix Table 3.A. Data Sources for Independent Variables

The data in this chapter are drawn from various sources. Data on the dependent variable is based on Vega Ruiz (2005), coded by the author according to the rules summarized in Table 2.A, above. Data for independent variables are drawn from the sources summarized below.

Variable	Definition	Source
Union Density	Union members as percent of nonagricultural labor force	Assembled from several sources, including International Labor Organization 1997; Martín Rama and Raquel Artecona 2002; various country-level and international reports
Years Schooling	Mean years of schooling in the total population aged 15 and older, 1985, 1995, circa 2005	Barro, Robert J., and Jong-Wha Lee 2000, accessed through updated dataset online
Manufacturing Employment	Share of total employment in manufacturing	Montevideo-Oxford Latin American Economic History Database, accessed at http://oxlad.qeh.ox.ac.uk/
Regime Type	Dummy variable for democracy, semidemocracy, or autocracy *In robustness checks:* Dummy variable for democracy or autocracy Combined Polity scale, with a range of −10 (autocracy) to 10 (democracy)	Mainwaring, Scott, Daniel Brinks, and Aníbal Pérez-Liñán 2000; with extensions by author Przeworski et al. 2000; with extensions by author Polity IV database. See www.bsos.umd.edu/cidcm/inscr/polity

Variable	Definition	Source
Government Partisanship	Percentage of total valid vote in elections for the lower or sole house of the legislature, for parties classified as left or right, averaged across all elections in the applicable decade	Coppedge, Michael 1998; 1997
Population	Natural logarithm of national population, averaged over each decade	World Bank, World Development Indicators (2007), author's calculations
Income per capita	Natural logarithm of GDP per capita, calculated using purchasing power parity, averaged over each decade	World Bank, World Development Indicators 2007, author's calculations
Trade	Total exports and imports as percent of GDP; averaged over each decade	World Bank, World Development Indicators 2007, Author's calculations
GDP Growth	Annual percent change in GDP per capita, averaged over each decade	World Bank, World Development Indicators 2007, author's calculations
FDI Stock	Total stock of foreign direct investment, averaged over each decade	Mosley and Uno 2007 replication data
FDI Flows	Flow of foreign direct investment, averaged over each decade	Mosley and Uno 2007 replication data

Chapter 4

Fragmented Individualism: Professional Labor Regulation in Chile

When thirty-three miners were discovered alive seven hundred meters under the surface of the earth in Copiapó, Chile, on 5 August 2010, after the collapse of a roof in the San José copper and gold mine, a world audience gained an unprecedented look into Chilean labor practices. They saw the whole nation rally around the cause of the miners, with newly elected president, Sebastian Piñera, personally overseeing the rescue effort. Millions watched live as all thirty-three miners were safely pulled to the surface, one by one, in the NASA-designed *Fénix 2* module, sixty-nine days after the initial accident. The arrival of Florencio Avalos, the first miner successfully rescued, evoked a massive cheer from the group of families and assembled rescuers outside the mine, and tears from the international viewing audience.

Chile put on display the complex and contradictory characteristics of its labor code, and underlying labor market institutions, throughout the affair. The nation's profound respect for the miners, and the dignity of work in general, was unequivocal. All over the country citizens expressed their respect for the sacrifice of the miners, working in the northern desert under the difficult conditions that characterize mineral extraction. An outpouring of solidarity was palpable, not least because of every Chilean's deep understanding of the importance of the mines—and the copper extracted from them—to the country's economy and social spending. Chilean miners' wages, which make them the highest paid miners in South America, are generally perceived by their countrymen as well-deserved remuneration for the onerous, yet critical, work they embrace (*The*

Economist 2006). Their rights were invoked as inspiration in the painstakingly urgent, and complex, work of the rescue effort.

Yet at the same time, the country's mixed results in protecting the dignity and safety of the miners were also evident. Chile's inspectors had fined the owners of the mine—the Compañía Minera San Esteban (CMSE)—forty-two times in the previous six years, and the San José mine itself had only recently been reopened, in 2008, after the death of a miner. It came to light that the country had only three inspectors dedicated to monitoring the Atacama region's 884 mines, and only sixteen safety auditors for more than 4,500 mines in the entire country (Govan et al. 2010). In fact, ladders required by the safety code, which would have facilitated the escape of the miners through a ventilation shaft, were missing.

And in spite of miners' high wages and respected position, their labor union's voice was weak and hardly heard. The Sindicato de la Minera San Esteban limited its demands to assurances of government assistance, first in providing lost wages and benefits to the trapped miners, and second in relocating the rest of the miners from the San José mine who had been in limbo since the mine's collapse. A wider movement of union outrage regarding the mining disaster did not materialize.

A year later, observers who continued to pay attention to the story's developments were surprised that the miners were entitled to return to their jobs. One year after the rescue, half of the group said they wanted to return to their underground jobs, and one had already done so (Sherwell and Alexander 2011). What they were seeing was a long-standing tradition in the Chilean labor market—the principle of immobility (*inamovilidad*), which presumes the right of a worker to keep his or her position. This principle is backed up in law; dismissing workers requires payment of a steep severance package—set at one month's wages per year of service—and at times in Chile's history, explicit justification of the dismissal. Workers, in formal sector jobs such as mining, have a strong presumption that they can continue in their jobs.

How did Chile develop this particular combination of labor laws? Individual labor relations are rigidly regulated, with significant restrictions on firing and extensive stipulations regarding workplace treatment. Unions are present and active, but existing legislation renders them weak and ineffectual. In the typology developed in Chapter 1, Chile can be described as a "professional" labor regulation regime, offering significant protection to individual workers, but also limiting the strength of unions. How did it develop this seemingly contradictory set of legal provisions?

In this chapter, I trace Chile's labor law configuration to labor market institutions in the late nineteenth and early twentieth centuries. The need to attract labor to the geographically isolated mines, and to skilled professions in the city, created incentives for workers to act as free agents, or in small, firm-level local organizations. In particular, I highlight the practice of *enganche*, the "hooking" of workers for work in the mines, as well as the development of crafts in Chile's Central Valley and coast, in shaping early labor legislation. Intellectually, this was reinforced by the prevailing strain of syndicalist thought imported from Europe, which saw the local firm, rather than the industry or economy, as the locus for contesting rights and privileges. Competition among these workers made later collaboration difficult, and created conditions ripe for labor laws that make union formation easy, but coordination across unions difficult.

This labor law regime has been remarkably persistent through time. The period from initial labor law codification, in the years 1924 and 1931, to the overthrow of the Allende regime in 1973, was largely given to deepening characteristics of the labor code that were already present. Strikingly, the military government headed by Augusto Pinochet did not fundamentally reorient the labor code. Rather, after an initial period of repression in which most labor code measures were suspended, it upheld the most typically Chilean aspects of the 1931 code, while seeking to liberalize them and add flexibility. The subsequent *Concertación* governments have brought back the features of the code that had been weakened by the Pinochet government, and tried to address problems of subcontracting and fixed-term employment that have become regularized means to circumvent the most rigid aspects of the labor code.

The chapter proceeds as follows. It first presents a brief overview of the main distinguishing features of the Chilean labor code. Next, it takes up four major historical periods in the development of the labor code: the era of early labor law formation, culminating in the 1924 social laws; the time of institutional deepening, from the enactment of the 1931 Labor Code to the Allende government in 1973; the years of military rule under Pinochet, from 1973 to 1990; and the return of democracy in the four *Concertación* governments of the 1990s and 2000s.

4.1. Overview: The Chilean Labor Code

The quantitative scoring of labor code measures in Chapters 2 and 3 placed Chile squarely in the "professional" labor law regime. It combines extensive, rigid provisions for individual labor relations with restrictive measures for labor union organization and functioning. From the outset, it is important to qualify that this does not mean that its laws regarding individual hiring and firing apply equally to all workers, or that they are perfectly enforced, or even that they are the most developed in Latin America (Winn 2004). Indeed, based on the evidence in Chapter 3, Chile is more or less centrally located among the upper half of the sample; Argentina, Uruguay, Costa Rica, and Mexico all have higher individual labor law scores. In this sense, Chile can help provide some traction on the ways that individual rights are enshrined in Latin American labor codes; it is not so much an outlier, as a representative case of countries that have extensive and rigid individual labor legislation.

These laws include a general presumption of continuous employment in a job, with a severance pay scheme that is sufficiently onerous to dissuade employers from unwarranted dismissals. They include, further, insertion of the worker into the national social security system. Sehnbruch (2006) summarizes well the way in which individual labor protections came to be seen as "acquired rights" in the Chilean labor law regime in the period prior to 1973:

> While other forms of contracting (such as fixed-term or short-term contracts) also existed in Chile from the outset, the open-ended contract came to be viewed as the norm, and labor legislation mostly concerned itself with regulating this norm. The period leading up to 1973 thus generated a certain type of standard job, which was highly stable, based on an open-ended contract (*contrato indefinido*), paid social security contributions, had regulated working hours, paid at least a statutory minimum wage and other statutory benefits, and offered the possibility of union representation. And the severance pay legislation established after 1966 for all workers (not just white-collar workers as before) came to be viewed as an acquired right associated with this "standard job" that protected workers against unfair dismissals as well as provided insurance against unemployment (Sehnbruch 2006: 54).

These rights also included the presumption of an activist state monitoring labor law compliance, setting minimum standards, and imposing fines or finding remedies for noncompliance.

Likewise, the scoring from Chapter 3 does not mean that Chile has no—or few—labor laws governing collective relations. Rather, it means that the laws that exist (and they are extensive) do not facilitate effective collective action among workers. The laws privilege liberty in labor relations, emphasizing the right of workers to freely associate, or to choose not to associate. The bar is set low for organizing and registering labor unions, but establishing a dominant union or federation is rendered extremely difficult. Multiple unions can exist in the same firm, and can compete with one another; workers can opt out of participating in any union, or paying dues; and collective bargaining has, in several periods, been limited to the firm level. As a result, organizing a broad-based comprehensive union movement has been extremely difficult, and the principal union confederation—the Central Unitaria de Trabajadores de Chile (the United Workers Central of Chile [CUT])—remains undersubscribed, underfunded, and politically weak. Further complicating matters, government oversight of unions—during most of Chile's history—has been quite strict. Union funds have been overseen by the Ministry of Labor, elections have been regulated and monitored, and strikes must receive prior approval from the Ministry of Labor. In short, laws governing collective labor relations in Chile promote an atomized labor movement, without a strong voice in economy-wide planning or national politics.

Chile's labor laws have been in constant evolution since their first introduction in the 1920s, but they display a remarkable continuity through time. In the sections that follow, I trace the extensive individual labor regulations to early labor market dynamics and to early currents in labor organization. The profile of the Chilean worker—in terms of skills (and the "skill" represented by willingness to move to distant inhospitable worksites)—shaped the demands for early labor regulation and legislation. Chapter 2 has already shown that Chile lagged behind the best educated countries in Latin America (especially Argentina) in the late 1800s, but that it had caught up by the turn of the century. These skill levels, in conjunction with the need for labor in distant mining camps and urban crafts, drove the demand for protective individual regulations. And the profile of early collective bodies of workers—which tended to be relatively small, firm-based, and syndicalist in orientation—shaped the development of a collective labor code that affords freedom and fosters disarticulated activity.

For reference, Table 4.A, at the end of the chapter, presents a chronology of labor law developments in Chile from the turn of the twentieth century forward. It breaks down the major individual and collective measures introduced in each period, so that the trajectory of each area of labor law can be observed, and ties the outcomes to the political regime that produced it.

4.2. The Origins of Labor Regulation in Chile

Chile's first social laws—a direct precursor to its first formal labor code—were enacted in 1924. Although they were passed rapidly in a unified package, they represented decades of "preincorporation" institutional development driven by labor shortages in key segments of the Chilean economy. In particular, in the late 1800s, two sectors were focal for labor organizing—the miners in the north and the urban workers and port workers in Santiago and Valparaiso.

Mining: Enganche and Union Fragmentation

After gaining rich nitrate deposits in its newly acquired northern territory after its victory in the War of the Pacific (1883), Chile needed to find sufficient labor to exploit the territory's economic potential. Numerous accounts describe the lack of available labor in the region and beyond (O'Brien 1996: 169). Indeed, the Chilean government even considered a plan to try to attract 25,000 European workers in a single year, but the costs proved prohibitive (Monteón 1979: 35). Instead, internal recruiting was undertaken to attract Chilean citizens from the Central Valley and coast to the north, using a system called *enganche*, which had first been used for railroad construction in the 1850s (Monteón 1979: 67). It was remarkably successful. Between 1885 and 1920, the population of the nitrate provinces expanded from 88,000 to 288,000 people; the nitrate industry itself went from employing just over 5,000 workers to more than 46,000 laborers during those same three decades (O'Brien 1996: 169). Over the single decade from 1880 to 1890 in the northern provinces of Antofagasta and Tarapaca, nitrate employment went from 2,848 to 13,060 (Angell 1972).

Enganche (literally, the "hooking" of workers) involved material incentives to attract workers away from capital cities and to the interior mines or fields (Monteón 1979; Ortiz Letelier 1985; Brass 1999). In its typical practice, employers contracted with an individual *enganchador*, a recruiter who would use an advance of funds from the employer to entice workers. This advance might be used to provide loans to workers to buy a home, finance a wedding or local feast, or to pay off outstanding debts. The worker became bound to the *enganchador* or employer, depending on the arrangement, until the loan had been repaid. In some cases, the cost of the workers' transport to the mines or fields was added to their debt.

Geographic isolation, and the obligations from *enganche*, colored the development of workers' demands in Chile. Since the mines were located more than two thousand kilometers from Santiago, an insular set of mining communities developed in the far north. The workers were doubly vulnerable. First, many came with *enganche* contracts that bound them to repay loans or transport costs to the northern territory. Workers were dependent on the mining industry as the only source of employment and income; other opportunities—even for private farming—simply did not exist. But they also lacked contracts guaranteeing them employment (their *enganche* contract only bound them to one particular *enganchador* or employer). They could be summarily dismissed in economic downturns, but they still owed their *enganche* debts. In 1896, for example, 6,000 workers were dismissed in the course of two months alone (Angell 1972).

Second, employers created several mechanisms to further bind the workers. Workers were often forced to live on credit, as they were paid only once per month. Wages were paid in the form of *fichas*, firm-issued scrip redeemable only in mine-owned stores and housing. The *fichas* had little or no value outside the particular firm; in fact, they were often written without any cash value, but instead stated a value such as a "pound of meat" or a "cart of ore" (Monteón 1979: 38, 89–90). Workers quickly incurred debt in other ways as well: they were charged for use of tools and other basic facilities. Finally, in some cases, employers and managers took advantage of worker illiteracy to misrepresent or even manipulate the amounts they owed, keeping them in a near perpetual state of dependence.

Nevertheless, workers were not completely trapped. There were a number of competing mines in the nitrate region, and workers developed informal networks to share information about employment conditions, wages, and job openings. Once workers had fulfilled their *enganche* obligations, they could shop around for better opportunities. Given the shortage of labor in the region, it was in the interest of the employers to compete to attract local miners. This was less expensive than hiring an *enganchador* to recruit and transport a new worker from the Central Valley, and a worker already residing in the north possessed some job-specific skills that would otherwise have to be imparted to a newcomer.

Thus in spite of the abusive aspects of *enganche*, workers in the north benefited from the relative scarcity of labor in the region. Wages rose, as firms sought to poach freed workers. And the workers themselves began to make demands of their own, consistent with the living and working conditions of the mines. The first of these called for guaranteed days of work (Bergquist 1986: 41). The workers had learned that, without such written guarantees, they could be left idle whenever mine operators chose, generally as a result of reduced demand or the absence of transport ships. The recognition of a guaranteed number of days of work was, in a sense, the first job stability measure introduced in Chile, and it would have a lasting impact; indeed, it stands as a very early precursor to later immobility laws. In addition, workers demanded payment in legal tender (rather than scrip), freedom to buy from noncompany shops, protection against illegal deductions from salaries, and safer working conditions (Angell 1972: 13).

Geographic isolation and the shortage of labor also provided opportunities for collective organization to develop among the miners. Far from home, lacking resources for the journey south, and without other employment opportunities in the inhospitable northern desert, they had strong reasons to organize to support each other. Shared housing and dining facilities and long hours together allowed leaders to emerge and to develop their skills and experience in fostering a new movement. Workers established *mancomunales* or brotherhoods—a type of mutual-aid and resistance society—as a way to pool their risk and resources, supporting one another through times of unemployment or illness (Bergquist 1986: 48). In many cases, these organizations became the seedbed for labor union organizing. But achieving recognition by their employers was not easy, since organization was seen as a threat to employer power. Workers thus began to turn to the state to establish provisions to ensure their right to meet and form associations.

The early decades of the twentieth century saw these workers become increasingly restive, and they met with a state that was alternately repressive and concessionary. For example, in 1907, 1,000 to 3,000 nitrate workers were mown down by the army in a school yard in Iquique while protesting against conditions in the mines and mass dismissals that had occurred in a recent slowdown in the industry (Angell 1972). Later, in 1919, facing a strike in El Teniente, the government showed restraint after sending in troops, and eventually mediated a compromise that provided for the strikers' demands for the eight-hour day and overtime. In return, the workers agreed that they would seek to arbitrate future disputes and that they would provide fifteen days' notice of any strike (O'Brien 1996).

In short, even before the development of a comprehensive labor code, and well before the well-studied "incorporation" period (Collier and Collier 2002), the principal features of the Chilean labor market model were on display. Individual workers in the northern mines—whose acquired skills and geographic presence made them a limited commodity—received significant protections for stable employment, guarantees of full payment of salaries, and compensation for workplace risks and injuries. And early labor organizations, centered on specific mines, exhibited the firm-level focus that would characterize most of Chile's labor history.

The Ports and Cities

Chile's ports functioned as important supply lines to the inland capital, but were built up with diverse sources of smaller-scale capital. As a result, two relatively weak kinds of labor movement took shape: a more organized, anarcho-syndicalist effort in the urban crafts and services (for example, in the leather, baking, construction, coal mining, tramway, metal, maritime, furniture, textile, printing, garment, and tobacco industries), and a more diverse and disorganized one in the capital-intensive metal mining, railroads, communications, glass, and beverage sectors (DeShazo 1983). Much like in the mines, the first urban worker organizations took the form of mutual aid societies, in which workers paid dues in order to have access to sickness and accident pay, dignified burial, death benefits to dependents, and in some cases, retirement payments; other societies also offered savings plans, night classes, cultural and social events, and consumer cooperatives (DeShazo 1983). The syndicalist approach of these organizations led to fragmentation: unions organized at the local firm level to resolve particular issues vis-à-vis their employers, while larger, industry-wide efforts were not undertaken. Internal divisions and competition for local leadership produced a "contestatory type" of union movement. Union leaders emphasized demand maximization, fragmenting the union voice and hampering collaboration across firms, even in the large-scale industries where it would have been most fitting and beneficial to workers (Valenzuela 1979).

In the early twentieth century, as electoral participation increased (it tripled in the early years of the new century), and strikes became more disruptive, political parties began to take an interest in workers and worker treatment. Couched in the language of the "social question" of urban labor, the two main political parties produced competing visions of labor law in 1919 and 1921. Conservatives emphasized plant-level unions overseen by government labor inspectors, in order to weed out agitators, while members of the Alianza Liberal (Liberal Alliance) preferred that workers be organized by trade or occupation. The two parties also differed on questions of union finance, with Conservatives preferring union participation in firm profits and Liberals opting for finance through union dues (Valenzuela 1979: 558). In other words, the Conservative proposal sought to fragment unions by restricting them to the local level and to limit their impact through close government supervision and intervention and restricted union funds. The Liberal initiative emphasized broader, cross-firm organization of workers by sector, and would have provided unions with a more reliable source of income. This divide, coupled with an even fiercer stalemate over issues of governance and church-state relations, prevented the Congress from reaching a consensus (Morris 1966: 35). The issue was only resolved when young officers from the military forced through legislation in an effort to contain worker mobilizations (DeShazo 1983: 222–23).

The 1924 Social Laws and 1931 Labor Code

The seven measures that were passed under military pressure in the 1924 Social Laws included pieces of both of the earlier proposals (Pace 1939; De-Shazo 1983: 218), laying the foundation for the particular form of labor market dualism that would predominate in the country. For individual workers, the labor laws provided significant new protections by regulating work contracts and the employment of women and children, establishing a social security fund financed with payroll deductions (one of the first in Latin America), and creating a workers' compensation fund.[1] However they also divided workers into blue-collar *obreros* and white-collar *empleados*; the latter received a generous package of additional benefits, including yearly bonuses based on profit sharing, a maximum forty-eight-hour work week, a guaranteed written contract, sick pay, a retirement fund, two weeks' annual vacation, and the right to a separation/dismissal payment. Among these benefits, the written contract and dismissal payment stand out: both are foundational to improved job stability. *Obreros* received none of these benefits.

The 1924 collective legislation also regulated cooperatives and the process to be followed in labor disputes (raising the bar for strikes), and established a legal division between craft-based professional unions and plant-based industrial unions. Both types had the right to federate, but were expected to negotiate only at the firm level.[2] Union revenues were closely supervised by the government; strike funds were not allowed, and union officials were not permitted to be paid on a full-time basis for union activities. As a result, the 1924 labor measures, while innovative for their time, "splintered the labor movement into isolated, impoverished . . . legal unions of negligible effectiveness in defending the economic interests of their members" (DeShazo 1983: 220). The legislation provided important support for union formation, especially at the firm level, but its protections were limited mainly to professionals, and many of its stipulations hindered the growth of united, national-level worker organization.

The 1924 Social Laws gained additional force when they were adopted as the nation's first Labor Code in 1931. The strong, centralizing government of General Carlos Ibañez used its authority to transform the Social Laws—which had been mostly symbolic—into an enforceable legal code. He saw it as a way to reign in the independent labor movement, whose infighting and social disruption had produced a turbulent succession of five presidents in three years. When he first came to office, in 1927, Ibañez implemented a systematic program of labor repression, arrest of union leaders, and the establishment of "official," government-controlled unions (DeShazo 1983: 242). He then shepherded passage of the 1924 measures as a comprehensive Labor Code in 1931, enshrining in law a set of limits on union activity that had previously been achieved through repression.

Thus the Chilean model under Ibañez sought to fragment union cooperation and ensure collective labor quiescence. As we will see, this approach to the labor code is very different from that pursued by other centralizing governments in Latin America. In Peru's main centralizing moment, the revolutionary military government sought to co-opt the labor movement by incorporating it into a new model of ISI-oriented industrial relations. And in Argentina, Perón created a network of preferred unions to support his own political movement, and invested them with considerable economic and political power.

Summary: Early Chilean Labor Regulation

In sum, Chile developed a deeply segmented labor code that divided workers along several lines: those with formal contracts and secure jobs from those without, those in the *obrero* sector from those in the *empleado* sector, and those with locally strong labor organizations from those who remained unorganized. This section has traced these outcomes to the country's early labor market recruitment institutions during the "preincorporation" period—involving *enganche* for unskilled workers in the mines, and European immigration for skilled workers in urban crafts and professions. In addition, it has highlighted how the presence of many mining firms in the north, and the adoption of a syndicalist strategy in the cities, led to fragmentation of unions in both areas and regularized government intervention and oversight over union finances. This basic pattern of labor contracting formed the template for the 1924 Social Laws and 1931 Labor Code.

4.3. Deepening and Increasing Professionalism: 1931–73

The period between 1931 and 1970 was marked by "continuity" in economic relations, institutions, and politics (Campero and Valenzuela 1984: 31). The first decades after 1931 saw the labor movement expand, but always under the constricting framework of the 1931 Code, which limited organization and collective bargaining to the firm level, divided *empleados* and *obreros*, and limited the ability to strike. One Chilean commenter has called the pre-1973 period a time of "complex legislation with a high degree of protection" (Velásquez Pinto 2009: 155). These protections were concentrated on individual workers' employment relations, securing their status against dismissals. But complex legislation hampered free union activity, and often led to the fragmentation of the labor movement's voice. Indeed, unions chose to link themselves to competing political parties, rather than to one another, and often fought at cross purposes.

Federations and Fragmentation

The economic weakness of unions, caused by their divisions and firm-level organization, gave them incentives to develop political ties and exploit any legal provisions that favored them. They made use of measures in the 1931 Labor Code—including those for compulsory unionization (once 55 percent of a firm's workforce had voted in favor of the union), dues checkoffs, and profit sharing—to build their membership and resources. This made them attractive as partners for small, often competing Marxist parties (Bergquist 1986: 72–73). Leadership was hotly contested among ambitious, firm-level leaders who sought to achieve benefits in wages or workplace treatment for their members.

Nevertheless, there were efforts to achieve higher-level union organization throughout the twentieth century. At least three major confederations arose over the decades, but they faced internal competition as well as external intervention from the government. The earliest large scale organization was the Federación

Obrera de Chile (the Workers Federation of Chile [FOCh]), founded in 1917. It built on the Gran Federación Obrera de Chile, which had been founded in 1909 among railroad workers, and had a communist orientation (Alexander 1962: 254). It was succeeded in 1936 by the Confederación de Trabajadores de Chile (CTCh), which sought to broaden the base of the FOCh, gathering together delegates from the FOCh itself and other major union confederations, including anarcho-syndicalists and socialists. It found a natural partner in the Frente Popular (1936–41) and Alianza Democrática (1941–46) governments, which likewise gathered a broad array of political parties—Radicals, Socialists, Communists, Democrats, and Radical Socialists. For a brief time, the CTCh even had a seat at the table in planning for development following the 1939 earthquake.

But the CTCh found itself riven by political divisions and ideological fights; even at its best moments, an uneasy alliance prevailed within its ranks (Alexander 1962: 257). By 1946, the movement was in crisis. When the Communists gained control of most unions, and the new president, González Videla, failed to bring the Communists into his government's coalition, the CTCh was dissolved (259–60). Just two years later, in an effort to stave off political unrest, President González Videla deported many of the union leaders and had the Communist Party declared illegal (260). The labor movement then entered into another period of decline and disarray.

A third attempt at economy-wide labor organization led to the 1953 founding of the Central Única de Trabajadores (CUT). Operating on the margins of the law, it sought to be a big-tent organization, uniting workers of all stripes—from the former members of the CTCh, to other confederations that had sprung up in the CTCh's absence. The Communist and Socialist parties had clear leadership within the CUT, however, and used their strength to hew out a more unified stance than had been possible under the CTCh. In its early years, it showed its strength through a series of general strikes (Barría 1971). But without a clear partner in government, it had to limit most of its demands to improving salaries, rather than addressing the weakness of the collective labor code.

In short, this period was marked by continued organizational weakness in the labor movement—divided as it was across ideological currents and political parties—that undermined further advances in the laws governing collective relations. Without a strong, centralized voice in discussions with the government, it could not present unified demands. And the existing labor laws further constrained the likelihood for better cross-union cooperation and coordination.

Permissive laws for establishing and managing unions made it easy for even small bodies of workers to retain a separate identity over time, and to draw resources away from concerted action. Nevertheless, we will see below that individual labor laws did not undergo weakening during this period (as might be expected given the weakness of the labor movement). Rather, they remained protective of job stability, consistent with the arguments advanced in Chapter 1.

Frei and Allende

Labor's fate shifted mightily in the second half of the 1960s. With a better organized CUT, and more receptive governments (first under Christian Democrat Eduardo Frei Montalva, and later under the Unidad Popular coalition of Salvador Allende Gossens), labor assumed a central place in government planning and unionization took off. After languishing around 10 percent of the economically active population for most of the century—mainly because union members were largely drawn from only a few productive sectors—the rate of unionization began to rise rapidly. Figure 4.1 presents unionization figures for the period from 1950 to 1989. The dramatic increase after Frei's inauguration in 1964 is clearly apparent.

A significant portion of the increase in unionization came as Frei legalized the organization of agricultural workers in 1967 (Law 16.625) (de Ramón 2003; Walker Errázuriz 2003: 162). This was an unprecedented move, and represented a massive departure from the pattern observed up to that point in Chile's labor code development. Agricultural workers were unskilled and had been left out of earlier legislation, but they represented an electoral prize too valuable to pass up. Further, bringing these workers into the fold fit well ideologically with the program of Frei (and later, Allende). In order to maximize their ability to mobilize these workers, regional-level bargaining (rather than farm-level) was implemented, and its outcomes were imposed even on unorganized farms (Silva 1988). Federations and confederations were permitted in the sector for the first time, and unionization went from virtually zero in 1964 to 33.9 percent of the sector by 1970 (Houtzager and Kurtz 2000: 409).

In addition, for the broader workforce, Frei introduced the expansive 1966 Immobility Law (*Ley de Inamovilidad*, Decreto Ley 2,200). This foundational law required an obligatory severance payment of one month's salary per year of employment and "prevented the dismissal of workers without a specific justified cause (*causa justificada*)" (Sehnbruch 2006: 53). Sehnbruch argues that "the

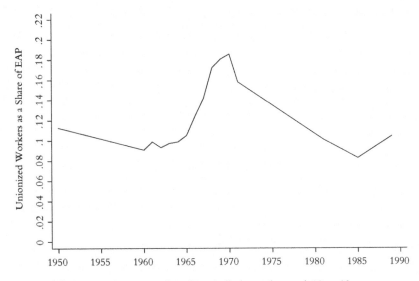

Chilean unionization rates have historically hovered around 10 to 12 percent,
but showed a dramatic increase during the governments of Frei and Allende.

Figure 4.1. Unionization in Chile, 1950–89. *Source:* Author's calculations based
on data from Zapata 1976, Ruiz-Tagle 2009, and the Montevideo-Oxford
Latin American Economic History Database.

importance of this law cannot be overemphasized" (53). It set a new standard for
job stability and protection against dismissal. And its implementation was as important as its formulation. "While on paper economic reasons were considered a
'just' cause for dismissal, in practice labor courts were biased in favor of workers
and tended to rule otherwise" (53). Armed with this kind of job protection, and
rising union membership, the panorama for labor was rapidly changing.

Under Allende, this trend continued. Given the circumstances of his election—with only 36.6 percent of the vote, only 1 percent more than his nearest
challenger—he felt an even greater need to build linkages to a broader base of
supporters. Workers were to be at the center of this effort. Through nationalization of manufacturing industries and copper mines, he gave workers a rapid
50 percent raise in their wages. The working class quickly perceived for itself a
newfound role in the economy and politics. As they adjusted their expectations
upward regarding working conditions and ongoing wage increases, they took
to the streets in a growing number of strikes, work stoppages, and rallies (Drake
1996: 122).

Perhaps the most important development came in the establishment of a formal link between the Allende government and the CUT. Just one month after taking office, the Allende government and the CUT agreed on a *Convenio* that would shape their relations throughout his presidency. It included the legal recognition of the CUT (remarkably, for the first time in its history) and the collection of 0.5 percent of workers' salaries to finance its activities (and the activity of associated federations). In addition, it put reform of Books III and IV of the Labor Code at the center of the government's program, facilitating the registration of new unions and the establishment of federations and confederations, as well as promoting the rights of labor in collective bargaining and in strikes. At the individual level, wages and pension payments were targeted for increases, and laws to protect job stability and reintroduce some aspects of immobility were proposed (Zapata 1976: 48). In addition, the *Convenio* accorded workers a role in management of their firms through "production committees," empowering workers with considerable say in the textile, mining, energy, steel, and transport sectors (50).

Unionization surged, both among rural and urban workers. Calculations in Figure 3.1 above put unionization at 19 percent in 1970, as a share of the economically active population, but other analysts place the rate as high as 37 percent as a share of the unionizable, employed workforce (Sehnbruch 2006: 52). Some sectors were organized at even higher rates, with more than 85 percent of miners and 60 percent of manufacturing workers unionized (52). Emboldened, they pushed for bargaining at the sectoral level, and by 1973 the majority of unions were participating in tripartite negotiation (Sehnbruch 2006: 52).

Nevertheless, little was achieved in terms of lasting labor law reform during this period. Attention was focused on raising wages to keep up with surging inflation and to make up for slow growth in previous decades. The divisions and inequalities in the labor movement persisted, keeping workers from coordinating their efforts on comprehensive reforms. Blue-collar *obreros* struggled to obtain treatment on a par with *empleados*. But this may have been counterproductive: the emphasis of *obreros* on achieving similar benefits to their *empleado* counterparts effectively distracted them from seeking better legal recognition of their collective organizing rights.[3]

In short, the late 1960s and 1970s saw an increase in both union membership and centralization, with numbers doubling and the CUT taking on a more prominent role, closely tied to the government of Salvador Allende. According to the theory developed in Chapter 1, this new configuration of labor power should have been particularly favorable to the development of collective labor regulation, and indeed it was—but only for the short term. Agricultural workers were permitted to unionize and federate, the CUT came to enjoy greater protection, federations and confederations across the economy enjoyed greater freedom, and mechanisms for regularized tripartite bargaining were implemented. But labor's favor rested almost entirely on the electoral needs and political project of the Allende government, and had little basis in the strategic importance of the newly incorporated workers in the economy or in the organizational strength of their unions (Silva 1988). The CUT thus proved incapable of uniting the movement as a whole, and considerable dissension undermined collective action, particularly among *obreros*. Recurrent, large-scale strikes and disruptions soon brought this worker-centered experiment to an end, with an impatient military stepping in to restore "order."

4.4. Disempowerment through Freedom and Fragmentation: Labor Law under Pinochet

When the military junta led by General Augusto Pinochet seized power in 1973, it sought to close spaces that had been opened for union organization and worker benefits under the Allende government. It proceeded in two steps.

First, it sought to deal with the economic chaos and crisis that it had inherited, using a combination of repression and repeal (or neglect) of existing labor code measures (Sehnbruch 2006: 55). Initial decrees "outlawed national federation and the CUT, denied all unions and their leaders most associational and bargaining rights, and forbade any collective or political activities" (Drake 1996: 129). The regime directly targeted and outlawed unions it found unsupportive: "[U]nderlying all these decree laws was the annulment, through regulatory means, of any syndical organization which might have an inspiration distinct from that of the regime" (Irureta 2009: 37).

The second period began in 1979, and consisted of the government's *Plan Laboral*. This set of measures essentially rolled back all the developments that had accrued—most notably during the Allende government—since the 1931 Labor Code, and even weakened some of the provisions found in that early code. Its principal architect, José Piñera, emphasizes that the *Plan Laboral* was essentially a reform (or refounding) of collective labor relations, and should not be confused with other reforms adopted separately that affected individual labor rights. It is "only and exclusively a syndical plan"; it applies only to the "norms about syndical organizations and about collective bargaining" (Piñera 1990: 49).

The new labor code was preceded by what Piñera calls "appetizer laws" that made "freedom" the centerpiece of collective relations. Unions were to be free to organize, and workers free to join them (or—importantly—*not* to join them). The new laws allowed unions to meet freely. But collective action also depended on the free choice of their members in giving resources to their unions; a majority vote of the members was required in order to collect union dues (Piñera 1990: 46–47). In short, the appetizer laws set the tone for a proliferation of atomized, structurally weak unions across the economy.

On this foundation, the *Plan Laboral* was erected with two major decree laws. Decree Law 2,756 governed syndical organizations, and Decree Law 2,758, stipulated the norms for collective bargaining (Piñera 1990: 100). *Empleados* had traditionally had the freedom to organize unions, while *obreros* were obligatorily unionized; the first decree law extended freedom to organize to the *obreros* as well, and established various categories of unions (Sehnbruch 2006: 55). The bar for establishing a union was purposefully low: only 10 percent of a firm's workers were required, with a minimum of 25 workers, and multiple unions could exist within a firm, as any group of 250 workers could form its own union. Indeed, this became the basis for "syndical parallelism," with unions competing, rather than collaborating, within the firm vis-à-vis their employers (Campero andValenzuela 1984: 134). The decree further removed the requirement that the employer be responsible for collecting union dues, and instead made the decision to pay dues the purview of the affiliated worker; workers outside the union who also benefited from collective bargaining were not required to pay dues. Closed shops were not permitted (Piñera 1990: 102–4).

In the latter decree law collective bargaining was restricted to the firm level, without regular government participation (Sehnbruch 2006: 55). Unions and federations were not permitted to participate in this plant-level bargaining; "enterprise workers committees" were charged with this task (Falabella 1981: 22). Discussions were limited to the issue of wages (other working conditions were not permitted to be the subject of collective agreements) (Pollack 1982; Frank 1995). Writing shortly after the reform, Ruiz-Tagle (1985) decried this new distinction, saying that "now unions can exist that do not bargain collectively, and collective bargaining [can exist] without unions" (46). Further, the right to strike was limited, and in the case of strikes that lasted sixty days, the labor contract was considered terminated without the right of a dismissal indemnization (Piñera 1990: 118). In short, in the early years, the Pinochet regime sought to homogenize and "molecularize the working class," so that the "labor movement would at most survive on the shop floor" (Drake 1996: 129).

In the arena of individual rights, the main reform concerned job stability. Decree Law 2,200 (1978) modified the principle of immobility (Law 16,455 of 1966), permitting employers to adjust unilaterally existing contracts and more easily dismiss disruptive workers or those involved in union activities (Campero and Valenzuela 1984: 128). The key innovation was the removal of the phrase "without express cause" from the prohibition on dismissals, which had stood as an acquired right since 1966. The law left intact the requirement to pay a severance indemnization, but the labor courts gave up their bias toward labor immobility, allowing firms to dismiss workers for reasons of economic redundancy (Sehnbruch 2006: 55).[4]

In sum, under the Pinochet administration, freedom was used to fragment collective labor strength, but individual labor rights were not as fundamentally undermined as might have been expected. Union organizing was first outlawed, and then saw its activity greatly restricted under the *Plan Laboral*. Unionization fell back to its historically low levels, and the CUT lost much of its prominence as the central coordinating body for labor. Nevertheless, the system of acquired rights and growing middle-class expectations remained. Somewhat surprisingly, severance payment schemes were capped, rather than removed, and no move was made to encourage or favor short-term or nonstandard employment contracts, as occurred elsewhere in the region (Sehnbruch 2006: 58). The removal of immobility was limited in its coverage to workers who were hired after the 1979 passage of the law. This is considerable evidence of the deference given to the Chilean worker. Even without solidarity across unions, and without a strong national representative, the hold-up power (and perhaps the symbolism of the Chilean worker) made reforms that would be undertaken elsewhere unthinkable in the Chilean context.

In a related measure, the Pinochet government privatized the Chilean pension system in 1981. This undermined one of the few solidaristic labor policies in the nation; prior to the reform, workers made pension payments into occupation-related "funds," creating at least a minimal level of shared industrial identity (to make up for what they lacked as a result of restricted industrial-level collective bargaining rights). But with the privatization of pensions, the workers' ties to both the state (as guarantor of the pensions) and one another (as members of shared industrial funds) were severed. Valenzuela and Goodwin (1983) have referred to this as a "market strategy of containment," in which market institutions and incentives were employed to fragment worker efforts at collaboration.

Nevertheless, in spite of its organizational weakness, the labor movement played a crucial role in the transition to democracy. Labor was the first non-church actor to oppose Pinochet publicly (Frank 1995). When opposition parties were outlawed, the unions provided opportunities for meetings and the planning of protests against the military government, and they helped mobilize voters for the "no" vote in the plebiscite on Pinochet's continuance in office. Yet, they remained extremely cautious—some would argue excessively cautious—in pursuing change in economic relations and labor laws, even as they supported political regime change. Inside the movement, there was a lasting fear of the instability that could be provoked by labor mobilization; the recent memory of the Pinochet coup against Allende made workers worry that their demands might provoke a new military intervention. Likewise, the parties of the nascent Concertación de Partidos por la Democracia (Concertation of Parties for Democracy) did not want to identify themselves too closely with labor (whose close ties with Allende were believed to have made him a target) (Frank 1995). And institutionally, labor faced steep restrictions on its political power. Pinochet had passed laws prohibiting union leaders from assuming party posts; if a leader wanted to enter the political arena, he or she had to give up the union post. Chile's binomial electoral system further ensured that representatives from the right would retain a sufficient share of the congressional seats to resist reforms that would expand labor protections.

4.5. Labor Regulation under the *Concertación*

The return of democracy brought conflicting pressures on Chile's labor regulation regime. As in the lead-up to the plebiscite, the *Concertación* was particularly sensitive to concerns about social order and the need to preserve the rapid growth that had been achieved under Pinochet. Their economic policy proposals thus displayed striking continuity with those pursued by Pinochet in the 1980s (Navia 2008). In addition, the labor movement had become, by 1989, one of the weakest in the region—structurally, institutionally, and politically (Drake 1996: 31). Undermined by deindustrialization and privatizations, its rights and resources had been curtailed by both legal reforms and direct government repression, and it enjoyed little decisive authority inside the *Concertación*. Industrial employment had fallen, as well, from 19.1 percent in 1972 to 13.8 percent in 1985 (Ruiz-Tagle 2009: 21).

Internally, the labor movement was divided among three groups, roughly corresponding to different skill profiles: a unionized, politicized old-guard, still seeking bargaining rights at the national level; a new group of more technical, nonpoliticized unions, which saw plant-level bargaining as best suited to their needs; and talented, more mobile workers who saw no need for unions and preferred to stand independently in the labor market (Drake 1996: 137). Embracing moderation, more and more workers abandoned communist leanings and aligned themselves with the Christian Democrats (Drake 1996: 141). This kind of dissension and disempowerment made concerted calls for major changes to the labor code highly unlikely.

The government of Patricio Aylwin—the first government after the return to democracy—came to office with twin goals: first and foremost, to show that it could achieve social order and tranquility, and second, to reform the economy in a manner that would promote equity, autonomy, efficiency, and economic growth (Cortázar 1993: 44). It quickly set out to negotiate a series of social pacts (*acuerdos nacionales*) with restive workers and businesses, raising the minimum wage to keep pace with inflation and building productivity into the calculation of future wage increases (Cortázar 1993: 40–41). Its hope was to continue the growth-inducing economic policies of the Pinochet regime, although with a more socially responsive outreach to the poor (Muñoz Gomá 2007). Indeed, much was made of the need to overcome the "social debt" that the military government's progrowth policies had engendered (Sehnbruch 2006: 59).

However, the demands for reform were moderated by a number of factors. The unions themselves moderated their demands "in a gesture of goodwill" to the new democratic regime (Campero 2000: 397, quoted in Sehnbruch 2006: 60). The business community was extremely fearful that the return of democracy—and the re-energizing of the labor movement through legal reforms—

would draw the country back into the chaos of the Allende years (60). And legislatively, the *Concertación* faced an implicit veto in the Senate, where lawmakers appointed by Pinochet gave the right a majority. In the face of this opposition, the *Concertación* adopted a policy of consensual democracy (*democracia consensual*); labor policy would be tested and vetted with the opposition before sending it forward for discussion in the Congress (61).

Nevertheless, the *Concertación* did carry out a series of cautious reforms to labor regulation. The maximum severance indemnity was raised from five to eleven months' salary, but, given a growing appreciation of the need for greater flexibility in employment relations, the principle of immobility was not reintroduced (Cortázar 1993: 41–49). Higher-level union federations and confederations were once again legalized at the national level, and multiemployer bargaining was permitted if all parties consented. The CUT was refounded, but now rebaptized as the Central Unitaria de Trabajadores. The organization of unions in midsize firms was facilitated by a change to the requirements for union affiliates. And at the operational level, unions were given greater autonomy in the use of their funds, and their leaders were guaranteed time off and protection from dismissal while dedicated to union activities (Cortázar 1993: 44–47).

These measures sparked a new burst in labor organization. Unionization rose from approximately 10 percent in 1985 to 15 percent in 1992 (Velásquez Pinto 2009: 163). Figure 4.2 details the evolution of unionization rates under the *Concertación* governments, from Aylwin to Bachelet.[5] They show that Chilean unionization jumped significantly at the start of the Aylwin government, as collective labor law reforms allowed for opportunities for union registration and affiliation. Nevertheless, as the 1990s progressed, unionization fell back to its historical trend of 11 to 12 percent (Sehnbruch 2006: 133).

It is striking that even with the reformed laws, intended to facilitate union membership and activity, Chile never approached the unionization levels of other countries in Latin America, especially its neighbor Argentina. The theory in Chapter 1, which places particular importance on labor's political and economic organizational capacity, helps explain this low figure. As throughout its history, the Chilean workforce remained divided along ideological and historical lines. Only 12.3 percent of unions were directly affiliated in 2002 with the CUT—which sought to function as the main interlocutor with the government in enacting reforms to labor law (Sehnbruch 2006: 134). In addition, 39.8 percent of the unions were not affiliated with any national-level federation or

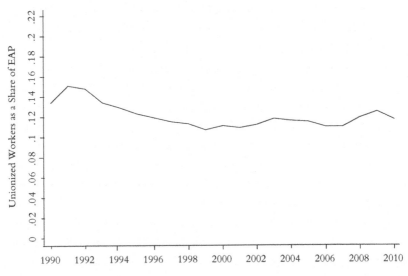

*After an initial rise following the return of democracy, unionization has
hovered between 10 and 12 percent under the Concertación.*

Figure 4.2. Unionization in Chile under the Concertación, 1990–2010. *Source:*
Gobierno de Chile, Dirección del Trabajo 2011.

confederation (134). Even the reforms to labor regulations, opening the possibility for unions to organize more easily and collaborate across firms and industries,
were insufficient to induce changes in the movement.

Similarly, although structural conditions in the Chilean economy have
changed dramatically over the course of the century, workers' preferences and
union activity remain startlingly consistent with those of earlier generations.
Surveys show that workers see the firm level as the most effective for promoting
their economic interests, but they also are concerned about how that dialogue
can become charged and counterproductive. Because of these fears, nearly 70
percent of workers either do not see the benefit of having a union or do not
believe that the union delivers more benefits than not having one. In addition,
they have largely adopted the competition-oriented rhetoric of the Pinochet
years. They feel that organized labor has failed to develop a persuasive vision for
labor relations in Chile in the globalized world. They cite the failure of high-
level labor organizations—especially the CUT—to address their grassroots concerns as a reason for its declining membership (Berg 2006: 43–51). Given these

preferences, it is not surprising that a more solidaristic, corporatist approach to organized labor has not taken hold in Chile, even in the more legally permissive years of the *Concertación*.

Individual labor laws underwent only minor revisions in the years of *Concertación* government. Under Aylwin, the principal of immobility was largely restored, as just cause was once again required for dismissals. In addition, the maximum severance payment was increased from five to eleven months' salary, with a 20 percent penalty for unjustified dismissal; the Frei government later increased this penalty even further. And workplace practices also saw worker-friendly changes. Aylwin extended the forty-eight-hour work week to additional categories of workers, and Lagos phased in a reduction from forty-eight to forty-five hours.

The most significant reorientation in individual labor policy occurred under President Michelle Bachelet (2006–10). While she did not undertake a comprehensive labor code revision—as some forces had desired—she did take decisive steps to introduce elements of universalism to social policy. This marks a significant departure from earlier, employment-based legislation. First, and most important, she introduced "basic solidaristic pensions," which provide a minimal level of financial support to individuals without sufficient retirement savings from the privatized pension system. A chronic problem of the privatized system had been that many of the poorest people had never made sufficient contributions to their pension funds to receive any benefits. Bachelet's initiative thus introduced basic pensions in July 2008 for individuals over age sixty-five that were in the poorest 60 percent of the population (Morales 2008; Garrido and Olivares 2008). Further, she enacted a supplemental state pension for those who had paid into the private funds but were not receiving adequate benefits.[6]

Second, Bachelet expanded coverage for the obligatory unemployment insurance (that had been first introduced in 2002), the *Seguro de Cesantía*, extending benefits to workers whose employment histories had not permitted them to make sufficient contributions to the insurance system. The new legislation was designed to include workers on temporary contracts, as well as to ensure that workers would receive a benefit regardless of the circumstances of their dismissal. However, even as it expanded coverage, it still did not include informal sector or independent workers, who make up approximately 30 percent of the workforce (Velásquez Pinto 2009: 164).

Finally, subcontracting has frequently been employed in Chile as a means to evade labor law provisions; it is another way by which labor law remains segmented in its application. Firms of all stripes, but especially those that are more prominent and likely to face labor inspections, have increasingly outsourced at least some of their production process to other, smaller firms in the local market (which may fail to make required social security contributions, or neglect to pay mandated severance pay, or may engage in other abusive behaviors). In 2007, in an effort to address these evasive behaviors, Bachelet introduced a law to require firms to verify the labor law compliance of their subcontractors (Velásquez Pinto 2009: 157). By making major firms responsible for their subcontractors, oversight of marginal employment has been extended considerably.

In sum, labor politics in Chile under the democratic governance of the *Concertación* bear considerable continuity with labor politics prior to the 1973 military coup (Buchanan 2008). And as we have seen in this last section, even though the *Concertación* governments did not introduce a new labor code to supplant the 1979 *Plan Laboral* and its associated measures, they did roll back many of the most damaging features. The principle of immobility has been largely re-established, albeit with seemingly more legal opportunities for evasion through subcontracting or the use of fixed-term contracts. Furthermore, the *Concertación* governments sought to address the reality of more vulnerable employment head-on. They forced firms to internalize the decision to subcontract, making firms liable for the abuses of their third-party suppliers. And the Bachelet government introduced basic pensions to better meet the needs of nontraditional workers. The institutional weakness of worker organization, however, has not been overcome. Unions remain as fragmented and divided as at nearly any time in Chile's history.

4.6. Conclusion

As suggested at the outset of this chapter, Chile's labor legislation constitutes an intriguing puzzle. First and foremost, it shows that all labor legislation is not of a piece. Individual regulations can vary independently of collective regulations. Individual labor laws can afford workers extensive legal protections, while collective labor laws undercut the organization, status, resources, and political power of unions. The strong presumption of the rights of workers can coexist with an equally strong presumption against the coordinated activity of unions.

This chapter has developed an explanation for this mix of labor measures. It has focused on the "preincorporation" experience of workers and employers in the geographically isolated northern mining regions, as well as the more skilled and sophisticated craft- and service-sector workers of the cities. In terms of the theory presented in Chapter 1, the fragmentation of the early Chilean labor movement, because of ideological differences and the lack of concentrated capital investments or geographically isolated industrial concentration, complicated and ultimately undermined the ability of labor to credibly threaten a holdup of the entire economy. Rather than demand legal protections of their right to organize, particular unions focused locally on more protective individual labor protections, initially granted by their employers at the firm level. As a result, those in the professional classes saw many of their demands met in labor laws. This legislation then became the template for later demands by *obreros* in other segments of the economy.

Military regimes in the 1920s and 1970s were willing to extend individual labor laws while ensuring that collective legislation gave unions few opportunities to collaborate across firms or organize broader political movements. As a result, relatively strong individual labor legislation, implemented and enforced for formal sector workers in semiskilled fields, coexisted with much more restrictive legislation on labor organizing and collective action. National federations remained weak in Chile, and universalistic labor laws and social protection measures were few. The recent Bachelet reforms sought to reach a broader, nonprotected population with solidaristic social policies; however, they remain limited in their benefit levels. And thus far, Chile has not moved forward on reforms to its collective labor protections; thus the institutional weakness of cross-firm labor coordination is likely to persist.

This analysis challenges many existing theories about labor law development. First, it reveals the importance of analyzing the components of national-level labor codes in a disaggregated way. The conceptualization of the labor law policy space in Chapter 1 highlighted the fact that individual and collective labor measures can vary independently, and the Chilean case illustrates the "professional" policy mix that affords extensive individual labor protections and minimal collective measures that would aid in large-scale worker coordination across the economy. The case history presented here shows that workers with important skills and characteristics were effective at achieving these individual protections but did not have the organizational capacity to create a broader movement that would have sought legal protections for its economy-wide activity. In other words, labor's "strength" has more than one dimension. At the individual level, workers may have skills or characteristics that make them essential to a local economy or firm, and that allow them to demand legal measures that protect their job stability and improve their working conditions. But at the collective level, those same workers may be "weak" in that they lack organizational capacity—leadership, a shared ideology, solidarity—to achieve legal protections that would support a national-level movement. In this case, ideological divisions and leadership competition kept workers divided, with ties to diverse political parties, and unable to develop a lasting, inclusive movement.

Second, this chapter suggests that regime type—autocracy or democracy—does not map onto labor law configurations in a straightforward way. On the one hand, autocratic regimes, and military pressure, have proven highly capable of implementing major changes in Chile's labor laws, first in 1924 and 1931, and later in 1979. Yet autocratic governments did not always pursue the same set of goals. In 1924 and 1931, military-influenced and controlled governments were responsible for establishing the basic protective features of Chile's "professional" regime. In 1979, however, the goal of the military-led Pinochet team was to fundamentally liberalize the country's labor laws, dismantling as many of its protective measures as possible. Nevertheless, several key features of the labor law configuration in Chile—a strong presumption of individual job stability and a firm-level focus on labor organization—proved remarkably resilient, even in the face of the Pinochet reforms.

In contrast, periods of democratic governance achieved only incremental change in the labor code, generally in the direction of increased individual protections and coverage. Admittedly, the governments of Frei and Allende were able to significantly increase unionization, but these reforms proved short-lived when Pinochet seized power. The *Concertación* subsequently implemented a series of cautious reforms to compensate for failures in the labor market—including better monitoring of subcontracting and additional financial assistance for the unemployed and the aged—but it did not introduce a new labor code of its own.

The Chilean case also implies that centralized, coordinated collective action is not absolutely necessary to achieve protective labor regulations, especially those that govern individual labor relations. Throughout Chile's history, the union movement has been fragmented, with competition a common occurrence among unions within the same firm and industry. Yet concerns about local production and working conditions were sufficient to raise consciousness about the "social question" in the 1920s. The skill levels and characteristics of the workers—both in the mines and in urban crafts—set the tone for the legislation that was eventually implemented. That legislation reflected the dispersed and divided nature of the labor movement, and sought to reproduce it, by ensuring individual rights but placing institutional constraints on the operation of unions and their collaboration.

Fourth, the Chilean case nuances our understanding of the role of government partisanship in the development of labor laws. While Chilean labor laws have seen expansions under left-leaning parties—including significant advances during the governments of both Frei and Allende and more muted ones under the postdictatorship *Concertación*—these have not been as fundamental or far reaching as might be expected. Left-leaning governments, especially the *Concertación*, were careful to temper their demands after the return to democracy. They have also been affected by the conflicting currents inside the labor movement, which tied unions to particular parties across the spectrum on the left, rather than into a unified, labor-allied left party. As a result, governments from the right have been the major enactors and enforcers of fundamental labor law provisions, and have had the greatest impact on the measures that govern labor law today.

Fifth, the narrative here suggests that policy legacies matter in a powerful way, exerting an influence not simply from the previous regime but also across long stretches of time. The laws implemented by the Pinochet regime were not simply a rejection of the Allende government's policies. In fact, the 1979 Labor Code was a reaction to more than a half-century of labor law development, and the Pinochet regime initially undermined provisions that dated to the 1920s. But it was not unconstrained in its reform project. It preserved features—such as syndical freedom, and a strong underlying bias toward job stability—that had been perennial features of the country's labor laws. Even the most significant reforms were "grand-fathered" in by the Pinochet regime, so that they did not apply to workers employed before the code. Reversals may be an important part of legal legacies, but they may be limited in their scope.

Finally, this chapter suggests that "critical junctures"—moments of decisive institutional change and development—take on their character not simply because of the political alignment that produces them (Collier and Collier 2002), but perhaps more fundamentally as a result of the structural economic factors that make them possible. The 1924 and 1931 labor code was not simply the project of a particular government that saw an opportunity to "incorporate" the labor force into the political system. Nor was it the direct translation of a unified workforce's demands on government. Rather, it was an effort to respond to a combination of production needs at the local level, labor market dynamics and institutions of recruitment, and punctual concerns about welfare and the social question. In other words, the underlying economic structure dictated the range of possible labor law measures that could be introduced. Similarly, the lasting impact of the critical juncture has much to do with the congruence of the labor code with the ongoing structural economic features of the country. In fact, critical junctures stand out, at least in part, because they "get things right" in terms of the economic balance of forces within a country. Those arrangements that do not achieve this coherence prove to be short-lived, or impossible to enact, as occurred with the reformist proposals of Allende.

The case of Chile also sets up well the analysis of Peru and Argentina taken up in the next two chapters. In both of those cases, structural economic factors fostered early labor market institutions, which served as the foundation upon which later demands for labor laws were made. The specific characteristics of workers—their skill levels, their willingness to undertake work in particular geographical and industrial contexts, their past experience—shaped their preferences for certain kinds of individual labor law measures. Argentine workers in key industries, especially those tied to the beef industry, and in urban crafts and services, bore many similarities in their demands to Chilean workers in the mines and cities. Peruvian miners actually behaved quite differently, in large part because of Peru's geography and labor market recruitment strategies. In addition, the organizational capacity of workers, which in Chile was diminished by fragmentation and in-fighting among unions, shaped the kinds of collective labor law measures that were undertaken. Peruvian workers experienced many of the same kinds of divisions that Chilean workers did, and developed a similarly weak collective labor code. In contrast, Argentina's unions showed early trends toward collaboration and cooperation, and later this was formalized in its labor code.

Appendix Table 4.A. Labor Policy in Chile, by Government, 1900–2010

Period	Party/President	Labor Policy Developments
1900–1923	Various	Piecemeal measures *Individual Relations:* Eight-hour workday and overtime provisions for some workers *Collective Relations:* Required workers to seek arbitration in labor disputes and give 15 days' notice for strikes
1924–31	Various Military Junta 1924–25 Presidents drawn from Military 1925–31	First social laws governing labor relations (1931). Set the tone for subsequent decades *Individual Relations:* Regulated work contracts. Regulated employment of women and children. Established a worker compensation fund. Divided workers into blue-collar *obreros* and white-collar *empleados*, with the latter receiving a written contract, 48-hour work week, regular bonuses, sick pay, vacation, retirement benefits, and a payment for dismissal or separation *Collective Relations:* Regulated cooperatives and the process for labor disputes, making strikes less likely. Established a legal distinction between craft-based professional unions and plant-based industrial unions. Mandated firm-level collective bargaining, unless employers agreed to industry-wide bargaining. Required government supervision of union revenues. Prohibited strike funds and paying union leaders on a full-time basis for their union activities
1931–64	Various	First Labor Code (1931). Cemented and gave force to the provisions of the 1924 social laws *Individual Relations:* Codified the dismissal indemnity at one month's salary per year of service *Collective Relations:* Regulated internal structure and activity of unions. Collective dismissal required prior authorization from the government
1970–73	Allende *(Unidad Popular)*	Effort to centralize labor union economic and political activity under the UP *Individual Relations:* Proposals to protect job stability and enhance some aspects of immobility *Collective Relations:* Gave legal recognition to the CUT. Made dues obligatory for all workers benefiting from collective bargaining. Mandated worker participation in management. Established tripartite commissions for industry-wide wage and working condition negotiations
1973–90	Pinochet *(Military)*	Deregulation, followed by introduction of the *Plan Laboral* (1979) *Individual Relations:* Overturned the Immobility Law (1981). Permitted at-will dismissals. Limited severance pay to maximum of 5 months' salary. *Collective Relations:* Limited collective bargaining to plant level negotiation of salaries, with coverage only for the parties to the bargaining, and excluded topics that would limit the ability of the employer to organize, direct, or administer the firm. Prohibited strikes for public employees and essential or temporary workers. Permitted replacement of striking workers. Automatic dismissal of striking workers after 60 days. Limited right of public workers and workers at new firms to organize. Subcontracting allowed without restriction. Temporary workers not allowed to join unions or bargain collectively

Period	Party/President	Labor Policy Developments
1990–94	Aylwin (*Concertación*)	Restoration of labor rights. First generation of reforms *Individual Relations:* Required justification for dismissals. Increased maximum severance pay to 11 months' salary, with a 20 percent penalty for unjustified dismissal. Extended 48-hour work week to additional categories of workers *Collective Relations:* Permitted multi-employer bargaining if all parties agreed. Abolished 60-day dismissal provision for strikes. Legalized national unions, federations, and confederations. Reduced number of workers required to register unions in medium-size firms. Protected job security of confederation leaders. Required nonunion members to pay 75 percent of union dues as bargaining fee
1994–2000	Frei Ruiz-Tagle (*Concertación*)	*Individual Relations:* Increased penalty for unfair dismissals *Collective Relations:* Recognized public employees associations. Expanded jurisdiction of the Labor Directorate
2000–6	Lagos (*Concertación*)	Second generation of reforms, with more protection and active labor market policies *Individual Relations:* Phased reduction from 48-hour work week to 45 hours. Penalized union-related dismissals *Collective Relations:* Opened up opportunities for temporary, seasonal, part-time, and apprentice workers to engage in some collective bargaining over wages and working conditions
2006–10	Bachelet (*Concertación*)	*Individual Relations:* Revised calculation of *semana corrida* salary measures, raising take-home pay of low-income workers. Introduction of basic solidaristic pensions, for workers who had not made sufficient contributions to the pension system to receive benefits. Requirement that firms investigate the labor law compliance of their subcontractors

Sources: Angell 1972; DeShazo 1983; Ruiz-Tagle 1985, 2009; Cortázar 1993; O'Brien 1996; Berg 2006; Sehnbruch 2006; Cook 2007; Velásquez Pinto 2009.

Chapter 5

Contradictions, Divisions, and Competition: Encompassing Labor Regulation in Peru

Investors and business owners complain bitterly about Peruvian labor legislation, which they claim imposes impossibly high costs on their production. Long vacations, high severance payments to dismissed workers, and the regular occurrence of strikes stand in the way of economic growth and development in Peru.

Nongovernmental organizations complain, equally bitterly, that Peru does not enforce its labor legislation, and that countless workers are mistreated, exposed to hazardous work conditions, paid poorly, and vulnerable to arbitrary dismissal according to the "junk contracts" the country allows. Even worse, statistics show that well over half of the workforce does not have formal employment; they undertake extralegal ventures and jobs that are completely untouched by the state.[1]

Can both of these sets of claims be correct? Peruvian economist Hernando de Soto sees a linkage between them (1989; 2000). He argues that informality and poor enforcement are a direct result of rigid labor legislation. Legal standards are so restrictive, he believes, that they encourage (even require) evasion. And the evasion comes at a tremendous cost to the economy—in quality of life for workers, in productivity for firms, and in overall development and institutional capacity for the state. The legal system reinforces a fundamental fracture in the workforce, between the skilled and unskilled, and between the organized and the unorganized.

Peru presents a striking contrast to both Chile and Argentina in the configuration of its labor laws, and a puzzle in its own right. According to the analysis in Chapter 3, postreform Peru had one of the weakest labor codes in Latin America in absolute terms, and thus stood at the opposite end of the spectrum from countries like Argentina and Mexico. However, this characterization obscures the underlying features of its labor regulation, which changed significantly during the reform period. In fact, as outlined in Chapter 3, the country moved from displaying many of the characteristics of a "professional" regime in the 1980s to those of an "encompassing" one in the 1990s and 2000s.

Prior to the reforms of the 1990s, Peru presented two divergent trends in the design of its labor codes. First, its individual labor regulations were among the most highly protective in the region—with "absolute job stability" enshrined in law even under diverse democratic and nondemocratic governments. Yet while this meant that workers who were covered by labor laws enjoyed strong protections of their jobs, it also created substantial pressures for employers to hire workers "off the books," without the costly requirements of legally mandated provisions. As a result, a small group of workers—mainly concentrated in the professional and state sectors—came to enjoy a full package of contract rights and privileges, while the majority of the workforce remained outside these legal protections. On the other hand, Peru's collective labor regulations were extremely weak, and largely designed to fragment the concentration of power in unions. Labor unions were small and frequently divided, and often shifted their allegiances among competing labor confederations; they lacked a single party interlocutor to represent their interests in government. How did this institutional mix come about, and how was it sustained through time?

In addition, what accounts for the rapid and lasting reforms undertaken in the 1990s? Peru is one of only two countries that saw significant decreases in the protectiveness of its labor codes, and then sustained that new equilibrium through subsequent governments. These reforms essentially reversed the previous labor law configuration, creating a system in which individual rights applied to an even more restricted few while collective rights moved toward greater protectiveness. The former were weakened by decreasing their coverage; the introduction of new "modalities" for temporary employment effectively excluded an even larger portion of the workforce from attaining job stability, long vacations, and high severance pay. Yet new legislation gave organized workers greater opportunities for engaging in strikes and diminished state intervention in their regular operation. Simultaneously, the reforms weakened labor unions by permitting even more competition among them, and raised the bar in terms of the requirements for forming new unions. Surprisingly, though, Peru's labor reforms were not univocally negative for labor. In short, the laws became stronger for covered individual workers, even as the number of workers who enjoyed the high protections declined. And they provided even more opportunity for labor organizing. How were some workers able to preserve their legal protections, while others saw theirs even further diminished?

This chapter argues that both labor regulation outcomes in the mid-twentieth century and in the reform period can be best explained through reference to Peru's relatively weaker skill levels and poorly organized union movement. The concentration of skilled workers in a small number of sectors gave these workers incentives to seek benefits restricted to themselves. And unions were divided even from the beginning, with one segment hewing a more communist line (the Confederación General de Trabajadores del Perú [CGTP]), while the other remained more pragmatic and maintained ties to the Alianza Popular Revolucionaria Americana (APRA) party (the Confederación de Trabajadores del Perú [CTP]). Thus no broad-based coalition of workers could emerge, and the small group of workers that was better organized had significant advantages in the shaping of the labor code. Both military and democratic governments catered policies to this small minority.

This chapter proceeds as follows. First it describes the distinctive features of the Peruvian labor code, which couples targeted individual protections, on the one hand, with permissive but fragmenting union regulations, on the other. The second section describes the origins of the Peruvian labor laws, indicating how a relatively small early endowment of skilled labor and late industrialization combined to make labor legislation a policy whose impact was restricted to a small subset of workers. In addition, it highlights how a lack of union organization and membership, as well as divisions within the movement itself and poor ties to organized parties, prevented the development of a more effective labor voice in the country. The third section traces the progression of labor code measures from the first laws until the end of the 1980s, describing how path-departing expansions of labor rights were introduced—and soon abandoned—by governments seeking to attract support from workers. These reforms promised a level of job stability that they could not deliver or systematically enforce. The fourth section details the massive reforms undertaken by Alberto Fujimori, which dramatically expanded fixed-term and nonpermanent employment, but also provided some new protections to unions. Section five concludes the chapter, highlighting the comparative strengths of the theory articulated in this book over other competing explanations of Peru's labor law development.

5.1. The Peruvian Labor Code and Its Anomalies:
The Puzzle to Be Explained

For most of its history, the Peruvian labor code has combined very strong protections of individuals with very limited coverage, on the one hand, and a permissive but weak approach to collective organization that facilitates union fragmentation and state intervention, on the other. Pasco Cosmópolis (2002) calls it a "profuse legislation, hyper-protective of the worker, whose emblematic characteristic was job stability, implanted with an absolute character to the point of becoming a virtual prohibition on firings, and the proliferation of anti-technical, anti-economic, and discriminatory benefits" (11). This section details the distinctive features of the Peruvian labor code, which the remainder of the chapter seeks to explain. As will be seen, job stability stands as a central feature in Peruvian labor law, always a point of reference even when it is not fully (or even partially) realized. And unions face fairly low hurdles for organization, but as a result are more likely to be divided and weak.

Peruvian Individual Labor Law:
From "Absolute" Job Security to Fixed-term Contracts

Somewhat surprisingly, several aspects of Peru's individual labor codes are among the most protective in Latin America. For example, workers on permanent contracts are entitled to thirty days' paid vacation per year, two yearly "gratifications" (extra wages in July and December), and they enjoy extremely large mandatory severance payments if they are dismissed without cause. But the fulcrum on which Peruvian labor law has traditionally turned is job stability. The "right" to job stability is central to the law's understanding of labor relations; it reached its high point in the military-imposed "absolute" job stability measures of 1970 and 1975, and was even enshrined in the Constitution of 1979. Employers who dismissed workers without grave cause were subject to fines, back pay, and criminal prosecution, in addition to being required to reinstate the worker.

The mechanism by which job stability is protected in Latin America, as seen repeatedly throughout this book, is severance pay. In Peru, current mandatory severance pay (a key component in ensuring job stability) is set at 1.5 months for each year of service; this is the highest in Latin America. Indeed, the figure is so generous that consumption by unemployed workers receiving severance pay is higher than that of workers who are presently employed (MacIsaac and Rama

2001). It is further augmented by an additional measure called Compensation for Time of Service (CTS, *Compensación por Tiempo de Servicios*). This is a one-time payment at the time of ending the employment relationship that effectively works as a combination forced-savings account and unemployment insurance for the worker. Employers make a monthly deposit in the CTS account of each of their workers (currently equivalent to 8.33 percent of the worker's wage). In theory, the worker has access to these funds only at the time of retirement, but various governments have chosen to relax this restriction in order to allow workers to use the funds for the purchase of homes, or in some cases, to weather financial crises. The large investment the employer makes into the CTS fund serves as a deterrent to firing the worker.

In contradistinction to these strong job stability provisions, Peru has since the 1980s adopted a wide-ranging set of nonpermanent employment "modalities"—fixed-term contracts that do not carry the presumption of absolute job stability. These were especially promoted during the latter years of the first García government and the early years of the Fujimori government, to bring informal workers and the unemployed into the formal sector by decreasing the costs of hiring (and firing) for employers. While provisions had previously existed for a period of apprenticeship or on-the-job training, these were generally restricted to short periods (three months), after which workers were to be considered permanent. But in the Fujimori reforms, the number of possible "modalities" was expanded up to nine main areas, allowing temporary contracts for a host of economic motives. At the same time, the probationary period was lengthened to five years and dismissal procedures were eased.

The combination of the strong job stability requirements and numerous fixed-term hiring regimes has created a regularized practice of evasion by employers. Workers are repeatedly hired on fixed-term contracts, or are fired and rehired numerous times before they reach the seniority necessary for high severance packages. Thus the labor laws reinforce, rather than combat, the precariousness of the labor market. Rigid laws and generous benefits effectively shunt many workers into the informal sector and into temporary contracts; the result is that only a small minority enjoy the full battery of individual protections. Only one in five private sector workers is legally entitled to severance pay, and only one in three private sector wage earners; additionally, the current system is distorted such that wealthier workers are covered more. These strong individual labor regulations create a clear bifurcation in the labor market between workers that have access to the full gamut of labor law protections and benefits and those that do not.

In short, the individual labor regulation in Peru is highly protective, with an emphasis on ensuring the absolute job stability of workers. However, this has resulted in a host of provisions that limit or circumvent that stability, either by legally steering workers into fixed-term contracts or by evasion by employers through firing and rehiring. It has also pushed workers into the informal sector, either as independent salespeople or service providers or as workers employed "off the books." Most survey estimates place the population covered by job stability measures—and all individual labor laws—at a stunningly low 15 to 20 percent of the workforce (MacIsaac and Rama 2001).

Peruvian Collective Labor Law: Fostering Fragmentation and State Intervention

The collective labor codes in Peru are not very extensive, and they tended to develop as a result of, rather than as a prelude to, the emergence of unions in the country. Indeed, unions existed for the first decades of the 1900s before having any legal requirement to register or seek government recognition, a provision that was only introduced in 1936. Ever since that time, three central features of the Peruvian collective labor code and labor organizing stand out. First, the bar for organizing unions is set quite low. This permits a proliferation of labor organizations, frequently resulting in competition or fragmentation among them. Second, the structure of Peru's economy—concentrated in small enterprises—effectively limits the possibility of unionization reaching beyond a small portion of the total working population. And third, the law allows easy government intervention in unions, limiting workers' ability to act, coordinate, and strike.

Peruvian collective labor law is set up to "privilege the firm [level]" of union organization, rather than sectoral or economy-wide confederations (Pasco Cosmópolis 2002: 23). While higher-level unions are not prohibited, little provision is made for them in the law or in their interaction with the Ministry of Labor. The main focus of labor legislation is thus on firm level unions, which are required only to have at least twenty members. In early periods, an additional requirement was that the unionized workers constitute a majority of the workforce of the firm. In later periods, however, the majority requirement was relaxed, making initial organization easier and, in many cases, permitting the organization of multiple unions within a firm or industry. In addition, confederations are easy to organize. As a result, several rival union confederations have existed, complicating coordination with political parties. Only one (Confederación de Trabajadores Peruanos [CTP]) has lasting linkages to a particular political party (APRA). Thus the collective labor law in Peru contributes to the development of a fragmented, competitive union marketplace.

However, union organization is also confined to a small portion of the workforce—not because of direct legal prohibitions on organizing, but as a result of the structure of the labor market. Peruvian firms tend to be small, so many workplaces do not have enough employees to meet even the low twenty-member requirement. Unions in the 2000s have called for this minimum to be reduced to ten workers in order to expand the possibility of unionization. Further, much of the Peruvian workforce finds itself full- or part-time in the informal sector, as independent small-business entrepreneurs or salespeople or service providers, day workers, or members of family businesses, making the pool of "union-izable" laborers even lower. Most estimates place unionization at approximately 20 to 30 percent of all workers. Given that the unions which exist have been competitive rather than cooperative, the small unionized sector is more likely to concentrate on the particular interests of individual sectors or firms. And those outside of unions are more likely to view them with suspicion; survey evidence shows that unions are among the least trusted institutions in Peruvian political life.

Finally, Peru's collective labor laws accord a central role to the state. The Ministry of Labor has broad powers to intervene in labor relations and limit union militancy. This role for the state begins with the recognition process, which gives the state veto power over unions that seem particularly conflictual or problematic. The Ministry of Labor must also approve all collective bargaining agreements, and exercises a role both in ongoing negotiations and when arbitration is needed to settle disputes. It also must give approval for all strikes and work stoppages. The law sets a high legal standard in terms of union voting requirements to authorize a strike, and facilitates intervention in the case of strikes.

In addition, unlike many other nations, Peru did not allow state-sector unions until relatively late. Government workers, including not only bureaucrats and administrators but also doctors, postal workers, and teachers, were not allowed to unionize until the 1960s (Law 11,377). The workers in the public sector, who make up roughly 9 percent of total employment, or about twenty percent of formal sector employees, were thus unable to engage in collective bargaining, and saw their wages and other benefits determined by the state government apparatus.

Summary

Peruvian labor law thus embodies several contradictions. It combines strong individual protections with limited coverage, and significant ease in forming unions with an environment that cannot support many of them. Table 5.A (at the end of the chapter) summarizes the development of labor laws by governmental period. Section 5.2 describes the "preincorporation" conditions that gave rise to Peru's first set of labor laws, which are detailed in Section 5.3. Section 5.4 examines the period of far-reaching reform under Alberto Fujimori, and Section 5.5 takes up the post-2000 governments' halting efforts to bring greater coverage or protectiveness to labor regulation. Throughout, I highlight the role of Peru's limited and concentrated skilled sector, on the one hand, and relatively small and fragmented union movement, on the other, in producing these labor law outcomes.

5.2. The Origins of Peruvian Labor Legislation

Unlike Chile and Argentina, which drew significant segments of their working populations from skilled or semiskilled European immigration, Peru's workforce was homogenous and low skilled in the early years of the twentieth century. Indeed, Chapter 2 showed that primary school enrollment in Peru lagged significantly behind that of its neighbors in the first half of the twentieth century, with only about half as many of its citizens receiving a basic education. This had far-reaching effects, as only 32 percent of the population were literate as late as 1925 (when Argentina already saw more than 60 percent literacy). But there was tremendous regional variation, with urban centers (such as Lima) achieving 50 percent literacy.

Labor recruitment practices, geography, and the structure of production also conspired against the development of extensive collective action by Peruvian workers. Peru faced labor shortages that were similar to those in Chile, but the results were very different. Mines and plantations tended to be located closer to population centers. When *enganche* was employed to attract workers, it did not exercise the same hold over them. Indeed, many workers would desert their jobs to go home for long or short periods, to tend crops or to be with family (Flores 1993). Worker organization was much more limited as a result. The transience of the mining and plantation workforce meant that early mutual aid societies were poorly funded, and early unions were smaller and weaker than observed in

Chile. Where Chilean workers had incentives—given by geography—to work together to improve their living and working conditions, Peruvian workers could simply leave and go home (Carnes 2014).

And since manufacturing was so slow to develop (as was seen in Table 2.5), Peruvian workers were slower to move to cities and find common cause with fellow citizens in factories. Indeed, until 1950, "industrialization had made less headway in Peru than in other South American countries of comparable size" (Thorp and Bertram 1978: 261). Employment remained concentrated in the agricultural sector well into the 1970s. Even as late as 1950, agriculture employed 58.9 percent of the economically active population, and this number fell only slowly over the next two decades, reaching 52.8 percent in 1961 and 44.5 percent in 1970. Given the geographically diffuse nature of agricultural production, there was very little opportunity for national-level collective action and very little threat of sustained hold-up in the economy. Disputes and strikes, while at times substantial in size, tended to be local, short-lived events. Over the same period, manufacturing employment showed almost no growth, moving from 13 percent of the workforce in 1950 to 13.5 percent in 1961 and 14.5 percent in 1970 (all figures are from Thorp and Bertram 1978: 259). Urbanization was still limited and had not yet created a critical mass of workers with shared interest in industry. The urban labor market displayed considerable slack, further hindering collective mobilization. In 1956, urban unemployment stood at 5 percent and underemployment at 25 percent; by 1967, these figures were largely unchanged at 31 percent combined un- and underemployment (Thorp and Bertram 1978: 273).

In addition, much of the early need for labor in Peru was filled by importing workers from China; roughly 87,000 workers entered the country between 1850 and 1874 (Chang Rodríguez 1958). By increasing the supply of available labor, these additional workers diluted the ability of Peruvian workers to make demands for better wages and working conditions. And since these workers were not considered citizens, and because of significant racial prejudice, there was little opportunity for building solidarity between them and Peruvian or European workers (Gonzalez 1989). The Chinese immigrants were not included when later labor laws were developed; indeed, their employment set a pattern for a kind of "extralegal" employment in Peru.

Finally, literacy and land-holding requirements for voting effectively disenfranchised both indigenous Peruvian workers and the imported Chinese workers. In the second half of the nineteenth century, electoral participation was around 1 percent of the population (Colomer 2004; Engerman and Sokoloff 2005; Paredes 2008), and this pattern would continue well into the twentieth century. Indeed, even as late as 1963, only 45 percent of citizens had voting rights, and literacy requirements were not removed until 1979. Thus worker interests were never a significant electoral concern to democratic politicians, and labor legislation was slow to develop.

Nevertheless, some workers did begin organizing during this "preincorporation" period, generally in isolated pockets in the cities (around crafts) or in some mining regions. The first calls for labor regulation came from the mines and the ports—much as in Chile—where workers sought the adoption of an eight-hour workday. In 1913, dock workers in Lima were the first to receive this protection; they were followed by other urban workers in 1919, in 1929 by sugar workers, and finally in 1931 by miners (Bernedo 1990: 24). Cook (2007) summarizes this period of piecemeal legislation by quoting Angell (1979): early "Peruvian labor law was 'a collection of scattered measures dictated by oligarchical regimes to favor the arbitrary action of the employers.'" She continues, "[T]he Peruvian labor movement remained relatively weak and did not pose a threat to government or employers until the 1970s" (106). Hold-up power was lacking. Peru's labor force was homogenously low-skilled and interchangeable. Union organization developed very late. And the state lacked the administrative apparatus and bureaucracy to competently take the lead in structuring a strong labor policy. The result was labor regulation that developed much later than that of other countries, and tended to be modeled on (and only applied to) the needs of the few well organized and best skilled workers.

5.3. The Evolution and Manipulation of Labor Laws, 1933–90

In terms of the theory developed in Chapter 1, the minimal labor law provisions that developed in the early twentieth century fit with the low-skill workforce and weak organizational profile of nascent unions. There were very few workers with skills sufficient to set them apart in the productive process; they could not make demands for extensive job stability or workplace treatment provisions. In fact, given the relative slack in the labor force, they may have feared that making labor legislation onerous would hurt their own opportunities for employment. Likewise, workers had not developed their organizational capacity to reasonably pose a hold-up threat to the economy. In isolated circumstances, they could present a credible threat of stopping production at their own firm, but linkages across worker organizations were too weak to coordinate broader action. And conversely, the state and holders of capital were capable of employing their repressive apparatus to squelch incidents of labor unrest.

Nevertheless, labor regulation did develop, and as we will see below, in some periods became extremely protective of employment stability. This was largely driven by the political interests of leaders seeking office or already in power, who sought to build a coalition of supporters from the labor force. These measures were wildly out of proportion to the productive capacity of the economy, and were repeatedly dismantled or diminished by subsequent governments. In the short term, they were able to have a meaningful impact on labor relations, but they were unsustainable in the long term.

The first systematization of a labor code came under the government of Oscar Benavides in the 1933 Constitution and 1936 Civil Code (Castro Rivas 1981: 13–15). The impetus came not from the concerted demands of a crucial and well-organized labor force but instead from growing international and domestic concern about the "social question" of just treatment for workers. The first laws guaranteed an eight-hour workday, weekend rest, prohibition of employment to children under fourteen years of age and limits on the employment of those under eighteen, equal pay for equal work, and compensation for workplace injuries (Castro Rivas 1981: 15).

Labor law development moved at a slow pace, commensurate with the slow industrialization of the country. Until the 1960s, Peru had only small, isolated pools of workers who were united by either interests or geography for undertaking collective action. Government policy did not encourage the formation of additional unions. In fact, early mining and manufacturing unions formed without any government oversight or support, operating without any legal status but in many cases achieving some regularization in their contracts. Federations and confederations developed opportunistically as well, with the communist-inspired Confederación General de Trabajadores del Perú (CGTP) emerging in 1929, made up of truck drivers, textile workers, graphic artists, motorists and conductors, dockworkers, beer workers, and miners. However, taken together, these workers constituted less than 20 percent of the labor force. Nevertheless, their early organizing efforts were sufficient to draw the attention of the military government of General Oscar Benavides, who created a registry of labor unions at the Ministry of Public Health in an effort to curtail union formation (Yepez del Castillo and Bernedo Alvarez 1985: 14–15). The economic growth of the 1940s led in 1944 to the foundation of a second major labor federation—the Confederación de Trabajadores del Perú (CTP)— that quickly came to ally itself with the APRA party. However, the military government of Odría (1948–56) brought severe repression, especially of the CTP, and set back the union movement significantly (Yepez del Castillo and Bernedo Alvarez 1985: 16).

Nevertheless, unionization began to reach a sufficient size to threaten serious losses in the event of work stoppages, and labor's organization made it attractive to successive governments seeking to cement popular support. But divisions in the labor movement made an alliance with a single political party or movement, as we will see occurred in Argentina, impossible. Both democratic leaders and military governments sought partners in the labor movement, and to woo them they offered considerable expansions of both individual and collective labor laws. The return of democracy saw the Prado-Ugarteche government grant a crucial organizing privilege: leave from work for union representatives to conduct collective bargaining. It also made the critical first overtures toward job stability, mandating severance pay.

But it was the left-leaning Revolutionary Military government of Velasco Alvarado that went furthest in creating opportunities for union expansion (Cameron n.d.).[2] With its *Plan Inca*, it sought to create a "capitalism of the state" (*capitalismo de estado*). Aggressively implementing ISI policies, cutting off imports and investing in industrial development, it greatly increased the size of the state by expropriating foreign-owned industries and expanding public-sector employment (Contreras and Cueto 2000: 326–31). Basic industry was to be under the monopolistic management of the state under the *Ley General de la Industria*, and workers were to be integrated into this development plan as part of the "industrial communities" that would participate in the leadership and profits of the state-run firms (Parodi Trece 2000: 105). These bodies presented ripe opportunities for organizing unions and exercising state control over labor in critical industries.[3]

During this period, labor was becoming (and intentionally being converted into) a big enough bloc—both for elections and public manifestations—that it could affect considerable segments of the economy. But labor did not coalesce into a single, organized force, and no single partner was able to capture its support; workers remained divided in several confederations. APRA would have

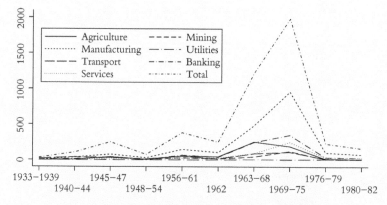

The growth of Peruvian unions was very slow until the 1960s,
when the Velasco Alvarado government promoted
industrial organization overseen by the state.

Figure 5.1. Union Organizations Receiving Government Recognition in
Peru, 1933–82. *Source:* Author's calculations based on Yepez del Castillo and
Bernedo Alvarez 1985.

been a logical political partner, because of its ideological affinity with labor's
interests, but it was outlawed during several periods. And even when APRA was
legally permitted to operate, it failed to command electoral majorities. Without
a lasting partner in APRA, labor's votes were sought by a succession of governments. This process set off incremental expansions of the labor code. And in general, once rights were granted in the law, they were slow to be dismantled by subsequent governments. The legal rights established during this period would have
a lasting impact, even if their coverage and enforcement would prove wanting.

Figure 5.1 shows the number of union organizations receiving government
recognition, by economic sector, in each of the governmental periods from 1933
to 1982 (data is from Yepez del Castillo and Bernedo Alvarez 1985). Unions expanded very slowly through the 1940s and 1950s, a time when Peru remained
heavily focused on agricultural production for export (unlike many of its Latin
American neighbors that had turned their economies inward in an effort to
industrialize). There is a significant upturn during the government of Manuel
Prado Ugarteche (1956–62), a conservative who had in a previous presidency
(1939–45) built a coalition with the left-leaning APRA party, and in this second
term was trying to draw their voters into his base.

Table 5.1.   Number of Strikes, by Government, 1957–84

Government	Total	Yearly Average
Prado 1957–62	1455	261
Military 1962–63	404	
Belaúnde 1963–68	2052	397
Military–Velasco 1968–75	3471	504
Military–Morales 1975–80	1875	469
Belaúnde 1980–85	2821	736

Source: Yepez del Castillo and Bernedo Alvarez 1985.

But with the arrival of the Velasco military government, union registration took off. Although manufacturing employment did not grow rapidly, manufacturing's share of total domestic product did (from 14 to 20 percent), and this created additional resources that could be shared with workers in industry. Workers could see that there was a prize worth fighting for. Manufacturing led the pack in this period of rapid union expansion, but other skilled sectors, including banking and commerce, also saw rapid organization of new unions. In fact, the growth in unionization was economy-wide, with even agriculture and services seeing a rise in registration of unions.

Another indicator of growing union capacity can be found in strike activity. Table 5.1 displays the number of strikes, by government, from the Prado government until the second Belaúnde government. Unions were clearly increasing their ability to mobilize and undertake action, but the large numbers of strikes also bears witness to the lack of coordination in the movement during this period. This disorganization undermined workers' ability to make coherent demands for labor legislation.

The legacy of division among union confederations prevented their acting solidaristically. Segments of the labor force acted opportunistically, with the CTP in particular taking advantage of ties to APRA to win benefits for itself during the Prado government. Observing the politics surrounding labor in the 1960s, Payne classically argued, "The labor movement in Peru . . . is politically oriented. This orientation is not primarily toward achieving favorable legislation through elected representatives and lobbying. Nor is it directed at the formation of a single labor party designed to gain control of the executive" (Payne 1965: 11). Relatively small, fragmented groups of unions often competed, rather than cooperated. The collective legislation that developed further supported this conflicted equilibrium: it made registration of unions fairly easy, but did not facilitate coordination to achieve shared goals.

The Origin and Evolution of Job Stability Legislation

As noted above, job stability formed the centerpiece of Peruvian individual labor legislation. These laws developed in a series of stages—they began in the severance pay measures established by Prado Ugarteche; they were promoted during the military government of Velasco Alvarado; they were weakened in the second phase of the military government, under Morales Bermúdez; they were once again strengthened substantially through their inclusion in the 1979 Constitution; and they were further emphasized and strengthened under the APRA-government of Alán García (Pasco Cosmópolis 2002: 13). They underwent their most significant reduction under Alberto Fujimori.

The high severance pay enacted by decree under Prado Ugarteche—equivalent to one month's salary for each year of service—provided significant job protection to workers by raising firing costs during the late 1950s and 1960s. A new standard was set, though, by the Revolutionary Government, which enacted Decree Law 18,471 (10 November 1970). This measure *guaranteed* the job stability of workers. It allowed workers to be fired only for "grave faults" committed by them or if the firm was completely shutting its doors or restructuring (and this required the authorization of the Ministry of Labor). Further, dismissed workers had the right to sue for reposition, and employers found in violation were required to provide back pay for missed work plus an additional three months' wages (later increased to twelve months' wages) and could face criminal prosecution (Castro Rivas 1981: 20–22). In the law's first years, employers responded by reducing their demand for new workers, on the one hand, and flooding the Ministry of Labor with requests to restructure and dismiss workers. But the government wanted to cement its relationship with labor, so it passed Decree Law 21,116 (11 March 1975), which conferred "absolute" job stability through the system of "compensation for time of service" (*Compensación por Tiempo de Servicios*, CTS) noted above, that made firing even more impractical for employers (Castro Rivas 1981: 25–27).

These 1970 and 1975 stability laws stand as the high point in individual labor protection in Peruvian history, and they became a constant point of reference for workers in later discussions. However, their "absolute" status was remarkably short-lived, for they were not congruent with the skill levels in the economy and they were only weakly calibrated with labor's ability to hold up the economy. Indeed, the laws were a blunt instrument. In seeking to construct a coalition with decisive industrial sectors, they offered the same rights to a broader swath of workers who could make no credible claim to organization, work stoppage, or even coordinated voting. Thus in 1978, the more cautious military government of Morales enacted Decree Law 22,126 (21 March 1978), limiting the application of the previous job security laws to workers employed prior to 1978. All new employees were governed by new stipulations, which stated that after three months' probation, workers were entitled to "relative job stability." This meant that in the period between three months' employment and three years' employment, they could be dismissed with ninety days' notice (Castro Rivas 1981: 29–30). Workers that attained three years of uninterrupted service with the same firm were entitled to the "absolute" job stability provisions. This set up two employment tracks, one of absolute stability for those workers who had passed the three-year minimum of employment and another for those who had not attained that longevity. It also created considerable incentives for employers to ensure that their workers did not achieve the fuller, privileged status: they could dismiss and rehire them, and thus avoid owing them "absolute" stability. For the government, these reforms divided labor between a protected traditional base and unprotected newcomers, who were less critical for maintaining power.

Finally, the Constitution of 1979, in its Article 48, recognized the right of the worker to job stability. This did not so much further extend the job stability provisions as make them a basic reference point in the legal code, stating that firing could occur only for "just cause" (Cook 2007: 115).

The return of democracy, and the return to the presidency of Belaúnde in 1980, now at the front of the moderate Alianza Popular, did not lead to a further expansion of labor rights. Rather, high unemployment, declining real wages, and the increasing resistance of employers to the job stability provisions produced a decade of decline in the power of organized labor (Cook 2007: 15). In addition, the ties that had developed between segments of the labor force and the military during the military regime made labor an uncertain and untrustworthy partner for Belaúnde. No significant labor regulation was passed, evasion increased on the part of employers, and informal employment was on the rise.

This pattern might have been expected to change under Alán García, the first president to come from the APRA party. To labor's delight, he enacted in June 1986 Law 24,514, which reaffirmed the job stability ideals from 1970 by restoring three months' severance pay for workers employed for less than a year (and increasing the severance pay to six months' wages for workers employed from one to three years, and to twelve months for those employed for more than three years). Yet, facing pressures and a mounting economic crisis, García also enacted an Emergency Employment Program that allowed employers to hire without requirement to pay benefits or ensure job stability (Cook 2007: 16, fn. 12), offsetting his job stability measures with a way around them.

This outcome set the tone for Peru's labor market in the post-absolute-job-stability era. On the one hand, the laws sought to continue to meet the needs of the traditional, industrial labor base, for which job stability was a particularly coveted prize. But on the other hand, they sought to address an increasingly heterogeneous group of nontraditional workers, some of whom were unemployed but seeking formal sector employment, some of whom worked primarily in the informal sector or in self- or family-employment, and some of whom mixed their economic activity among these possibilities. Thus García played to the interests of the higher-skilled workers in industry and professional services and government by restoring full job severance packages, while reaching out to lower-skilled workers who found themselves unemployed or in the informal sector with the employment promotion plan.

By the 1980s, limited union membership and limited coverage of labor laws was the norm in Peru. Table 5.2 displays the rate of unionization in 1981–82. As noted above, although the bar is set low by regional standards for registering a union, unionization remains quite low. In the late-industrializing, small-firm, high-informality context of Peru, most workers do not find themselves in firms where union membership is even a possibility. The first column in Table 3 shows that unionization is quite high in firms where unions are possible—67.8 percent in the country as a whole, and 73.4 percent in Lima. But, as a percentage of all salaried workers, the figures are much lower—39.1 percent in the economy as a whole, and 52.8 percent in metropolitan Lima. And finally, as a percentage of all workers in the economically active population, union membership only reaches 17.5 percent. This factor, combined with the divisions in unions previ-

Table 5.2.   Unionization in Peru, 1981–82

	As share of union-eligible workers	As share of all salaried workers	As share of all workers
Total	67.8	39.1	17.5
Lima	73.4	52.8	
Rest of Country	60.9	28.3	

Source:Yepez del Castillo and Bernedo Alvarez 1985.

Table 5.3.   Coverage of Collective Bargaining Agreements, by Sector, 1981

Sector	Share of Economically Active Population	Sector	Share of Economically Active Population
Agriculture	6.2	Construction	78.9
Mining	39.0	Transport	16.3
Manufacturing	45.1	Commerce	18.8
Electricity	51.8	Total	31.5

Source:Yepez del Castillo and Bernedo Alvarez 1985.

ously noted, means that the modal worker in Peru is neither unionized nor in stable, formal-sector employment.

Similarly, coverage of collective bargaining agreements is also limited. As Table 5.3 shows, less than a third of the economically active population has its wages or working conditions decided in collective negotiations. However, there is significant variation in the coverage by economic sector—industrial, utility, mining, and construction workers are far more likely to have collective bargaining than are workers in agriculture, transport, or commerce. While collective bargaining coverage is not a perfect proxy for the application of all labor laws, it does give some sense of the portion of the workforce that sees its fate as tied to the collective action of worker organizations. Taken together, the data in Tables 5.2 and 5.3 suggest that labor law application is limited to between one-sixth and one-third of all Peruvians; yet, in sectors where it applies, it is quite important.

In sum, the Peruvian labor code and labor market by the 1980s displayed several divergent trends and contradictions. First, individual labor law was highly protective for those on permanent contracts. The military governments of the 1970s and the García government had made job stability the foundation for Peruvian individual labor law. However, this rigidity was complemented by measures to promote employment on temporary contracts. And a significant side effect was increasing evasion on the part of employers and the growth of informal employment. In collective labor law, unions were relatively easy to form, but divided into several confederations and thus quite weak in their political impact. Two competing goals coexisted in the labor code: one focused on permanent employment and significant worker organization, and the other centered on flexibility and worker turnover.

5.4. The Fujimori Reforms

The government of Alberto Fujimori—who came to power in the midst of economic and political chaos, and who increasingly accrued powers to himself by dismissing Congress and governing by decree—represents a decisive turning point in the labor legislation of Peru.[4] Indeed, Fujimori's labor measures represent the fullest legal embrace of the bifurcated labor market that has come to characterize Peru, divided between secure formal-sector employment and vulnerable short-term employment. In the individual labor regulation arena, it created permanent legal means for hiring workers on temporary contracts. Thus it fundamentally altered the law's primary orientation toward job stability. And in the field of collective labor regulation, it established the principle of union pluralism and privileged firm level collective-bargaining, thus further weakening and fragmenting union organizations. Fujimori's success in implementing these reforms is attributable to four factors: (1) a strategy of rolling out reforms so that they only came to touch insiders last, (2) the small group of insiders and low public support for unions, (3) the fragmentation of those unions, and (4) his own popularity after restoring the nation's economic fortunes and combating the Shining Path guerillas.

In attacking the principle of job stability, Fujimori strategically rolled out the reforms in two phases. In 1991, Decree Law 728 introduced nine new "modalities" of short-term contracts—including those for the start of a business, for reconverting a business, and even for the broad category of "market necessities" (Vega Ruiz 2005: 99).[5] These effectively gave employers wide latitude in hiring workers on temporary contracts. In addition, Fujimori chipped away at job stability measures by removing them for workers hired after 1991 (Cook 2007: 122). Thus he avoided angering workers already in protected jobs, and he simultaneously catered to the unemployed, who were eager to find even temporary employment.

By the mid-1990s, Fujimori had brought inflation down from 139 percent in 1991 to 15 percent, and the economy was growing at a rate of 12.5 percent (Cook 2007: 121). On the basis of this economic improvement, he felt he could undertake a second round of reforms. His 1993 Constitution removed the principle of absolute job stability from the earlier 1979 Constitution, instead requiring only "adequate protection against arbitrary dismissal" (Cook 2007: 123). And Law 26,513 in 1995 did away with job stability for all workers, not simply those hired after 1991. Thus by the mid-1990s, Fujimori had effectively eliminated the principle of job security from the labor code. As will be seen below, severance pay remained fairly high, but even it was reduced, and it came to cover only about a fifth of the population.

Fujimori also undertook a broad reform of the collective labor code. Early on, he weakened unions by removing protection for union leaders when in office or carrying out their union duties (the *fuero sindical*). This, of course, hindered their ability to organize opposition to his first round of reforms. And in 1992 he introduced a Law of Collective Relations (25,593), which further fragmented unions, by allowing more than one union at the firm level, and by complicating the procedures for collective bargaining and strikes (Cook 2007: 123). Fujimori also dealt decisive blows to state-sector workers, reducing employment in federal jobs from 633,349 to 294,979 between 1990 and 1993 (Mejía 1998: 24).[6] Thus by the mid-1990s, while unions were easier to start (given the new provision for union pluralism at the plant level), most collective bodies had a harder time negotiating contracts and taking broad-based action through strikes.

In addition to riding the wave of his successes at bringing inflation under control and making significant headway against the violence and terrorism of the Shining Path guerillas, Fujimori was aided in his labor reforms by several factors. First, the reforms were poorly understood; in a 1996 poll, 47 percent of respondents said they were not informed about the labor law modifications carried out by the government. Perhaps as a result, disapproval of these labor laws was only 51 percent, and curiously, the young (age eighteen to twenty-five)—who were most likely to experience the effects of the reforms—were also the most likely to be uninformed, and to approve of the reforms (Grupo Apoyo: November 1996). The complexity of the measures may have made possible negative consequences less apparent to them (such as the foreclosed opportunities for job stability), while the promise of "flexibilized" opportunities to be hired attracted their support.

Second, unions enjoyed very little public confidence in Peru, and their status only diminished in the public view during the 1990s. Indeed, during this period,

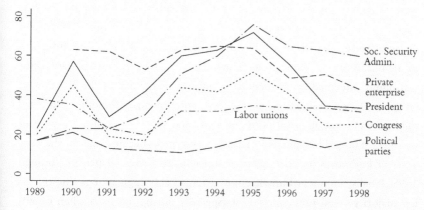

*In the 1990s, unions were among the least trusted political institutions in Peru.
Private enterprise, in contrast, was highly respected, as was President Fujimori,
especially in the middle of the decade.*

Figure 5.2. Confidence in Peruvian Political Institutions, 1989–98. *Source:* Polls
administered by Grupo Apoyo.

unions were among the least trusted political institutions. Figure 5.2 displays
polling data on the confidence of Peruvians in various public actors and collective bodies. For most of the period of Fujimori's government, unions were the
second least trusted group, surpassed only by political parties (which enjoyed
less than 20 percent support). This was a deadly combination, for it undermined
both of the crucial actors that could underwrite labor-friendly laws: unions
which could hold up broad sectors of the economy and parties that could ally
with them to enact policy.[7]

By the end of the 1990s, union members clearly stood as a group apart within
Peruvian society, and for this reason it is not surprising that many nonunionized
workers did not trust them. Union workers were "more likely to be more educated, older, and with significantly longer tenures than non-unionized workers.
They were also more likely to work in a large firm and to have a permanent
contract" (Saavedra and Torero 2002: 13). In addition, after Fujimori's reforms,
temporary workers had an even lower probability of working in a unionized
firm (Saavedra and Torero 2002: 14). In short, little likelihood existed for solidaristic behavior between these two groups of workers.

In contrast, the main social actors promoting the liberalization of labor laws were extremely popular. Private enterprise had embraced a more public, political role during the Fujimori years, taking on a strategy consisting of "finance of electoral campaigns, effective lobbying work in Congress, and greater influence in the means of communication" (Durand 2006). The corporate, private sector was highly esteemed by the general population at the end of the 1980s, with an approval rating of 63 percent. State-run enterprises, on the other hand, had only a 34 percent approval rating in 1990, and this figure fell to 16 percent in 1991.[8] The public appraisal of private enterprise began to fall in the later years of Fujimori's presidency, but it still remained over 50 percent through 1998. Finally, Fujimori himself enjoyed remarkably high ratings throughout the majority of his presidency, most especially during the years when he was most forceful in facing the Shining Path and in passing his sweeping economic reforms.

This does not mean, however, that labor law changes always went unnoticed or unopposed. The case of severance payments provides a good example of organized resistance. Mandatory severance payments were intended to be decreased in 1996, from one month's salary per year of seniority of the worker being dismissed to one-half month's salary per year. However, when the draft regulation made its way into the news, the public outcry was so great that the government conducted an abrupt about-face: it announced that the proposed decrease in severance pay was in fact a *typographical error*, and that their true intention was to increase severance pay by a half. The result was a more generous, rather than less generous, severance pay calculation (Saavedra 1999; recounted in MacIsaac and Rama 2001).

This incident concerning mandatory severance pay is highly revelatory of the politics surrounding labor regulations in Peru. First, it shows that the appeal of severance pay is broader than its coverage. Even workers who do not meet the requirements to be eligible for it (including sufficient time in a particular job and "permanent" status) are willing to mobilize around it, or at least express their outrage. This may reflect their expectation that they will eventually achieve permanent status in their jobs and enjoy the protection of the severance pay provisions. Second, it makes clear that the government recognized the threat posed by dissatisfied workers, even if many of these are not directly included in these policies or many are not unionized.

Finally, it may indicate that these measures, while popular, are less costly than they appear. Since coverage is limited to about one in five private sector work-

Table 5.4. Collective Bargaining Agreements and Their Coverage, 1990–96

Year	Number	Coverage	Year	Number	Coverage
1990	1762		1994	883	
1991	1402	27.8	1995	803	
1992	401		1996	623	7.4
1993	1059				

Source: Rueda-Catry, Sepúlveda-Malbrán, and Vega Ruiz 1998.
Coverage figures are for workers in Metropolitan Lima only.

ers (and one in three private-sector wage earners) (MacIsaac and Rama 2001), increases in this policy do not affect most employers. Arguably, the previous policy was high enough that the firing of long-time workers was highly unlikely; adding to the figure did not make the firing of any of these workers (and being subject to the required severance pay) any less or more likely. And since fixed-term contracting options provide many opportunities for hiring workers without incurring the cost of high severance pay, employers could anticipate that they would not suddenly be burdened with a large number of severance-pay-eligible—and demanding—workers.[9]

Unions are hurt, too, by their divisions and inability to coordinate. As Yepez del Castillo and Bernedo Alvarez (1985) summarized for the 1980s, "The existence of parallel unions is still observed in important sectors. This is the case of workers in the metals industry, in which there exist two federations and union division has impeded a unified response by the workers in one of the sectors most hurt by the recession. The ongoing confusion between union and party in some sectors of the left [has] led them to forget the character of a unique front of unions" (93). At the end of Fujimori's government, one commentator called the unions "totally disarticulated and broken" (Romero Montes 2002: 96).

Thus the effects of the Fujimori reforms were substantial and far-reaching. The use of fixed-term contracts increased, significantly reducing costs to employers but also raising the "precariousness" of employment relations for workers. Unions saw a drop in their membership numbers, while collective bargaining declined in both the quantity and quality of the measures it considered, frequently introducing productivity requirements for wage increases and overturning long-standing legal protections for workers (Pasco Cosmópolis 2002: 26–27). Table 5.4 presents the number of collective bargaining agreements from 1990 to 1997, making clear the pattern of declining numbers. Unlike in Argentina, where the decreased number of total (mostly firm-level) agreements was compensated by greater use of sector-level agreements (Etchemendy and Collier 2007), in Peru no such substitution occurred. Collective bargaining declined by approximately two-thirds under Fujimori, and coverage of these agreements declined by three-quarters, so that only 7.4 percent of the workforce had their employment relations governed by collective bargaining agreements in 1996.

5.5. The 2000s: Hints at Change, but No Substantial Reforms

Since 2000, Peru has made only marginal changes in its labor laws. While Chile saw gradual expansions of rights under the *Concertación*, and Argentina (as will be seen below) witnessed a significant revindication of privileges for organized labor in the early years of the Kirchner governments, Peru never implemented significant enhancements of its labor code. It continues to provide strong job security measures for a fairly small subset of its workers—roughly one-fifth of them—and leaves the remainder of workers in temporary contracts or the informal sector. Collective labor law, although marginally strengthened, perversely creates additional opportunities for division in the labor movement, and has not fostered unified pressure for further changes in the labor code.

Worker divisions and a "low-skill trap" (Schneider 2009) greatly complicated effective mobilization for labor law improvements. The Peruvian labor market in the 2000s was highly bifurcated between those covered by full labor protections—estimated at 21 percent of private wage earners with stable job contracts—and those who are not (García 2004).[10] A vicious circle emerged: with permanent, higher-skilled jobs so scarce, workers were discouraged from pursuing the education or training that would make them eligible for them. And few employers were willing to invest in training for nonpermanent workers; high-rotation industrial firms, which make extensive use of temporary contracts, had only a 28 percent chance of investing in worker training compared with their more stable counterparts (García 2004: 31). Thus the restrictive, bifurcated system tended to replicate itself.

Thus conditions similar to those that existed in earlier periods—relatively homogeneous skill levels and limited and poor labor organization—complicated any change in the labor laws inherited from the Fujimori years. While educational levels rose, employment on permanent contracts did not keep pace; better-skilled workers seemed to be absorbed into temporary, rather than permanent, jobs. Labor unions remained divided—principally between the CGTP and the CTP—and lacked a strong political party partner, and thus were often unable to present a unified front vis-à-vis employers or the state. As a result, both the Toledo and García governments that came to power in the 2000s made only marginal changes to the labor regulations; indeed, the latter introduced several measures but failed to see them through the congressional approval process.

Alejandro Toledo: 2001–6

After Fujimori stepped down and was succeeded by the brief care-taker government of Augustin Paniagua, Alejandro Toledo came to power. The political campaigns of both 2000 and 2001 revealed how Fujimori's rule, and his inclusion of measures in the 1993 Constitution geared toward participative and more direct democracy, essentially undermined the role of parties in the nation. Tanaka summarizes the weakness of parties in the Peruvian system: "[F]rom the middle of the 1990s onward, in Peru there exists a politics without parties: politics is carried out by actors marked by dis-ideologization; personalism; volatility, improvisation, and precarious leadership; short-term thinking; excessive pragmatism; all of which have as a consequence the impossibility of making calculations about the medium- and long-term, and complicates the development of collective activity" (Tanaka 2005: 22). This lack of viable, meaningful parties with long-term orientations meant that labor had no institutional means to bring its demands for a softening of the Fujimori reforms into the restored democratic arena.

Toledo was a particularly unconnected political player. Formerly an academic and consultant to the World Bank, International Labor Organization, and other international organizations, he had entered politics in the 1995 presidential campaign, gaining just 3 percent of the vote. In 1999 he was still polling just 6 percent support. But as the campaign developed, he postured himself as the candidate who could best complete the "democratic transition" after the Fujimori years. Although he failed to win election at that time, his 37 percent of the popular vote (second to Fujimori, amid allegations of electoral fraud) made him a top contender after Fujimori was forced to allow a second election in which he would not participate. In that set of elections, Toledo won a run-off with Alán García, with 53 percent of the vote to García's 47 percent (Tanaka 2005: 24). His centrist party, Perú Posible, won only 45 of the 120 seats in the Congress, so he had to ally with the more conservative Frente Independiente Moralizador (the Independent Moralizing Front—FIM, as it is abbreviated in Spanish).

Thus Toledo came to office without ties to labor and with a coalition that allied him more directly with the representatives of business. To the extent that labor had tied its fate to a party, this had been with APRA. Unlike in Argentina, where the returns of democracy frequently unleashed significant labor-friendly reforms in response to pent-up demands, in Peru the democratic government of Toledo did not place an emphasis on reaching out to labor. This was in part a reflection on the coalition that had elected it, and in part the result of the much weaker status of labor in making demands of the state. But after five years of declining strike activity, unions took to the streets in increasing numbers in each of the first three years of Toledo's government (Tanaka 2005: 34). However, this growing strike activity was still lower than had been experienced in the Fujimori years.

Changes to labor laws were confined to marginal changes in the laws inherited from the Fujimori years. On the individual labor regulation front, Toledo permitted employers to expand the workday and work week for individuals not employed at the maximum time (Supreme Decree 007–2002-TR of 2002). His government also gave workers greater opportunities to use 80 percent of their accumulated savings in the CTS system for the purchase of a home (Law 28,461 of 2005). Also, further legal oversight of temporary, training contracts was provided in an effort to ensure that these be used in a genuinely formative—and not exploitative—way (Law 28,518 of 2005). A law against sexual harassment in the workplace was passed (Law 27,942 of 2003).

Collective labor relations under Toledo saw greater organizing potential and protection given to unions, and the restoration of many freedoms that had been foreclosed by Fujimori. Law 27,912 of 2003 removed the prohibition on political activity by unions. Further, it allowed workers to join unions more easily, eliminating a job tenure requirement, and reduced the number of required workers to begin a new union from one hundred to fifty. Greater union freedom in choosing leadership was granted, again through eliminating requirements for longevity in the firm. In addition, collective bargaining at the sector level was expanded, but only to unions representing the majority of workers and firms in the industry; otherwise, collective bargaining was restricted to the firm level. Finally, the law facilitated strikes by removing the requirement for a secret ballot of union members prior to undertaking the strike.

Alán García: 2006–10

García's return to the presidency, at the head of the traditionally more left-leaning APRA party, seemed to augur opportunities for more labor friendly labor legislation. However, the process of rehabilitating himself as a viable candidate, and his tightly contested race with the nationalist Ollanta Humala, resulted in García's adopting a much more centrist, or even center-right, political stance. Labor unions, although divided, looked at him with a certain amount of suspicion, and they brought pressure to bear for a revisiting of both the pension privatizations and the labor contract flexibilizations of the 1990s. García gave both of these issues significant play in the electoral campaign, and immediately brought them into discussion once elected. However, these efforts did not result in significant changes in Peru's labor legislation.

In an early overture to better-off, formal sector workers, he quickly assembled a plan to allow the "free disaffiliation" (*libre disafiliación*) of workers in the privatized pension system. This private system had become the object of much dissatisfaction. Even though it covered only 15 percent of the population, 60 percent had expressed their lack of confidence in the private funds.[11] Much like the initial Kirchner plans in Argentina, this initiative was to allow workers to "revisit" their decision to join the private pension funds, and if they so desired, switch back into the public pension system. However, after much fanfare, the proposal was limited to only those workers who could demonstrate that they had been defrauded in the initial decision to join the private pension funds. The government projected that only 1,400 workers would be eligible, including 800 miners. In a system of 3.7 million private pension fund affiliates, and a total of roughly 28 million people in the country, this amounted to an almost inconsequential measure (even though the government estimated the cost of the reaffiliation of workers to the state system to be $1.4 billion) (*El Comercio* 2006a).

More attention was given to a reform of the labor law (a new *Ley General de Trabajo*), which promised to be deeper than those changes undertaken by Toledo. Unions called for a return of many of the privileges they had enjoyed under earlier governments—including the possibility of reinstatement for improperly dismissed workers (although unions were divided over whether this should involve a return of "absolute" job stability or not), increasing the maximum severance pay (from one to two years' salary, at which it had been capped under Fujimori), and collective bargaining at the sectoral level (*El Comercio* 2006b). Employers opposed these measures as onerous, and stalled discussions in the National Labor Council. The minister of production, Rafael Rey, argued that the reform should be opposed because it would apply only to 14 percent of the workforce—those who were unionized and in permanent contracts (*El Comercio* 2006c). By 2007, the discussion of the new labor law was said to be approximately "85 percent" complete, but it eventually remained frozen in Congress without approval (*El Comercio* 2007).

Thus the García administration did not make significant inroads in reversing the trends of the Fujimori labor reforms. As Chapter 3 made clear, Peru stands out as a nation that underwent one of the most pronounced reforms in the region in the 1990s and then has not seen substantial modifications since.

5.6. Conclusion

This chapter has presented both an overview of the principal features of the Peruvian labor code through time and an explanation of the contrary currents in that labor code that have emerged to meet the need of a bifurcated labor market with weak, fragmented union organization. Peru's strong individual protections, and especially their emphasis on job security, bolstered by high severance payments, developed in embryonic form when APRA coalitions brought labor interests to bear in the legislative process. However, their greatest expansion occurred relatively late, when Peru embraced ISI policies under the Revolutionary Military government of Velasco Alvarado. This government sought to use labor legislation to cement a coalition that would underwrite its other economic reforms. Opposition from employers eventually led to some rollback on "absolute" stability but did not fundamentally change the prolabor orientation of labor legislation.

Massive reform came under Alberto Fujimori, who was less beholden to labor because he enjoyed such high popularity after bringing inflation under control and containing the violence of Shining Path guerrillas. In addition, polling evidence suggests that many people were not well informed about the complex legal changes he was making, and that this shielded him from significant opposition. And perhaps most important, while the labor law reforms reduced protections for the portion of the labor force that enjoyed them, they also included advances for labor in its collective relations and they facilitated the hiring of workers from the informal sector on temporary contracts. Thus the 1990s reforms, although often considered harsh, actually catered to the interests of unemployed and informal sector workers, who in Peru make up over half the population. This helps explain why they have persisted, and why opposition in recent periods comes mainly from concentrated groups of workers in protected sectors—such as doctors in the state-run medical system.

One important contribution of this chapter is to challenge, or at least add additional nuance to, the literature on ties between left parties, unions, and labor legislation. Although Cook (2007) argues that "[t]hroughout the middle decades of the twentieth century, Peruvian labor's fortunes rose and fell with APRA's relationship with power" (106), and Collier and Collier (2002) describe Peru as a case of "party-incorporation" of the labor movement, the relationship between labor and APRA was in fact far from close or lasting. Indeed, one simple reason behind the linkage is the lack of other long-term parties in Peru; many parties have been extraordinarily short-lived, especially in more recent decades as Peru's party system has collapsed. While governments in Peru that affiliated with APRA were more generous in their response to labor in the early decades, they were not the exclusive suppliers of benefits to the workforce. Indeed, in the case of labor regulation, this chapter has shown that military governments have been the greatest innovators and agents of expansion (and contraction) of labor protections. The hallmark "absolute" job stability measure was passed under the Revolutionary Military government of Velasco Alvarado and saw its greatest enforcement and coverage during his and the subsequent military government of Morales Bermúdez. It would seem that the strategy of striking bargains with the labor force is not the restricted province of left-leaning parties, but in fact may be advantageous to any political agent seeking to gain office or stay in office.

APRA has also failed to capitalize on its earlier, close ties to labor. The fragmentation that occurred in the 1960s under the Belaúnde government, as APRA became both opportunistic and particularistic, allowed for the emergence of rivalry among labor unions—the APRA-affiliated CTP and the communist-inspired CGTP—ultimately weakening the impact of the labor movement. And finally, during the periods in which APRA has controlled the presidency, the results on labor legislation have been at best mixed. The first García government had two contrary trends in labor legislation, with the return of job stability as a basic principle but a policy of employment promotion that effectively bypassed that principle. And the second García administration was not effective at enacting stronger labor provisions, even though these were raised and brought to

Congress. In both cases, the García governments were plagued by other problems—economic adjustments during the 1980s and the 2000s, and Shining Path violence in the earlier period. Why has the party that has the strongest linkages to labor also been one of the least likely to implement labor-friendly labor laws? The answer lies in the small size of the skilled labor force, and the poor coordination among labor unions, as this chapter has highlighted. These prevent labor from acting as a cohesive and coherent political force in Peruvian society.

In sum, the Peruvian labor code stands at one extreme of the possible labor law configurations predicted by the theory in Chapter 2 of this book. With a very small skilled labor force and small, fragmented unions that have little permanent linkage to political parties, the country does not have a unified labor movement or political expression of labor demands. Expansive labor laws have been enacted only under authoritarian regimes, and these laws have reinforced the patterns of skill acquisition and distribution, limited union membership, and fractured union solidarity. The current low levels of unionization and protection under individual labor laws for job stability and severance pay are not a new development, but a logical extension of the bifurcated labor movement that has characterized the nation for most of the last century. Given these deep economic structural roots, further proposals for redesigning the labor code are unlikely to produce meaningful change or lasting results.

Appendix Table 5.A. Labor Policy in Peru, by Government, 1933–2007

Period	Party/President	Labor Policy Developments
1900–1933	Various	Piecemeal measures *Individual Relations:* Eight-hour workday for some workers
1933–39	Benavides	*Individual Relations:* Guaranteed an eight-hour workday, weekend rest, prohibition of employment to children under 14 years of age and limits on the employment of those under 18, equal pay for equal work, and compensation for workplace injuries. Some severance pay prescriptions *Collective Relations:* Registration of unions with Ministry of Public Health
1939–45	Prado Ugarteche *(promised APRA recognition)*	*No significant new labor legislation.*
1945–48	Bustamante y Rivero *(alliance with APRA)*	*Collective Relations:* Fostered union recognition and wage gains

Period	Party/President	Labor Policy Developments
1948–56	Odría *Military* *(APRA outlawed)*	*Individual Relations:* Guaranteed sick workers the right to return to job *Collective Relations:* Required Ministry of Labor approval for collective dismissals
1956–62	Prado Ugarteche *Movimiento* *Democrático* *Peruano-Convivencia* *(alliance with* *APRA)*	*Individual Relations:* Set severance pay at one month per year of employment *Collective Relations:* Gave union representatives leave from work to carry out collective negotiations
1962–63	Godoy *Military*	*No significant labor legislation*
1963–68	Belaúnde Terry *Acción Popular* *(alliance with* *APRA, which* *fractured as APRA* *joined conservative* *UNO coalition)*	*Collective Relations:* Increased opportunities for union organizing
1968–75	Velasco Alvarado *Revolutionary* *Military Govt. –* *First Phase*	*Individual Relations:* Created Industrial Communities to give workers participation in firm governance and profits. Decree-Law of Labor Stability, increasing legal sanctions (fines and back-pay) for dismissal and allowing dismissal only for just cause and with government authorization, applied to workers after three months seniority
1975–80	Morales Bermúdez *Military Govt.—* *Second Phase*	*Individual Relations:* 1978 Decree-Law eased dismissals for workers up to three years' seniority, but raised cost of firing after three years. 1979 Constitution incorporated the principle of job security as an economic right
1980–85	Belaúnde Terry *Alianza Popular*	*No significant labor legislation, but high unemployment and wage declines, as well as division among labor unions.*
1985–90	García Pérez *APRA*	*Individual Relations:* In 1986, restored job stability through increased severance pay scale, but also started Emergency Employment Program that allowed employers to hire without paying benefits or assuming job security requirements
1990–2000	Fujimori *Cambio 90* *Perú 2000*	*Individual Relations:* In 1991 Law of Employment Promotion, introduced short-term contracts, youth contracts, flexible scheduling. Ended job security for post-1991 contracts. Broadened the possible causes for dismissal and facilitated collective dismissals. Promoted subcontracting of services. Weakened severance protections. In 1995, lengthened time of short-term contracts. Replaced absolute job security with "adequate protection against arbitrary dismissal." In 1996, raised severance pay *Collective relations:* In 1992 Law of Collective Relations, established union pluralism. Promoted decentralized collective bargaining. Increased strike restrictions. Favored small unions over large unions. Gave more government oversight for unions *Social Policy:* Established private pension system in 1993

Period	Party/President	Labor Policy Developments
2000	Paniagua Corazao *Acción Popular*	*No significant labor legislation.*
2001–6	Toledo *Perú Posible*	*Individual Relations:* Permitted expansion of work day. Allowed use of 80 percent of worker's CTS funds for house purchase. Expanded legal oversight of formative (apprenticeship) contract terms. Adopted laws against sexual harassment in the workplace *Collective Relations:* Removed prohibition on political activity by unions. Allowed workers to more easily join unions, and reduced the number of required workers to begin a new union. Allowed greater union freedom in choosing leadership. Limited collective bargaining at sector level to unions representing the majority of workers and firms in the industry—otherwise, collective bargaining restricted to firm level. Facilitated strikes by removing requirement for secret ballot of union members
2006–7	García Pérez *APRA*	*Individual Relations:* Proposal to increase maximum mandatory severance pay from 1 to 2 years *Collective Relations:* Proposal for greater freedom for sectoral collective bargaining

Sources: Castro Rivas 1981; Contreras and Cueto 2000; Collier and Collier 2002; Vega Ruiz 2005; Vilela et al. 2006; Cook 2007.

Chapter 6

Integration and Incorporation: Corporatist Labor Regulation in Argentina

The month of January stands out in the Argentine calendar, and particularly in Buenos Aires. Schools and businesses shut down as the city's working residents—especially those in unionized jobs in the public and private sectors—flood out to the beach resorts of Mar del Plata or interior destinations around Córdoba. Normal commercial activities all but stop in the capital, and unions decamp for the summer and play host to their members in the social clubs and low-cost hotels they own and operate in both locations. A full fifteen days or more of vacation with family are part of the annual summer rhythm for workers as diverse as doctors and lawyers and plumbers and truck drivers, as well as technicians and factory workers and bankers. Labor leaders and union members from far-flung provinces rub shoulders and enjoy hours-long *asados* of the beef for which Argentina is famous.

Just a few weeks later—beginning in February and March—the season of labor mobilizations begins, when unions call on their members to take to the streets in anticipation of collective bargaining over wages and other benefits. Relationships built in the annual vacations foster solidarity and increase attendance at rallies, helping the unions show their strength and signal their capacity to hurt the economy if their demands are not met. Annual salary increases, always calibrated to exceed increases in the cost of living, are among their chief demands. Successful campaigns are celebrated in the winter vacation season, when schools again shut down and many workers make use of their mid-year *aguinaldo* (a salary bonus mandated by law—one of two given each year—equivalent to a half-month's paycheck) to visit the capital and enjoy its theaters, parks, museums, and restaurants.

Even if the numbers who enjoy these month-long vacations has fallen in recent decades, the overwhelming presumption in Argentina, both in the law and
in popular thinking, is that workers are entitled to them (Neffa 2004). Chapters
2 and 3 have shown that the country stands out for having one of the most
protective combinations of individual and collective labor regulations in Latin
America—a "corporatist" labor code in the terminology of this book. Indeed, its
labor regime has been called "the most important union movement of the New
World" (Galiani and Gerchunoff 2003: 133). Workers across the economy—especially in the manufacturing, transportation, professional, and public sectors—
enjoy job security, annual bonuses, paid maternity and disability leaves, and retirement benefits.[1] Unions are granted expansive rights to organize, coordinate,
and manage immense resources.

This chapter undertakes two tasks. First, it traces the historical development
of Argentina's labor code, highlighting how the hold-up power of skilled and
organized workers made its laws robust and resilient despite several attempts at
reform. It begins in the late nineteenth and early twentieth centuries, when the
foundations for later labor regulation were laid. It then examines labor law development during Argentina's three periods of Peronist government—under Perón
himself (1946–55), under Carlos Menem (1989–99), and under Nestor Kirchner
and Cristina Fernández de Kirchner (2003–present). These have been the most
significant moments of labor law expansion, reform, and re-establishment, and
they have given continuity to the labor code despite significant efforts at change
undertaken by nondemocratic and non-Peronist governments.

Second, it examines one of the most enigmatic aspects of Argentine labor
politics: the enduring, but often uneasy, relationship between organized labor—in particular, as represented by its main confederation, the Confederación
General de Trabajadores (CGT)—and the powerful Peronist Party (Partido Justicialista—the Juticialist Party [PJ]) (Crassweller 1988). It has frequently been
assumed that their tight relationship would make their fates rise and fall together,
but this chapter shows that there is actually a *nonmonotonic* relationship between
the electoral strength of the PJ (and its presidents) and the legal benefits enjoyed
by its supporters from organized labor. In other words, rather than simply and
continuously representing the interests of organized labor, the Peronist Party has
calibrated its approach to labor law based on the electoral support its candidates
enjoy. When the party, or its candidates, have faced electoral competition, it has
seen labor regulation as a way of attracting labor's votes and strengthening party-

union ties. Conversely, when Peronist politicians have ruled without meaning-ful rivals, they have been most likely to enact reforms that hurt labor's interests (Murillo 2001, 2005).

As a reference for the reader, Table 6.A, at the end of the chapter, presents the historical evolution in labor laws and related social policy measures from approximately 1900 forward. The table first gives an overall characterization of the relationship between the government and labor, and then explains the out-comes of the period on each of three indicators—individual rights, collective labor relations, and social policy. For simplicity of presentation, the following sections of the chapter focus on four key periods of significant labor law con-testation: the "preincorporation" period before Perón, Perón's first two terms in office (1946–55), the Menem years (1989–99), and the governments of Nestor Kirchner and Cristina Fernández de Kirchner (2003–present). Other periods, which include both moments of military and opposition rule, are treated only in passing because of their limited effects on the long-term trajectory of labor code development.[2]

6.1. The Origins of the Argentine Labor Code

Many analysts trace the Argentine labor code to the first government of Juan Domingo Perón, but recent scholarship shows that most of its measures had al-ready begun to take shape before his ascent to power (Torre 2006; Carnes 2014). At the close of the nineteenth and beginning of the twentieth century, orga-nized workers in key productive sectors were beginning to demand and achieve significant protections. As this section will show, decades prior to Perón's ascent, these "preincorporation" workers had protections against arbitrary dismissals, forced overtime work, and unsanitary conditions, and their unions had been granted legal status and significant bargaining capacity.

Argentina's labor market prior to the twentieth century was extremely tight and its production processes were characterized by significant bottlenecks. Throughout this period, the country experienced "an acute shortage of labor" (Galiani and Gerchunoff 2003: 126). With vast, far-flung territories dedicated mostly to cattle-raising and agriculture for export, it required a significant influx of workers, many of whom needed to be willing to travel seasonally following crops. Employers faced frequent labor shortages, and workers shouldered the high cost of regular relocation and frequent bouts of inactivity. Employment was thus irregular and impermanent, carried out in an effective "spot market," in which jobs and wages were agreed upon for a day or brief season without formal contracts (Galiani and Gerchunoff 2003: 127).

European immigration—in three waves, including 1880–90, 1903–15, and 1924–33—brought additional workers, but still in insufficient numbers to meet the demand of the growing economy. The Spaniards and Italians who made up roughly half of these immigrants were generally unskilled (but were often marginally better skilled than native-born Argentines), and many of them worked only seasonally and then returned home each year. They came attracted by Argentina's relatively high wages, which were double those in Italy in both the 1880s and early 1900s (Cortés Conde 2005: 37). Indeed, the high wages attracted higher-skilled craft workers as well; these would become the first sets of workers to organize. In 1870, printers founded the nation's first union, and in 1878 they held their first strike (Collier and Collier 2002). Both of these groups of workers also brought with them a familiarity with European labor ideologies. Anarchism was most prominent in early organizing, but this gave way to a more syndicalist orientation over time (Matsushita 1983).

We have already seen in Chapter 2 that these workers were better skilled—both in terms of literacy and education—than workers elsewhere in the region. And in comparison with Chile and Peru, they particularly stood out. Argentina had undergone an educational revolution from the 1840s forward, when Domingo Sarmiento famously traveled abroad to study European, North American, and African education. He gave impetus to a massive reform of the educational system during his presidency (1868–74) that quadrupled state spending and created a culture of literacy and education in the nation. In the latter half of the nineteenth century and the early twentieth century, Argentina had a considerable lead on its neighbors in terms of primary school enrollment. As a share of population, Argentina enrolled 50 percent more of its citizens than did Chile. In absolute terms, this meant that Argentina had 387,000 educated workers with an educational base of literacy and numeracy, compared with only 157,000 such workers in Chile. Peru had only 92,000. And literacy stood at 60 percent by 1914, when most other countries still had less than half their populations capable of reading and writing (Engerman et al. 2012: 138).

Simultaneously, Argentine industrial development was creating conditions ripe for workers to organize themselves. Workers were concentrated, both geographically and economically. They were drawn to rapidly growing factories, and the cities in which the factories clustered, as well as to the junctions of new railways. A fifth of the economically active population worked in the manufacturing sector, where they had the opportunity to discover common cause in issues of workplace treatment and organizing rights. And because the country depended so heavily on production in a few key industries, which often exhibited production bottlenecks—most notably, beef for export—these workers had substantial power to make demands of their employers, and later the state.

The case of meat industry workers in the economically crucial *frigoríficos* (refrigeration plants) in Berisso is particularly illustrative of these organizational dynamics. Berisso is located a short distance south of Buenos Aires, and the work in the refrigeration plants was critical in ensuring Argentine beef exports to Europe. It saw a substantial influx of immigrants—Italians, Poles, and Ukrainians—as the refrigeration plants expanded their capacity. Thus it possessed a workforce with hold-up power over a crucial industry, and with the ideological experience of labor organization from their home countries. A remarkable transformation took place in their employment conditions. Prior to 1900, these workers were hired on only a temporary basis, often for a single day. But by the early decades of the new century they began to receive some additional compensation from their employers. This began with an infirmary in 1912, a dining room in the 1920s, and a new medical service in 1936. Later, in the 1940s, these workers began calling for greater wage stability and insurance that they would be employed a minimum number of working hours in each pay period (Lobato 1998, summarized in Galiani and Gerchunoff 2003). Thus these crucially located workers set the terms for early labor law development, with emphasis on job stability and better workplace treatment. By the 1940s and 1950s, when vote-seeking governments would come to power, these meat industry workers had years of experience of organizing and were ready to engage in a call for the government to extend broader legal protections for labor.

In the early years of the twentieth century, other sectors drew on this experience, and unionization quickly expanded throughout the economy. Table 6.1 displays the unionization rate in various industries over time.[3] The earliest observations—from 1936—show that unionization was especially concentrated in transportation (primarily railroads). Because transportation is a bottle-neck—limiting the ability to get supplies to production centers, and products to market—unionization in this sector gave its workers immense "hold-up" power

Table 6.1.   Union Density in Argentina, Various Sectors and Years, 1936–2007

	1936	1948	1954	1964	c1986	1995	2001	2007
Agriculture	–	–	6	5.2	11	–	–	–
Manufacturing	6	51.5	55	60.2	–	–	–	–
Industry, Mining, Elec., Gas, Water	12	–	–	79	67	–	–	–
Construction	–	15	41	3.8	35	–	–	–
Commerce	–	21	29	57.9	60	–	–	–
Transport, Communication	79★	101	117	66.4	95	–	–	–
Services—public & private	–	–	–	30.2	54	–	–	–
Services—state	–	2	51	–	–	–	–	–
Services—personal	–	17	30	–	–	–	–	–
Total	10	30.5	42.5	35.7	56	38.7	44.2	44

Sources: Data on industrial unionization in 1936 are from Torre 1990: 45. The figure for total union density in 1936 is from Galiani and Gerchunoff 2003: 135. Data for 1936 (railroads and manufacturing) and 1964 are from Torre 1972. Data for 1948, 1954, and 1986 are from Godio 2000. Data from 1995 are from the International Labor Organization 1997. Data for 2001 are from Groisman and Marshall 2005. Data for 2007 are from Etchemendy and Collier 2007.
   ★ The 1936 figure for Transport and Communications includes only Railroads.

in the economy. Stopping the railroads would effectively stop the economy, so both employers and the state had an interest in establishing norms and laws that kept growth and transport humming. Railroad worker unionization increased in subsequent years, and the sector came to be a perennial standout for its union organization.

   Transportation served as a vanguard in labor organizing, as workers in other sectors observed the treatment and status of its workers, and adopted similar demands. By the mid-1940s, unionization in Argentine manufacturing had also taken off, reaching 51.5 percent. The Peronist incorporation of labor, discussed below, saw further unionization across the economy; by 1954, the majority of workers in manufacturing, transportation, and state services were unionized, and the economy as a whole had 42.5 percent of the workforce in unions. From that point forward, unionization never dropped below 35 percent, and generally remained above 40 percent. These levels of union membership, sustained over decades, made Argentina stand out in the region. With such a massive, and largely united, base of organized workers, labor was able to demand, and receive, remarkably protective treatment in the labor code.

   Based on the demands of its relatively skilled workforce, and its early union organizing, Argentina developed its first labor laws in the early 1900s. These measures were created in a piecemeal fashion, largely in an effort to preserve uninterrupted production and supply chains, and ensure against labor unrest.

They were also driven by a growing concern over the "social question" in Latin America and in the industrialized economies of Europe. The nation's first formal labor law came in 1905, prohibiting work on Sundays in the Federal District; in 1913, this same limit was extended to the entire national territory.[4] In 1907, the employment of children under ten years of age was prohibited. By 1915 a law was introduced to regulate workplace accidents and illnesses. Laws in 1929 and 1934 legislated the maximum workday and workweek (eight hours per day and forty-eight hours per week) and the length of maternity leave (thirty days before and forty-five days after childbirth).

Job stability measures were also introduced, establishing high levels of severance pay to cement workers in place. Initially granted in 1933 to workers in the trade sector to compensate for the international price volatility they faced, the first severance payment law set mandatory benefits at one month's wage for each year worked with the firm. While intended to assist a worker in relocating after being dismissed as a result of international competition, the law quickly came to function as highly effective job protection for workers, especially those who had worked for a few years or more for the firm. Faced with the cost of several months' wages should they dismiss a senior worker, employers generally preferred to retain the worker. Thus the high dismissal indemnity established a stability standard—one that was very attractive to other workers in the economy. Indeed, the following decade saw the extension of similar severance pay statutes for additional sectors, first for bankers and then other industries.

In sum, the earliest labor laws in Argentina established principles that would later be extended widely across the economy and amplified in their generosity. Although they were initially a hodgepodge of special provisions based on the risks and economic characteristics of particular occupations, they set the tone for later political contestation and economic development. Job stability for individual workers, and a recognition of the rights and role of organized unions, would be at the center of labor relations for the next century.

6.2. The Consolidation of Argentine Labor Legislation under Perón

When the Grupo de Oficiales Unidos (the Group of United Officers [GOU]) seized power in 1943, they immediately realized the "hold-up" threat industrial workers could present to the economy. They were especially wary of communist and socialist elements within the working class, who might foster broad-based opposition to their rule. They thus targeted such unions for repression, successively infiltrating and disbanding them (Godio 2000: 818).

Two of the generals in the junta—Perón, as president of the Dirección Nacional de Trabajo (the National Department of Labor [DNT]) and Mercante as the officer in charge of the intervention in the national railroad unions—sought to use the interventions as an opportunity to draw labor into the regime. Within his first month in the DNT, Perón converted this body into the Secretaría de Trabajo y Previsión (the Secretariat of Labor and Prevision [STP]), increasing its role from the monitoring of labor law compliance to include a vast array of state social assistance measures, including pensions, public health, housing finance, unemployment insurance, and immigration (Godio 2000: 818–19). This gave Perón control over a set of high-impact governmental spending measures that directly tied labor's fate to his decisions.

Perón adroitly used his position to remove labor leaders whom he saw as impossible to sway, on the one hand, and to co-opt those he believed could be won over, on the other. This expanded the military-industrial alliance that had supported the coup into a military-industrial-labor coalition, and he would soon seek to channel labor's participation through a single representative interlocutor. Decree 2669 of 1943, and then the Law of Professional Associations of that same year (Law 23,295), formed the centerpiece of this effort. Regulating the organization, registration, and recognition of bodies representing workers, the Law of Professional Associations strategically limited *personería gremial* (legal union personhood) to only one union in each craft or industry. The result was a system of monopoly unions, each chosen (in principle) for having the highest number of affiliates in that industry.

Further, these unions were to be organized into a single set of second-level federations, and all these into a single confederation that could dialogue with the regime. Worker skills and organization were crucial when Perón selected which existing national union confederation to incorporate into the regime. Based on these factors, the Confederación General de Trabajadores (CGT) proved an obvious choice. It was not only the largest confederation, but it was also made up mostly of skilled and semiskilled workers, and it included the highly organized meat industry and railroad workers described above (Epstein 1979: 449). Perón then gave the CGT a tutelary role toward unskilled workers, whom he encouraged to unionize and affiliate with the CGT. Other well-organized unions with long histories outside the CGT, such as that of the printers in Buenos Aires, were eventually brought into the Peronist fold through interventions (Di Tella 2003: 153–79; Torre 2006).

By 1944 and 1945, Perón had begun to fashion the CGT into a personally responsive body, and used social benefits and government recognition to attract former communist union members into his fold. It provided support for Perón's policies within the military regime by staging pro-Perón and progovernment demonstrations, culminating in the decisive call for his release from prison on October 17, 1945 (Collier and Collier 2002: 340). And it was crucial to his rise to the presidency; in 1946, unions organized into the newly formed Partido Laborista (the Labor Party [PL]) "played a central role in the mobilization of voters," giving Perón 54 percent of the popular vote in his victory over his Radical rivals of Tamborini and Mosca (Gerchunoff and Llach 2003: 169).[5]

Seeking to centralize the mobilizational capacity of organized labor further, Perón mandated, under Decree Law 23,852 in 1945, that employers take responsibility for collecting the union dues from their workers and transferring them directly to the unions (Galiani and Gerchunoff 2003: 163). This measure gave the dominant, monopoly unions (represented by the CGT) financial resources that far exceeded those of any potential competitor. (Later, collective bargaining in the 1950s extended the financial resources of the dominant unions even further, giving them the right to administer the workers' health insurance system, called *obras sociales*.)[6] However, the legislation of this period was formulated to keep unions docile to the regime as well. The 1949 Constitution, which was expansive on several dimensions, did not give unions the right to strike. Any unions that did so without government approval—most of which were dissident unions— met with intervention, "mass arrests, strikebreakers, or even martial law" (Lewis 1990: 163).

Perón instituted a highly protective individual labor code to parallel the collective labor code. His approach was to draw on the existing early labor code provisions from the earlier preincorporation period, expanding their coverage to the unionized labor force as a whole. In short order, he extended mandated severance pay (Law 12,921), paid vacations (Decree Law 1,740), and the thirteenth wage (an annual bonus paid to workers prior to the Christmas holiday) (Decree Law 33,302) to all workers.[7] In the 1949 Constitution, he further enshrined the rights of workers to a job, healthful working conditions, vocational training, social security, and even "economic betterment" (Perón, quoted in Altamirano 2001: 193–95). His direct role in these measures cemented workers into the growing Peronist movement, which he himself termed a "syndicalist state" (Lewis 1990: 162–63). With severance pay set so high that it served as effective job protection, and labor courts that made firing more difficult, these workers could feel secure in taking to the streets in support of the regime. Effectively, they became "insiders" in not only their firms but also in the larger Peronist movement, with benefits and influence guaranteed them by the jobs they held.

The "incorporation" of labor extended to salary negotiations, as well. By law, wage agreements came to apply *erga omnes*, to all workers in the firm regardless of their unionization status.[8] In addition, the various collective bargaining agreements—negotiated at roughly the same time in the fall and winter months of each year—over time came to have an unofficial coordinating function with a strong top-down orientation. National-level collective bargaining at the industry level generally established the floor for local-level wage bargaining for each unionized firm. And even employers outside of the unionized sectors used these agreements as a reference point for their wage modifications (Galiani and Gerchunoff 2003: 139–40). Thus although unions served as the central actors in collective negotiations, their agreements set the benchmark for the vast majority of other workers in the economy.[9]

Beyond extensions of labor law, Perón also sought to deliver palpable wage gains to further cement the loyalty of labor. Figure 6.1 presents real industrial salaries for the period 1940–2004; the massive wage gains for industrial workers—25 percent in 1947 and 24 percent in 1948 (Skidmore and Smith 2005: 86)—in the first years of Perón's presidency are clearly apparent. Labor's share of the national income increased by 25 percent between 1946 and 1950 (86). Public expenditures also rose dramatically; real total public spending in 1948 was 285 percent of its 1941 level (Gerchunoff and Llach 2003: 179); much of the increase was targeted to the new social programs administered by Perón's wife, Evita, through the foundation she established in 1948.

In sum, Perón's early years in office witnessed a definitive integration of the CGT-dominated labor movement into his larger political following. The relationship reached its apex when the CGT was given an explicitly political role. The so-called *tercio* system institutionalized labor as one of the three major corporate units within the Peronist movement, and conferred upon the CGT the right to name one-third of the candidates to office within the party (Levitsky 2003: 83). Within the CGT, the core "62 Organizations" emerged as the focal

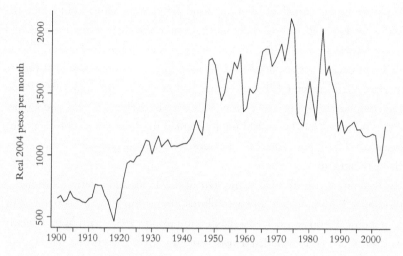

Figure 6.1. Real Industrial Salary, Argentina, 1900–2004. *Source:* Calculated by author using data from Ferreres 2005.

point of the movement, and by 1957 they were recognized as the voice of organized labor within the Peronist party (González 2004: 21). Labor regulation was expertly employed by Perón as the foundation to attract and secure the support of labor; combining generous individual and collective labor provisions, he made labor the centerpiece of his ascendant political movement.

A Reversal: From Cultivating Ties to Labor to Controlling It

A point of inflection occurred in Perón's later years in office, beginning in 1951. At this point, his political dominance allowed him greater freedom in dealing with labor. Where before his ascendance and that of labor had gone hand in hand—in an almost linear, monotonic way—now, at the height of his political power, he became far less generous toward labor. In fact, he would ask labor to bear the costs of economic adjustment.

In 1951, Perón scored a decisive victory in his bid for reelection, garnering 62 percent of the popular vote. With a huge majority in the Chamber of Deputies (Perón's Labor Party and other left parties had gone from holding 68 percent of seats in the chamber in 1946 to winning 90 percent of seats in the 1952 election) and control of all seats in the Senate (both in 1946 and 1952), Perón and his party held an effective monopoly on power.[10] Labor suddenly found its crucial role as a swing constituency diminished, and it lacked credible political alternatives.

No other option existed for labor to pursue its interests—either from within the left, as the Labor Party was so dominant, or from the right, as the Radicals and Conservatives were at a historic low point in their influence. Further, Perón's ability to declare strikes illegal, and his use of intervention in dissident unions to place them under CGT trusteeship, "meant that by the mid-1950s Perón had consolidated nearly total control over organized labor" (Collier and Collier 2002: 341–42). Thus Perón had unprecedented freedom, not only to continue to cater to his supporters but also to enforce wage moderation and other policy changes on them.

Declining terms of trade at the start of the 1950s and a series of droughts threatened both industrial and agricultural production (Godio 2000: 878–80). In response, Perón announced a stabilization plan in 1952 that was particularly hard on workers. It included a two-year wage freeze, decreased state spending, lowered domestic consumption, and increased exports (Collier and Collier 2002: 343). In real terms, workers saw industrial wages fall by 9 percent each in 1951 and 1952 (Ferreres 2005). Food prices, especially for beef, which is a staple of the Argentine diet, rose. Nevertheless, workers directed their dissatisfaction not at Perón but at the CGT leadership. The few wildcat strikes that occurred during this period did not undermine labor's allegiance to Perón. And in fact, the death of his wife, Evita, in July of 1952 provoked an enormous outpouring of support for him, one that was divorced from policy quid pro quos and gave him an even freer hand toward labor (Collier and Collier 2002: 343).

The trajectory of Perón's first tenure in office thus follows the theory advanced in Chapter 1. Prior to his rise, the labor movement had a significant and well-organized presence in key sectors of the economy—in particular those that involved higher skill levels and could threaten industry, transport, and the export of beef to the European market. The hold-up power of these workers found its complement in Perón, who cornered the market in the GOU regime for labor policy. Perón sought to co-opt the major organized labor currents, and did so through the expansion of a legal code that would manage and respond to labor. He thus rose to power on legislation that was labor friendly and provided regular wage increases, and the early years of his presidency continued this pattern. The result was a fusion of the major strand of the labor movement into his Labor Party, tightening the alliance and producing stability and rapidly increasing benefits to the CGT through the party.

However, when at the height of his power, facing an economic crisis, Perón was able to enact policies that were detrimental to labor without undermining their overall support for him. Because union representation was monopolistic, with financial resources doled out by the government, and because no alternative party or union confederation could offer similar benefits under the law, labor had no choice but to remain loyal. In the end, the only alternative to Perón's monopolistic control of the benefits of policy was an extraelectoral and extra-judicial one that did not come from the labor sector: a coup led by the military. Indeed, the CGT remained supportive of Perón right up until he was toppled from power (Godio 2000: 931).

Between Peronist Presidencies: Two Reversals, 1955–73

The period between Peronist governments saw three years of military rule, then eight years of bitterly contested Radical rule (under a succession of leaders from the two branches of the party), and a return of military rule from 1966 to 1973. The military government that came to power in 1955 sought to bring order to state spending and to limit the legal concessions to labor that it felt were out of control. Between 1955 and 1958, successive leaders enacted laws that effectively revoked nearly all the major union-friendly legislation from the Perón presidency. The rights of unions to strike and to negotiate collectively were suppressed. The state was given an arbitrage role in regulating contracts, thus further empowering it to intervene to overturn measures adopted during the Peronist years. A policy of "sindical freedom" (Decree Law 9,270, later written into the 1957 Constitution) effectively eliminated the privileged status of the monopoly unions.

With the return to democracy and the Peronists outlawed, the Radicals restored basic labor and union rights, but in a far more limited fashion than under Perón. By introducing greater oversight of union finances, they further restrained labor's freedom and sought to undermine competition from the Peronist movement. But they soon fell to a coup in 1966, and once again the military implemented an even more repressive policy toward labor, severely limiting the role of unions in collective bargaining and the scope of negotiations. In addition, the military seized the opportunity to universalize the *obras sociales* system (Fescina 2004), undercutting one of the landmark sources of union revenues by establishing a new market for private providers of health care (Alonso 2000).

In short, military rule repeatedly undermined labor legislation and worker organization. The military's perception of a significant threat posed by labor gives testimony to the integration that had developed between labor and the larger Peronist movement. The Radicals had to respect the economic hold-up potential of the skilled and semiskilled workers, but the military could crush it, and did.[11]

6.3. The Second Peronist Period in Power, 1973–76

In March 1973, the election of Héctor Cámpora, a stand-in for Perón, ushered in the return of Peronist rule. Receiving 49 percent of the vote, he enjoyed far greater popular support than the anti-Peronist Ricardo Balbín, of the Popular Radical faction (Unión Cívica Radical del Pueblo—Radical Civic Union of the People [UCRP]). Likewise, Peronists won 50.6 percent of the seats in the Chamber of Deputies, more than double the number held by the reunited Radicals. Nevertheless, a number of smaller national and provincial parties had also emerged, together accounting for more votes than the Radicals. Thus the electoral marketplace, while dominated by the Peronists—competing in elections for the first time since 1954—offered a greater set of choices for labor's allegiance than in Argentina's past. Leftist guerillas offered another, outside alternative. Cámpora sought to reincorporate labor into the political arena after its years under attack by military and Radical governments, and in doing so, he sought to recement labor's lasting support for the Peronist movement. Thus he brought together both the CGT and the Confederación General Económica (CGE—the Peronist-affiliated employer's association) to enact a *Pacto Social*, stabilizing prices and increasing workers' earnings for a year (Godio 2000: 936).

After just six months, Perón swept back into power, this time winning with 62 percent of the vote to the Radicals' 24 percent (Mainwaring and Scully 1996: 242). He moved quickly to restore labor laws that had been weakened since his last period in office. A new Law of Professional Associations (20,615, in 1973) renewed the sindical model from his earlier government, but invested greater "power and homogeneity" in the union movement (Galiani and Gerchunoff 2003: 163). Further, Decree 1,045 allowed unions to charge their sindical fees to all the workers in the industry who benefited from their negotiations, not just those who were registered as union members. Thus unions' power grew as they enjoyed resources beyond their numbers from these additional fees.

Perón sought to deliver benefits to workers on the individual level, as well. He enacted a new Contract Law of Employment (Law 20,744 in 1974), reinstating (and increasing) former Peronist provisions for annual leaves and severance pay. In addition, he made the firing of workers even more difficult, enshrining in law a strong presumption for the continuity of employment contracts, such that "almost every article in the law was based on the most favorable legal anteced-ent for workers" (ibid.). And to further sweeten the deal, he oversaw real wage increases for industrial workers of 8 percent in 1973 and 11 percent in 1974 (see Figure 6.1, above).

However, economic improvement—and implicit trust between organized la-bor and the regime—was short-lived. The 1974 international oil crisis drove up prices and hurt Argentina's balance of payments. At the same time, labor union discipline began to fracture, with several labor unions seeking to negotiate new wage contracts, in violation of the *Pacto Social*. Perón chose to support the unions in this effort, eventually giving large year-end bonuses to all the CGT unions. This had the effect of driving up inflation, and undermining the wage gains as quickly as they could be given.

The labor-friendly equilibrium was further destabilized when Perón died in July 1974, leaving his third wife, Isabel, who had been serving as vice presi-dent, to assume the presidency. With the economy threatened by inflation and growing leftist violence, she vacillated between taking a hard line toward the left and reaching out to it. In 1975, when unions negotiated wage increases of 100 percent or more, her loyalties were not as true as her husband's, and she annulled the settlements. However, a series of strikes led her to reverse this measure, reinstating the wage gains and exacerbating the problem of inflation. On wage policy, her unenviable legacy was a decline in average industrial wages of 4 percent in 1975 and 34 percent in 1976 (Ferreres 2005).

In terms of the theory from Chapter 1, two findings about the second Per-onist government's labor regulation stand out. First, the labor union movement was far more divided—internally and externally—than it had been in the years of Perón's first government. This was due, at least in part, to the weakening of the ISI measures that had begun in the 1960s and 1970s; economic pressures and competition decreased the privileged status of industrial labor. Further, ef-forts by Augusto Timoteo Vandor to reassert the role of the 62 Organizations in the CGT had left the confederation weakened, and had led Perón to empha-size other aspects of the Peronist movement—especially the youth and political wings—to the detriment of labor. Labor ceased to be the only credible partner to the PJ. The rise of leftist guerillas and wildcat strikes gave options on the left outside of the CGT and the Peronist movement. The Peronists made significant overtures through the labor legislation, but these were overshadowed by the other labor-restrictive wage policies they enacted. Indeed, the *Pacto Social* actually gave workers much less than they had been demanding; further, it gave wage increases at the cost of collective bargaining, which was suspended during the first two years of Peronist government (Torre 2004: 33). The leadership of the major unions was so weak politically that they could not generate any meaningful resistance to Perón and extract concessions (35).

Second, the alliance was largely personality based. Perón was the only leader who could marshal the full resources of the Peronist movement politically. He held the movement together by force of will, but in his return he embraced the need to attract foreign capital by opening markets to imported inputs, controlling inflation, and limiting wage gains. He was perhaps the only actor with sufficient political standing to implement these policies. Once he was removed from the scene, the Peronist-CGT alliance all but dissolved. By 1976, the Peronist movement had lost both its economic and political strength; facing widespread discontent from both left and right, another military intervention was all but inevitable.

Military Rule and the Return of Democracy under Alfonsín, 1976–89

The second post-Peronist period mirrored the first in that it consisted of a military regime, with frequent turnover of presidents, succeeded by a Radical government. This time, the military was more repressive, employing disappearances and political violence to deal with leftist guerillas and re-establish order. It sought to reverse the course set by the Peronists by adopting a decisively export-oriented model of development; however, it fared little better than its predecessor, running a huge fiscal deficit and exposing Argentine industry to a level of competition for which it was not prepared. This set of policies was called by one commentator "the worst possible responses to the challenges and opportunities of globalization" (Ferrer 2004: 331). Coupled with the disastrous invasion of the Falkland Islands, this economic failure paved the way for another return to democracy.

The Radical government of Raúl Alfonsín that took office in December 1983 had to deal with political and economic legacies that left it little room to maneuver (Gibson 1996). Inflation surged, contributing to a 50 percent fall in real wages over his five years in office; unemployment and underemployment doubled (McGuire 1997: 186). In an effort to reach out to both labor and capital by promoting growth and easing unemployment, Alfonsín sought to achieve a new "concertation" between employers and workers. However, he met early defeats on these proposals, and was especially constrained by the renovated CGT under the leadership of Saúl Ubaldini, which carried out a series of general strikes (Quiroga 2005: 37–39). In the face of this labor strength, he had to scale back his policy goals and focus on simply achieving economic stability.[12]

Alfonsín's labor legislation consisted of the passage of a new Law of Professional Associations (Law 23,555, of 1988). This law reinstated monopoly unions in each craft or industry and awarded *personería gremial* to the union with greatest membership. In addition, a new Law of Collective Bargaining (23,545 and 23,546, both of 1988) was modeled on the Peronist Law 14,250, with collective agreements extended *erga omnes* to all workers in the industry. Thus the Radical Alfonsín, facing a renewed labor movement that could exert hold-up power over the economy in the tenuous years after the return of democracy, oversaw the adoption of a collective labor code very similar to that of the Peronists prior to the military dictatorship.

Alfonsín's approach to labor fits with the predictions of the theory in Chapter 1, which emphasized stability and resilience in labor codes. Argentina's relatively skilled labor force, and the ongoing organization of workers in key sectors, combined with the development goals of the nation, earned a privileged place for industrial labor. Even though Alfonsín's Radical Party did not have institutional ties to labor, or an ideology particularly conducive to labor's interests, he could not ignore this vital economic force (and its hold-up power over the economy).

6.4. The Return of Peronism: Turning against Labor, 1989–99

By the end of Alfonsín's term in 1989, hyperinflation had gripped the economy, and public distress and disorder were on the rise. In the presidential election, the Peronist Carlos Menem was perceived as a standard bearer for change—especially by organized labor—and he swept into office with 47 percent of the vote (to the Radicals' 32 percent). But the situation proved so severe that Alfonsín struck a deal to hand over the presidency to Menem early, announcing on June 30 that "the depth of the socioeconomic crisis required not only energetic efforts but also permanent ones" (Quiroga 2005: 64).

In these circumstances, Menem found himself with political capital that exceeded even the significant electoral plurality by which he had won the presidency. As part of the agreement to assume office early, he received implicit guarantees from the opposition and conservative elites that he would not be challenged. On the other side of the spectrum, labor instinctively looked to him as *their* representative, given his Peronist credentials, and expected him to restore their fortunes (especially since they had provided the votes that helped see him elected).

To their surprise and dismay, however, once in office Menem enacted a sweeping set of neoliberal reforms that undercut the interests of his working-class supporters. Indeed, his presidency represents the greatest Peronist challenge to the movement's labor base in its history. First, he removed many of the ISI-inspired barriers that had shielded Argentine producers from competition, slashing tariffs on imported goods, privatizing state-owned industries, and introducing favorable treatment for foreign investment. In a direct frontal assault on the country's labor legislation, he decreed the Law of Administrative Emergency (23,696) and the Law of Economic Emergency (23,697) in late August and early September. These made it a priority to "flexibilize" employment, creating a range of "modalities" under which workers could be hired, many of which did not involve the full range of previous legal requirements. These laws also reduced (or eliminated) employers' mandated social security contributions, simplified (or removed) procedures for dismissals, and suspended the indexation of wages to inflation (Basualdo 2006: 287). In short, these measures undermined the legal basis for labor's privileged treatment, and represented a challenge to its organizational unity. Shortly, the CGT fragmented between radicals and moderates (Senén González et al. 1999).

The Reforms under Menem

Menem's reforms sought to flexibilize the labor market at both the individual and collective levels. His Employment Law of 1991 (24,013) introduced several new modalities for fixed-term contracts in the case of young workers, new businesses, and new entrants in the economy. These contracting provisions entailed no payment of severance pay or other benefits to workers employed under them. They were aimed to reduce unemployment by making the hiring of new workers less expensive for employers. The law also created the first unemployment insurance fund Argentina had known, albeit on a limited basis (Lo Vuolo and Barbeito 1998: 206). Later in 1995, Laws 24,465 and 24,467 created additional fixed-term modalities, including those for part-time, apprenticeship, and probationary contracts, as well as mandated special, lower-cost contract terms for small- and medium-size businesses. Since the firms would not need to pay the full complement of payroll taxes for these workers (as such workers do not receive the full benefits of the law during their probationary period), it was hoped that they would take on a larger workforce. Simultaneously, the mandated amount of severance pay was capped, thus reducing the future risk to employers of hiring additional workers in the present. Finally, in 1996, Law 24,635 made conciliation necessary prior to appeal to labor courts. All of these measures effectively reduced the protections available to workers—most especially those in temporary contracts, but also those in longer-term positions who might wish to challenge unfair dismissal or treatment.

Likewise, the marketizing project of the Menem reforms set its sights on the collective labor codes. After limiting the right of unions to strike in Decree 2184 in 1989, Menem made a concerted effort to reduce the centralization of collective bargaining. Decree 1334 (1991) carried out this goal by limiting wage increases to changes in productivity. Since productivity can only be measured and calculated at the local, firm level, wage negotiations were effectively removed from any higher-level discussions. Later legislation, such as Decree 2284 (1991), facilitated decentralized collective bargaining, and Decree 470 (1993) established "articulated" bargaining at the firm and industry levels, a significant departure from the former legal deference to higher-level collective bargaining. It is important to note that most of these measures were carried out by presidential decree, effectively bypassing the Congress with the rationale that rapid action was necessary given the economic emergency the nation was facing.

Studies show that these labor laws had many of their intended results. The use of temporary contracts rose from 8 to 17 percent of total employment between 1995 and 1998, and at their peak in 1997 they constituted 80 percent of the new contracts issued (Berg et al. 2006: 139). The hazard rate (probability of job loss) increased by 40 percent for workers during the trial period of their first three months of employment; after three months, the increase in hazard rate was about 10 percent (Hopenhayn 2004: 497–98). Further, while the temporary contracts did not help the least educated workers find jobs, or reduce informal employment, they did increase the probability of workers moving from temporary to permanent jobs. In fact, this probability was significantly higher than that in OECD countries, and was greatest for the most skilled workers (Perelman 2001).[13] Unskilled workers and those not registered with the state experienced more frequent periods of unemployment and shorter periods in particular positions (Beccaria and Maurizio 2005: 90–91). Likewise, because collective negotiation had been weakened by being decentralized, and wage increases were to be based on productivity gains rather than an inflation index, workers began to experience greater wage dispersion (Marshall 2002). Thus the Menem flexibilizing measures effectively undermined worker solidarity, offering new opportunities for the most qualified workers to follow independent career paths—through which both their likelihood of getting a job, and being better paid, were increased.

Finally, one of the greatest threats to organized labor came in the battles over pensions and *obras sociales*. In 1993, Law 24,241 restructured the pension system in Argentina, setting up private capitalization funds for workers alongside the traditional, state-administered defined-benefit pension system.[14] This made workers into economic free agents in saving for retirement, and exposed them to greater risk of poverty in old age. Since all decisions and results are individual, the new system militated against a solidaristic approach to pensions, and to labor organization more generally.

In what would have been an even more far reaching policy change, the Menem government initially sought to privatize the *obras sociales*—a proposal that would have taken the massive funds out of the hands of the unions that controlled these health care providers. Union opposition was resounding, and it was successful in forcing Menem to back down. Nevertheless, he did achieve his goal of promoting competition among *obras sociales*, decreeing that workers could freely choose among *obras sociales* and switch affiliation between them (Decree 9/1993 and Decree 1141/1996).[15] And importantly, private *obras sociales* were permitted, creating an alternative to unions in one of the key areas where they had enjoyed an absolute monopoly. In another substantial way, the solidarity of the organized labor movement was threatened.

In sum, Menem presided over a remarkable marketization of the economy during the first several years of his presidency, significantly rupturing the relationship between the CGT and the PJ. The explanation for this transformation flowed not only from his own personal charisma and deal-making, but also from the structural conditions he inherited (a crisis economy in transition toward greater openness) and from his early success in lowering inflation. This gave him enormous political capital, and a broad spectrum of support that allowed him to enact labor reforms that would never have been anticipated from a Peronist president. Furthermore, globalization and pressures from international financial institutions accentuated the pull toward market liberalization. As predicted by the theory in Chapter 1, the weakness of organized labor, its inability to provide a decisive electoral base, and the demands of providing relief for hyperinflation all conspired to permit the labor-weakening reforms of Menem.

Menem's Reversal—Reinstating Labor Protections

However, the story of the Menem years does not stop in 1995, for he undertook a second reversal of course in the later years of his presidency. Where his earlier reforms had been founded on his unrivaled political power, this second set of reforms was motivated by his weakened electoral support, which was increasingly apparent in the lead-up to the 1999 presidential elections. Widespread dissatisfaction with the temporary contracts—which covered larger numbers of workers each day, and which were often used to avoid dismissal costs (by hiring and firing workers at intervals)—placed Menem in considerable electoral jeopardy.

Once again, Menem returned to the traditional Peronist base to shore up support (Berg et al. 2006: 139–40). To win their favor, he introduced a new reform in 1998 (Law 25,013), which effectively reversed many of the earlier reforms undertaken just five years before. It restored centralized collective bargaining at the industry level by shifting negotiation to higher-level unions, and mandated that contract renegotiation was to occur every two years.

Even more fundamentally, Menem eliminated most of the specially promoted fixed-term contracting measures introduced in Laws 24,013 and 24,465. He reduced the maximum probationary period from three months to just one month, effectively moving workers onto the permanent payroll more quickly.[16] And he also lowered the mandated severance payment for new hires, thus making the more rapid movement of temporary workers into the permanent force more palatable to employers. As a result, the use of temporary contracts returned to its historic trend of 5 percent (Berg et al. 2006: 140). In general, then, the final labor code of the Menem years sought to incorporate more workers into the formal labor market, through which they would enjoy more of the benefits of the labor law. But at the same time, it also weakened some of those benefits.

In a final set of non–labor code concessions to workers, union debts were subsidized by the Menem government, and a proposal to reform the *obras sociales* was tabled (Murillo and Schrank 2005). Thus several of the key features of classic Argentine labor code were returned in the 1998 labor reform under Menem: collective laws once again ensured the status and resources of the unions, and individual laws returned job stability and other benefits to workers. Even in the face of the most sustained challenge it had ever seen from inside the Peronist movement, the symbiotic relationship between the party and labor would prevail. Unions showed that they could provide the crucial support needed to win and retain office, and Menem eventually was forced to return the favor with job protection and legislation that preserved their institutional privilege.

However, this grudging support would not last long, and the PJ was soon riven with new divisions, especially as the debt burden of the 1990s and slowing growth pushed the country into economic and political chaos.

6.5. Labor Law and Policy under the Kirchners: 2002–Present

In 2002, Nestor Kirchner—like Menem a decade before him—took over a nation in crisis, but he did so from an extraordinarily weak position. Economic stagnation, unemployment, and a massive debt burden from the 1990s had caused economic and political chaos, and a rapid succession of presidents had proven incapable of restoring order. The PJ was sharply divided internally, so much so that it could not settle on a single candidate for the presidency to succeed Duhalde in 2002. The party allowed three candidates to run, giving none the party's official endorsement. Kirchner and Menem were the top vote-getters in the first round, but Menem chose to withdraw before the run-off election was held. Thus Kirchner's popular mandate was never given an electoral stamp of approval; he had actually received only 21.8 percent of the popular vote compared with Menem's 23.9 percent in the first round (Godio 2006: 28).[17]

Given his vulnerability, and the vulnerability of the PJ and the presidency itself, Kirchner needed to reach out in search of support, especially from the supporters of his rivals within the PJ in the presidential election. He quickly convoked labor leaders of various stripes, inviting them to play an important role in his government by participating in discussions of minimum wages and labor policy. He sought the support of the unemployed *piqueteros*, appointing one of their leaders as a cabinet minister, and invited the dissident Central de los Trabajadores Argentinos (the Argentine Workers Central, Argentina [CTA]) labor confederation (which includes some unemployed members) into discussions with the Ministry of Labor.[18] The tight CGT-PJ alliance had been called into question under Menem, and it had been all but undermined in the 2001–2 crisis. Divisions in the labor movement meant that the CGT unions were not able to function as a monopoly source of support for Kirchner, who had to cultivate ties to segments of the labor movement to build up his political base. To win them over, and promote the CGT as his primary interlocutor, he allowed the return of industry-level collective bargaining, encouraged wage gains in unionized sectors, and eventually began to restructure social security commitments.

In his principal labor law reform (Law 25,877), Kirchner extended both individual and collective labor provisions. At the individual level, his government confirmed the previously established maximum on probationary hiring at three months, but now added a prohibition on further extensions. In addition, the severance pay was increased for new hires, and incentives were given to small- and medium-size firms to hire additional workers. These measures gave workers more opportunities to enter the formal sector, and to stay there, and thus increased the population for whom labor law was an important outcome. These individual labor law reforms represented an attempt to devise a new equilibrium in the labor market in Argentina, one that would respond to the needs of both formal sector, unionized workers, by increasing job stability measures, and to the needs of unemployed workers or those who worked mainly in the informal economy, creating a path into formal employment (Carnes and Mares 2013).

At the collective level, Kirchner allowed the reactivation of collective bargaining. One of the most important provisions in this legislation was the reestablishment of *ultractividad*, the principle that previous collective agreements remain in effect without renegotiation. This allowed workers in many industries to retain (or reassert) labor-friendly provisions from collective agreements originally negotiated in the second Perón regime in the early 1970s. And it permitted a wider range of negotiating options through "articulated" bargaining at different organizational levels; by mutual agreement of the parties, collective bargaining could occur at the local firm level or at the federation or confederation levels. Ultimately, in the case of conflicting resolutions, the agreement most beneficial to the employees prevailed. Thus collective bargaining—one of the perennial marks of the Peronist labor legislation—reassumed its central role in the legal regime pursued by Kirchner, but in a new form that may be more flexible and useful for workers outside the traditionally powerful union sectors.

The legal changes under Kirchner had a dramatic effect on the pattern of collective bargaining in 2001–5. The total number of CBAs made a remarkable recovery in 2002 and 2003, and significantly surpassed the levels predominating in the 1990s (Etchemendy and Collier 2007). Indeed, total CBAs rose from an average of 190 per year during the 1990s (1991–99) to an average of 293 per year in the period from 2000 to 2005, or more remarkably, an average of more than 380 per year if only the postrecovery years of 2002–5 are considered (Novick and Trajtemberg 2000). In short, collective bargaining resulted in more than twice as many agreements as occurred during the reform years under Menem. Industry-level, peak-style bargaining grew in importance since 2002, moving from a low of 13 percent of all CBAs to nearly 36 percent in 2005. Further, since industry-level agreements have greater reach in the economy—affecting multiple firms each—the importance of industry-level bargaining was actually underestimated by these figures.

Union activity in the late 2000s affected "44 percent of the working class" (Etchemendy and Collier 2007: 43). While this is a minority of all workers, it represents a coveted electoral prize for political candidates, and it is comparable to the unionization rate in the first Perón government. These union members are also more willing to take to the streets. Strike activity, a traditional measure of labor union militancy and power, underwent a marked increase in the years after the Kirchners took office (Etchemendy and Collier 2007). Their efforts have not been in vain. In Figure 6.1, above, we see that the mid-2000s period of collective bargaining has yielded improved wages in industrial sectors, which tend to be the most highly unionized in the Argentine economy. Of course, these recent gains are overshadowed by the huge losses of the late 1980s and the later decline in 2001–2, but they mark the first reversal in the trend since 1990.

In addition, Nestor Kirchner—and his wife and successor in the presidency, Cristina Fernández de Kircher—presided over remarkable changes in the private pension system that were of benefit to workers in the years 2007 and 2008, culminating in the renationalization of the pension system. In February of 2007, Kirchner pushed a bill through the Argentine Congress to allow periodic "free dis-affiliation" from the private system into the public one. This opening up of the social security system moved over 1.1 million Argentines back from the private pension system to the state-run system, or from facing their retirement relying on only their own savings to being covered by government promises of old-age assistance. Cristina Fernández de Kirchner, once in office, undertook an even more fundamental restructuring of the pension institutions in 2008, seizing the assets of the private pension funds and transferring them to the public pension system. This gave the state a central role in the welfare of all formal sector workers (who also tend to be unionized), and further drew organized labor back into the Peronist fold.

Additionally, the evidence from the Kirchner years shows that organized industrial workers have consistently outperformed other sectors in terms of wages and employment—as expected by the theory outlined in Chapter 1. Figure 6.2 shows the pronounced difference in wage levels across sectors during this period. Workers in utilities and financial services—the first of which has strong unions, and the latter of which has high levels of human capital—enjoyed the highest wages, exceeding the average wage by 40 percent or more from the mid-1990s through 2004. Transport and manufacturing—the other two highly unionized sectors—also surpass average wages, although by a more modest amount. And the largely nonunionized sectors—including services, commerce, and construction—earned the lowest wages. Further, it is the utilities and manufacturing sectors that see an upturn in their wages at the end of the period, reflecting the increase in collective bargaining in those sectors.

Industrial sectors also tended to be more moderate in their job losses during the economic crisis of 2001–2 than did construction or services (Ministerio de Trabajo, Empleo, y Seguridad Social 2003: 6). Again, the concentration of labor unions in industry is likely to have played a role here. Unionized workers have better job protections than their nonunionized counterparts. Further, there is an element of selection bias. The firms that were large and stable enough to experience labor organization in earlier decades are also more likely to be large and stable enough to weather economic downturns with less dislocation in the present. What is remarkable, however, is that industrial firms did not take the crisis as an opportunity to permanently shed workers, but instead rehired workers in the recovery and increased the overall employment in the sector. Thus union-

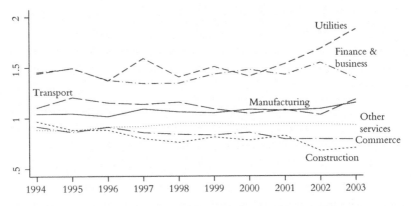

*Sectors with higher levels of human capital and more extensive
unionization enjoyed higher wages in the 1990s, and suffered less
in the 2001 economic crisis.*

Figure 6.2. Wage Level Comparison as Multiples of the Average Salary,
by Economic Sector, Argentina, 1994–2003. *Source:* Author's calculations,
based on Dirección General de Estudios y Formulación de Políticas de
Empleo 2004.

ized workers have benefited from the greater stability (and job protections) they
enjoy.

To summarize: one way of understanding the Kirchner and Fernández de
Kirchner presidencies is in terms of which social actors they privilege. Initially,
in the first postcrisis years, Nestor Kirchner reached out not only to the CGT,
the traditional Peronist labor arm, but also to the newly formed CTA—which
represents dissident unions, state workers, teachers, and a small number of the
unemployed. He sought support from as broad a base as possible. But as his
status grew, he resolutely resisted granting further roles (and legal rights) to the
CTA. The CGT became once again the principal labor interlocutor for the PJ
in Kirchner's presidency.

The cementing of the Kirchner-CGT relationship continued after December
2007 in the presidency of Cristina Fernández de Kirchner, but with a new twist
as her power increased. During the campaign, she directed her appeals to the
traditional bases of Peronism, largely turning her back on the *piqueteros* who had
been convoked to participate in the coalition of her husband's early years in the
presidency. In the election, it was voters with the middle range of educational levels that turned out to bring Fernández de Kirchner to power; these are precisely

the workers that make up the bulk of the industrial sector and unionized labor (Szusterman 2007). Thus labor seems to be upholding its end of the traditional Peronist bargain in the transition between Kirchner presidencies.

Commentators have noted that in spite of her initial distrust of Hugo Moyano, leader of the Confederación General de Trabajadores (CGT), "[Fernández de Kirchner] needed him." In 2009, he promised to be an "unconditionally loyal" leader, particularly useful to her government that sought to avoid "social and union conflicts." Her husband, Nestor Kirchner, had ratcheted up negotiated salary increases with unions by 16 percent prior to her 2007 election, and she followed suit with increases of 20 percent in 2008 (Laugé 2008a). In addition, she initially followed the trend of the later years of her husband's presidency by opposing dissident union efforts for government recognition of the rival CTA, further increasing the power of the Peronist-tied CGT (Laugé 2008b). And by decree in January 2008, Fernández de Kirchner increased by 300 million pesos the funds destined to the *obras sociales* health care systems, administered by the CGT-affiliated labor unions, effectively increasing the resources at the unions' disposal (Laugé 2008c).[19] Moyano returned these favors by containing wage increase demands to 19.5 percent (*La Nación,* 4 March 2008) and delivering a disciplined yet supportive labor movement.

The close, yet mutually demanding, relationship could be detected in remarks at a 2008 celebration of Moyano's twentieth anniversary at the head of his union (Camioneros).[20] Moyano paid lengthy homage to Nestor Kirchner's largesse toward organized labor, and then reminded Cristina of her statement, while a senator, that she "would never vote for a law that would hurt the workers."[21] In her remarks at the event, Fernández de Kirchner emphasized the work of labor leaders in continuing the postcrisis measures begun by her husband, and especially at containing the demands of workers for unbridled wage gains.[22] The implicit "alliance" between the PJ and the CGT thus deepened and took on greater prominence (*La Nación,* 4 March 2008). The silent presence on the dais of Nestor Kirchner, who as president of the party dedicated himself to rebuilding the PJ into a monolithic political force after its fractious experience of recent years, signaled the centrality of organized labor in the new Peronism.

Nevertheless, the relationship has shown strains as Fernández de Kirchner's power has grown. After the untimely death of Nestor Kirchner, Fernández de Kirchner was catapulted to a second term in office in October 2011. Elected by a landslide with an unprecedented 53 percent of the popular vote (35 percent more than her nearest rival), she began her term by increasingly turning her back on the CGT. Hugo Moyano had become increasingly demanding during the campaign—for union representatives to be put forward high on the Peronists' lists, for higher wage increases in the face of inflation—and after the election he called for a special year-end bonus for workers. Since Fernández de Kirchner had such a broad popular mandate, she felt the freedom to marginalize Moyano. While still preserving the rhetoric of the centrality of workers to the Peronist movement, she snubbed Moyano by refusing to invite him to political rallies, and commentators began to speak of a rupture between the president and the labor leader (Obarrio 2011).

6.6. Conclusion

This chapter has traced out a political explanation for the ongoing expansion and limited retrenchment of labor policy over time in Argentina. The concentration of skilled and organized workers in key economic sectors led to the development of early labor laws that favored job stability and sanctioned union activity. Later, Perón sought to cement his power through an alliance of the labor movement with his emerging political movement (eventually the PJ), and used the extension of labor laws to draw workers into his fold. This alliance effectively constituted industrial labor and state sector workers as a privileged, "insider" group—with special privileges over nonunionized, agricultural, or informal sector workers. The subsequent breakdown of ISI, coupled with division within the Peronist movement, led to shallower pacts between Peronist leaders and organized labor insiders, but never to a fundamental dismantling of many of the features of Argentine largesse toward labor. This pattern holds true throughout Peronist periods in government.

It is important to note that the political alliance that developed between labor and the Peronists does not imply that there was a continuously harmonious relationship between them. A completely peaceful integration has never been the norm, and often there have been open tensions between leaders in both realms. The key feature in the relationship has been that neither side could credibly commit to another partner. Thus historians have commented on "three Peronisms" or "four Peronisms," corresponding to the party's periods in government, each with a different configuration of the labor-party balance

(Horowicz 1991; Sidicaro 2002). But in each configuration, a significant sector of organized labor has continued to have both the specific skill levels for the nation's desired economic development and growth and the organizational capacity to remain a critical political actor. And the PJ has shown that it is incapable of long enduring without a labor base. The aspects of Menem's market reforms that most directly threatened labor had to be rolled back. Similarly, the development of an alternative, clientelistic network by the PJ (Levitsky 2003) has not precluded a concerted effort by the party to regather its labor support—beginning under Menem but continuing under Duhalde and especially the Kirchners.

Labor's political importance extends beyond this alliance, although that is where it is most clearly observed. Indeed, even when the Peronist party was outlawed under military governments, the CGT (or segments of it) was able to mobilize strikes and credibly threaten to hold up the economy. Both military and Radical governments had to take this political bloc seriously. For the former, this meant suppressing "dissident" leaders and intervening in union finances and government; for the latter, it meant providing a basic menu of labor protections and laws. The "insider" status that labor had achieved made it impossible to completely exclude from the nation's economic and political model.

This chapter also offers a nuanced and coherent account of the changing fate of labor in recent decades. It explains why Menem was initially less beholden to labor interests—he inherited the presidency from a discredited opposition and lacked significant internal competition within the PJ—but had to backtrack on the most damaging of his reforms to labor law. It also provides a rationale for the resurgence of the CGT in the early 2000s, arguing that Kirchner reached out to labor in response to the political climate he inherited, marked by economic crisis, a vulnerable presidency, a weakened labor movement, and a divided party. Labor unions provided a particularly ready source of political support, based on their long-standing historical ties to the party. And even as Fernández de Kirchner pushed back against a presumptuous CGT, she still recognized its central importance to her government. Thus contrary to earlier findings in the literature (Levitsky 2005), the Peronists remain the party of labor—albeit in an evolving, contested, and less exclusive way—and it is impossible to imagine either of these two actors without the other.

Appendix Table 6.A. Labor Policy in Argentina, by Government, 1946–2007

Period	President	Labor Policy Developments
1905–43	Various	First efforts to address labor relations issues in law *Individual rights:* Sunday work prohibited, child labor (under 10) prohibited, workplace accidents and illnesses regulated, maximum workday and workweek established, maternity leave, severance pay for workers in trade-related sectors *Collective rights:* Registration procedures for unions
1946–55	*PJ* Perón	Cultivation of strong ties to labor movement by Perón and then PJ *Individual Rights:* Expansion of minimum wage, paid holidays and vacations and severance pay, restricted the dismissal of workers, mandated a year-end bonus amounting to one month's wage *Collective labor relations:* Law of Professional Associations established single, monopolistic unions in each industry with greater independence. Pattern of industry-level bargaining *Social Policy:* Accident insurance introduced
1955–58	*Military* Lonardi Arumburu	Efforts to dismantle the Peronist labor code *Individual Relations:* Set equal pay for the same tasks across genders *Collective Relations:* Suppressed collective agreements. Established sindical freedom by eliminating trade union representation. Established an arbitrage role for the state in collective conflicts
1958–66	*Divided Unión* *Cívica Radical* *(the Radical Civic* *Union—UC)* Frondizi Guido Illia	Reversal of most of the military antilabor laws. Return of the distinctively Argentine labor law system *Individual Relations:* Established national council to set minimum wage. First law governing individual labor contracts *Collective Relations:* Re-established the Law of Professional Associations in a manner similar to under Perón. Regulated the auditing of trade union finances
1966–73	*Military* Onganía Levingston Lanusse	Attempt to limit union strength while preserving international legitimacy *Individual Relations:* To comply with ILO resolutions, regulated minimum working age and the working conditions for women and children *Collective Relations:* Established that collective bargaining should not be used for wages. Limited wage increases to the inflation rate plus productivity gains *Social Policy: Obras sociales* systematized by state for all workers

Period	President	Labor Policy Developments
1973–76	*PJ* Cámpora Lastiri Juan Perón Isabel Martínez de Perón	Initial reinstatement of labor-friendly policies, followed by growing chaos *Individual Rights:* New contract of employment law—increasing annual leaves, severance pay, assumed continuity of employment Initial wage increases decreed by Peronists, followed by wage freeze *Collective Relations:* New Professional Associations Law, reinstating and expanding many earlier privileges. Increased the strength and solidarity of the union movement. Called for a social pact among firms, unions, and government in establishing wages and controlling inflation. Allowed unions to charge sindical feels for all members of industry even if not union members Collective bargaining frozen for two years. Some bargaining at firm level. Isabel fluctuated between support for collective bargaining and rejecting it
1976–83	*Military* Videla Viola Galtieri Bignone	Strong antiunion movement in reaction against the second Peronist government's policies *Individual Relations:* Limited some of the worker-friendly provisions of the Peronist 1974 Contract of Employment Law *Collective Relations:* Suspended the right to strike and collective bargaining. Established a system of reference wages that were used until collective bargaining restored in the late 1980s. Eventually suspended all union activities. Removed provision allowing unions to charge dues of nonunion members in industry
1983–89	*UCR* Alfonsín	Initial caution in return to democracy, but eventual re-establishment of basic lines of Argentine labor law model *Individual Relations:* no significant changes *Collective Relations:* New Law of Professional Associations, largely along the lines of the Peronist Law, with monopoly unions for each industry. New collective bargaining law, making agreements *erga omnes*
1989–99	*PJ* Menem	Elected with labor support, then strong marketizing reforms that divided labor *Individual Rights:* Measures to "flexibilize" the labor market, including new temporary hiring contracts (1991 and 1995). Reduced severance payments In 1998, most of the new, fixed-term contract measures were eliminated *Collective Relations:* Restricted wage bargaining to productivity advances, which promoted firm-level collective bargaining *Social Policy:* Privatized pensions, created unemployment insurance system

Period	President	Labor Policy Developments
1999–2001	*UCR/Alianza* De la Rúa	Promarket reforms, but within the context of Argentine protective legislation *Individual Relations:* Reformed the Law of Employment Contracts, increasing maximum probationary period. Rewarded employers who gave indefinite contracts with a one-third reduction in their social security contributions *Collective Relations:* Attempt to decentralize collective bargaining, by allowing bargaining at any level of representation (without requiring deference to higher-level union bargains). Required workers from the firm's internal commission to serve in the negotiations *Social Policy:* Mandated worker contributions to pension system reduced from 11 to 7 percent. This emergency measure persisted into 2007
2001–3	*Crisis* (Puerta) Rodriguez Saá (Camaño) Duhalde	No major changes in labor policy Emergency decrees used by Duhalde to increase wages throughout economy
2003–7	*Divided PJ* Nestor Kirchner Cristina Fernández de Kirchner	Rebuilding traditional Peronist linkages to labor *Individual Relations:* Reformed the contract law, limiting extensions on temporary contracts, increasing severance pay for new hires *Collective Relations:* Re-establishment of regularized collective bargaining, with greater freedom to bargain at the industry level. Labor union participation in minimum wage negotiations. Re-established *ultra-actividad*, through which expired collective agreements remain in force. Limited the right to strike for industries that provide "essential services" *Social Policy:* Workers permitted to move between the public and private pension systems

Sources: Adapted from Galiani and Gerchunoff 2003, 160–65; with additional information from Epstein 1979; Senén González and Bosoer 1999; Godio 2000; Vega Ruiz 2005; Cook 2007; Argentine labor codes (various years); and newspaper articles in *La Nación* (various dates).

Conclusion: Politics and Labor Regulation in Latin America

Labor policy is among the most far reaching of government interventions in the economy, affecting the working opportunities and livelihood of nearly every citizen and potential employer at some point in their lives. Regulations for contract terms, provisions for collective bargaining and union activity, and programs to deal with social security, unemployment, and health seek to protect workers and ensure economic stability. At the same time, they shape the decisions of firms and individuals about employment and consumption. Only recently have political scientists and economists begun to study why nations adopt the kind of labor policies they do, and why these policies evolve with such great variation through time, especially in the developing world.

This book has examined the development of labor regulation in Latin America. It has shown that the labor codes have been among the most protective and resilient measures within the larger welfare policies of the region, and that they have proven highly stable in the reform period. Indeed, the long-term trend of stability in labor policy is an outcome that can only be appreciated now, after other policy areas have undergone sweeping transformation.

This concluding chapter undertakes three tasks. First, it discusses the major contributions of the book, highlighting its comprehensiveness and comparative scope. It also describes the theoretical innovations of the book, in particular the development of a coherent, integrated explanation of both the origins of labor regulations and their reform. Second, it discusses the implications of the project for the literature on Latin American social policy, political economy, and corporatism. Finally, it suggests further extensions of the project.

Contributions

This book makes significant contributions on three fronts: in the scope of its comparative approach, in its integrated theoretical perspective, and its historical analysis of the Chilean, Peruvian, and Argentine cases. First, this book employs an innovative, comprehensive comparative approach to the political dynamics of labor regulation in Latin America. With a research design that is intentionally both cross-sectional, including the eighteen major Latin American nations, and intertemporal, with data on labor codes across the three last decades (and seven decades, in the cases of Chile, Peru, and Argentina), it significantly increases our understanding of the range and dynamics of labor code variation. It thus moves beyond earlier studies that examine only particular aspects of labor codes, such as labor law reforms and modifications (Murillo 2005; Murillo and Schrank 2005; Cook 2007; Murillo et al. 2011). Further, by examining a single region with similar institutional legal origins, it sheds light on the important effects of coalitional dynamics, political competition, unionization, and the structure of employment on labor code design—all of which are washed out in cross-regional studies (Botero et al. 2004). This permits it to dialogue with earlier work in the discipline on the role of labor in the political arena (Collier and Collier 1977, 2002; Schmitter 1979). In fact, the strength and lasting power of that pioneering work becomes all the more apparent as the legacies of labor's incorporation continue to have crucial effects.

The theory developed in this book also makes a significant contribution. First, it constructs a coherent framework that can explain both the origins of Latin American labor regulations and their change through time. Most earlier work can at best explain only one of these processes. Indeed, there is a clear bifurcation in the literature between scholarship that examines the establishment of interventionist state policy (Thorp and Bertram 1978; Godio 2000; Alexander 2001; Collier and Collier 2002) and that which describes globalization and the liberal reforms to that policy (Murillo 2001; Levitsky 2003; Madrid 2003; Weyland 2007, 2004, 2002).

Second, the theory draws on sets of explanatory variables that are often studied independently by economists and political scientists, without sufficient appreciation of their inter-relationship. Thus this book brings together several strands of the political economy literature on the welfare state, much of which was developed to understand OECD countries, and applies it to the Latin American cases. It suggests that structural variables—most importantly, the distribution of skill levels of workers—play a crucial role in shaping the later cleavages that develop. Thus politics is not completely detached from economics, but neither is the economic structure completely determinative. Indeed, without sufficient organization and ties to parties, the demands of workers, regardless of their skill level, are unlikely to get translated into policy. The inter-relationship, then, of economics and politics that a political economy perspective can bring to bear is crucial for untangling the determinants of labor law.

Further, the theory in this book adds nuance to two of the important sets of theories of the welfare state. First, it extends our understanding of the power resources (for example, Mesa-Lago 1978) and left-party literatures (Huber and Stephens 2001, 2012), arguing that party ideology is less important to understanding labor regulation in Latin America than is the opportunity for political gain and linkages between parties and workers. The relationship is not simply a reflection of similar beliefs, but instead emerges from political and economic exigencies. In earlier periods, this was the need of new governments— most often authoritarian ones—to ensure that critical sectors of the economy would not be held up by their workers; they crafted marriages of convenience that have endured through time, albeit with a fair amount of conflict and change through the years. The lasting connection has not been ideological, but instead pragmatic, as labor still can provide a decisive electoral force even after many reforms.

Similarly, the literature on economic "insiders" is enhanced by this book (Rueda 2005). It argues that these insiders achieve their status through their carefully constructed, and ongoingly negotiated, relationships. Thus insiders are not simply thugs or elites who can structure the economic or political world to their liking, but instead must create lasting, interlocking linkages with other actors to the benefit of both (and the exclusion of others). Indeed, recent work has shown that labor market insiders were very much supported by, and supportive of, insiders in the capital market (Pagano and Volpin 2001).

Likewise, this book builds on recent literature that has emphasized that "legacies" of either past policies (Etchemendy 2011) or historical experiences (Cook 2007; Etchemendy and Collier 2007) shape the kinds of reform that were undertaken. By stressing the long-term influence of structural economic and political variables, it suggests that legacies come from the same dynamics that govern the reform process. Rather than representing radical departures from pre-existing equilibria, recent reforms have been remarkably consistent with the underlying economic and political balance.

Finally, the book has shown that labor regulations are not simply a technical matter, as some economic studies or policy briefs can suggest, especially those that seek to "get it right" for growth, employment, competitiveness, or some other ultimate goal they espouse. Rather, labor laws are essentially political. If reforms are to have success, they must address this essential fact; otherwise, they are likely to reinforce, rather than undermine, privileged treatment for segments of the workforce at the cost of others.

Implications

This book raises a number of issues that have relevance for our study of labor and social policy, on the one hand, and our understanding of Latin America in the reform and postreform period, on the other. First, it directs the attention of analysts to a largely neglected dependent variable among social policy measures: labor regulation. In the past, government expenditures have been the outcome of choice in large, cross-national studies of policy-making and social policy, perhaps because these are by definition quantitative and comparable across cases. However, these figures can include spending on defense, infrastructure, and a host of other measures. More recently, spending on pensions, health care, and education have been disaggregated, and this has permitted a far better appreciation of the distinct political dynamics that shape the development of each policy area. In terms of policy design, the last several years have seen work on pensions and health care regimes—with special attention on the reform processes of each and the move toward greater privatization of services.

This book has shown that labor laws are important dependent variables in their own right, which cannot be explained simply with existing explanations drawn from the literatures on pensions and social spending. The laws first reflect, and then come to shape, coalitions of insiders that can be surprisingly resilient even through changes in other aspects of social policy. Indeed, at least part of the reason that Latin American unions and the left have repeatedly returned to prominence is that labor laws have preserved a special status for them during the reform process; when they lost on other fronts, they retained a crucial role in the economy and in the electoral coalitions that could bring their associated parties to power. Where they did not have this power, as in Peru, they have not been able to stave off economic reforms that threatened their status.

Second, the story of labor laws calls into question the collective wisdom on the final effects of the neoliberal reforms of the 1980s and 1990s. The literature had come to assess these as "retiring the state" (Madrid 2003). This was most apparent in the privatization of pensions—where the state, in many countries, literally removed itself from the old-age insurance business. Yet even during the reforms that appraisal was not quite true, as many countries retained mixed or parallel systems of private and public pensions. And this study has highlighted the region's recent pension-policy reversals. The first, now-classic privatizer, Chile, has extended a public pillar to cover those left out by the private funds. And even more radically, Argentina has done that which was considered unthinkable: the renationalization of its pension system. Beyond pensions, the 1980s and 1990s were thought to have severely limited, and even eliminated, government intervention in the economy. Labor laws, however, did not follow this rule; rather, the laws actually became, on balance, more protective in the vast majority of the countries that undertook reforms.

And in fact, if one starts to scratch the surface in most Latin American countries, other government involvement in the market becomes apparent—from price setting on tortillas in Mexico to energy subsidies in Argentina. The sea-change that had overtaken the region in the "reform" was neither as final nor as unidirectional as most commentators would have us believe. Further, the "swing to the left" of the 2000s is not nearly as surprising as it has been portrayed, once we appreciate that the reforms were not as deep as previously thought. Indeed, taking the longer view, the region may be returning to a long-term equilibrium rather than entering a new, unique (and implicitly in the literature, extreme) phase of economic and political relations.

If indeed politics and economics are coming full circle, then students of Latin America would do well to rethink their appraisal of the earlier literature on corporatism and labor-party ties in the region. Corporatism, while admittedly diminished from its peak in the 1940s and 1950s, continues to exert a legacy on economic and political relations. Laws that were "captured" in that period, by elements of labor and capital and parties associated with them, continue to provide an institutional status that has not been undone with other reforms. While these actors do not control the apparatus of the state completely, they still can preserve significant benefits for themselves. In fact, the trend of recent years—suggested by this book but needing further exploration—is toward labor regulations that apply to smaller and smaller portions of the workforce. To the extent that informal employment has grown over the last several decades, by definition labor laws have come to apply to a smaller segment of the labor force. The unionized sectors, which tend to be industrial, state, and some professional workers, thus become the chief beneficiaries of the labor laws. The division between insiders and outsiders is widened, as a result, with an ever more restricted set of high-skill and mobilized insiders and a growing mass of low-skill, unorganized outsiders.

In sum, this book has significant implications for the study of economic and social policy, pointing to a new dependent variable that requires further, more systematic study across countries and time. And it also forces us to reconsider earlier characterizations of the impact of neoliberal reforms in Latin America during the 1980s and 1990s, for these were not as unequivocally marketizing as they seemed at the time. Finally, it suggests that the legacy of corporatist institutions is deeper than had been thought, and that these measures continue to shape political coalitions (that now are becoming even more restricted and selective).

Future Work

Several issues have fallen outside the scope of this project, but present particularly promising avenues for future work. First, this book has built much of its intuition on fieldwork conducted in Chile, Peru, and Argentina, and a careful reading of those countries' histories. While the hypotheses developed in the theory chapter have met with initial confirmation in the econometric testing, and been further borne out in the carefully chosen case histories presented here, there is still the danger of having overgeneralized based on these limited cases. Of the cases, Argentina and Peru present extreme values on the key independent variables, especially during the early phase of labor law development, with Argentina high on both skill levels and union organization and Peru low on both. In addition, they show extreme values on labor law scores, with Argentina among the most protective and Peru among the least. Chile is an intermediate case, with a relatively skilled labor force but a fragmented labor movement. Close examinations of additional cases from the region are needed to further test the mechanisms described in this book.

Second, the theory developed in this book is not specific to Latin America. It has been crafted to be portable, and testing its hypotheses in the context of other developing countries holds particular promise. The East Asian "tigers" that had such success in the period of market reforms seem particularly apt cases to test. Among the crucial factors in the more heavily regulated Latin American cases seem to be the overlapping presence of midlevel and high-skill workers and some organizational experience among unions, often brought from Europe. To the extent that these are lacking in other cases, the theory developed here may struggle to explain their labor codes, or may indicate that other, alternative paths to union organization and labor law formation exist.

Third, as was noted in Chapters 1 and 2, the question of endogeneity and the causal relationship between the main independent variables highlighted here (skill levels and the organizational capacity of labor) and the dependent variable (labor laws) is best resolved through historical process-tracing. Ideally, this involves isolating times when changes to skill levels or union organization were unrelated to the labor law environment, and thus any effects they have on labor laws can be taken as independent and causal. I have carried out this sort of focused historical analysis for the period of initial labor law adoption in the Chilean, Peruvian, and Argentine cases in Chapters 4, 5, and 6. However, additional testing could examine times when exogenous shocks led to changes in skill levels or union organization (perhaps resulting from international campaigns, unrelated to the particular country's labor law environment), and then see how these changes in the independent variables affected labor law design and reform processes. This would add confidence regarding the theory's applicability not only in the period of labor law origins but also in their evolution through time.

Fourth, the book has made only limited reference to the issue of enforcement of labor codes, which is very uneven throughout the region. Unfortunately, measurement of enforcement is extremely difficult, and in many cases historical data simply does not exist. However, recent studies have begun to construct measures of labor law enforcement and compliance. These generally take one of three approaches. First, some scholars examine violations of labor codes, by reviewing media reports, legal cases, or monitoring by the UN International Labor Organization or other NGOs (Mosley and Uno 2007). Of course, this work presents particular problems of bias: the countries that are bigger and richer may report more violations on a per capita basis simply because they can dedicate more resources to monitoring. A second set of studies examines the resources dedicated to enforcement, measured as either the number of labor inspectors (per million workers) or the number of labor inspections (per thousand workers)

(Ronconi 2012). This compensates for the bias of studies of violations, but still cannot distinguish the effectiveness of inspectors or inspection (some of which might be more or less competent, or prone to corruption, and so forth). Finally, household surveys have been employed to collect individual-level reports of labor law violations (Ronconi 2010). These provide remarkably fine grained evidence but are very sensitive to question wording, and cannot yet provide extensive time-series data. Thus, while there are important new efforts to gather data on enforcement and compliance, analysis is hampered by how little is known across time and countries.

Nevertheless, limitations on data should not keep us from further exploring the political aspects of strategic compliance or noncompliance. Labor law enforcement has recently begun to enter regularly into international trade agreements, and states may choose to increase their commitment to the monitoring of labor laws in order to win beneficial trade relations (Greenhill et al. 2009). Governments from the left, and democratic governments in general, seem to dedicate more resources to enforcement (Ronconi 2012). On the other hand, strategic nonenforcement seems to increase under governments from the right, perhaps as a way to compensate employers who feel hurt by restrictive labor laws. In these regimes, the state may seek to give organized labor and concerned international NGOs what they want, by enacting protective laws, but simultaneously give employers what they want, by systematically not enforcing the laws it passes. This suggestive evidence points to the need for further theoretical and empirical work on the scope and strategy of labor law enforcement.

Conclusion

Labor laws in Latin America are not neutral "rules of the game" governing employment relationships, but in fact are highly susceptible to targeting, selectivity, and "capture" by some workers, to the exclusion or detriment of other workers. This book has explored the political determinants and dynamics of labor regulation in Latin America, showing that the distribution of worker skill levels and union organization together explain the variations in the region's labor regulations.

This book began by noting a puzzling divergence in the fates of workers in Latin America. Some, including a fortunate group of pensioners in Chile, continue to enjoy job security and generous pensions. Others, including medical workers in Peru, have seen legal protections erode and have become much more vulnerable to job loss and bouts of poverty. In the end, I have argued that this divergence should not be so surprising. It is rooted in the economic structure of production of each country, which changes only slowly, and which has in fact pushed countries back toward long-term labor market equilibria. Skill distributions tend to reproduce themselves, and limit the likelihood of lasting change to labor market institutions. Likewise, where labor's organizational capacity has been greater, lasting political linkages to political parties and the state have dampened possibilities for path-departing reforms.

In short, this book suggests that in fact the underlying political relationship of labor market insiders and political parties had not changed. Thus the "resurgence" of labor, and the "turn to the Left," are not so much a new development as the reflection of long-term dynamics in the region. Students and commentators who emphasize the impact of globalization, and ignore this long-standing political arrangement, do so at their peril. For all of its touted effects, globalization has not fundamentally broken the political-labor nexus in Latin America.

Notes

Chapter 1

1. Botero et al. (2004) represents a significant exception, as it codes a variety of labor law provisions for a broad set of countries. However, it is atheoretical in its approach to labor law configurations; it employs a single continuous measure of labor laws, without distinguishing how combinations of laws may function when considered together.

2. Regulation need not be either labor friendly or business friendly. Nevertheless, an asymmetry exists between workers and owners of capital in an unregulated market in the "state of nature": individual workers have less bargaining power than do capital owners (since capital ownership implies owning surplus capital). Thus, the introduction of labor legislation implicitly provides labor with a status, rights, and enforcement mechanisms that it would otherwise lack. Increasing legislation further limits the discretion of employers, or carries additional specification of worker rights.

3. While the origin indicates a labor market with no legislation, there is no corresponding theoretical "maximum" of labor regulation.

4. Note that collective action is not ruled out in the professional regime, and indeed workers may choose to form professional associations. But these associations are not regulated or protected by law. Instead, individuals enter into the associations freely, with only the provisions of the "individual" labor code to protect them—as individuals—against arbitrary dismissal or other retaliatory action by employers.

5. Somewhat surprisingly, the "legal origins" literature—which argues that colonizing powers' legal regime set the parameters of all future labor law development—fails to address these pendulum swings and variation that have occurred through history. Instead, its analysis draws observations only from very

recent years, when the region's labor codes have been uncharacteristically calm and relatively homogenous.

Chapter 2

1. Table 2.1 presents only a subset of the variables included in the dataset, which includes measures of twenty-three variables for eighteen countries. Descriptions of all the variables and coding rules may be found in the appendix at the end of this chapter.

2. These measures do not lend themselves to simple presentation in real-world numbers (such as hours of work or days of rest), as in Table 2.1 above, so I do not present a table here to summarize them. Full coding rules, however, are presented in Table 2.A at the end of this chapter.

3. In additional examination of the dataset using factor analysis, as suggested by Rosenthal and Voeten (2007), it is apparent that (within the individual-labor rubric) several variables load onto two factors—one concerning *job stability and flexibility*, and another concerning *employment conditions*. For this reason, while I use the broad categories of "individual" and "collective" labor laws in my econometric analysis—as has become customary in the literature—I pay particular attention to issues of job stability, flexibilization, and employment conditions in my qualitative study of historical cases.

4. Earlier work has highlighted this consistency across a subset of cases and with regard to particular elements in the labor code (Murillo 2005; Cook 2007), but has not documented it systematically for the entire region or for labor codes taken as a whole.

5. In addition, all three countries are in the upper half of countries in the region for efforts at labor law enforcement. Based on calculations of the number of labor inspections per thousand workers in the 2000s, Chile stands out among the highest in Latin America (17.4), and both Argentina (5.0) and Peru (7.3) are above the median (Ronconi 2012: 94).

6. Of course, primary school enrollment is at best an imperfect measure of skill levels in the economy. Since it is measured as a share of the population, it is dependent—at least in part—on the shape of the demographic pyramid. Further, the effects of primary enrollment only enter into the economy after a certain lag (as students transition into the workforce). For this reason, I also employ a measure of literacy below as an additional proxy for the availability of relatively skilled workers in the economy.

Chapter 3

1. This chapter makes use of a dataset of twenty-three author-coded labor law provisions for eighteen Latin American countries, as described in the previous chapter. It employs as its source Vega Ruiz 2005. Complete coding rules can be found in Table 2.A, above.

2. Differences in labor law provisions can have enormous economic and political effects, and a significant literature in economics has developed around these impacts of labor codes (see, for example, Edwards and Lustig 1997; Heckman and Pagés 2004; and Restrepo and Tokman 2005).

3. Of course, over time these endowments become endogenous to the pattern of investment and economic development pursued within the territory, and may be affected by international trade and investment flows. But fundamentally altering resource endowments is extremely difficult, and patterns of production persist over many decades (especially in developing countries).

4. This years of schooling measure is drawn from Barro and Lee 2000, with additional updates on-line.

5. Studies of European cases have shown how vocational training and industrial employment provide specific skills to workers in particular sectors, thus changing their preferences regarding labor policy (Iversen 2005).

6. Union density data is extremely difficult to compile (see, for example, Roberts and Wibbels 1999). I have used the one generally reliable cross-country comparison of union density figures—the World Labor Report of the International Labor Organization (ILO) from 1997 to 1998, which reports figures from the mid-1990s—as a benchmark for other studies that provide data for previous or later periods. Further, Rama and Artecona (2002) provide data on a number of countries that they link with the ILO data. I then use country-level studies to complete my dataset, in each case examining the observations for consistency with the ILO figures and cross-referencing with other sources wherever possible.

7. I employ the regime-type dataset developed in Mainwaring, Brinks, and Pérez-Liñán 2000. My coding rule has been to code each country-decade observation according to the regime type it had for the majority of the years in that decade, and then include a dummy variable for "democracy" in each of the models developed below. Alternative coding rules and model specifications, including a proportional score for each country based on the proportion of years in the decade that they were coded by Mainwaring et al. as "democratic," and the inclusion of dummy variables for authoritarian or semidemocratic regimes, do not substantially change my results. In additional robustness checks, results for analyses using both the Przeworski et al. (2000) data and the Polity IV data were consistent with my findings using the Mainwaring et al. (2000) data.

8. Data on partisanship are drawn from Coppedge 1997. These data indicate the "percentages of total valid vote in elections for the lower or sole house of the legislature." I construct a measure for the vote share of left parties, averaging the results across the total number of elections in the decade.

9. Substantive effects were calculated using the *Clarify* statistical software in Stata (Tomz, Wittenberg, and King 2001).

10. In addition, the small number of observations in the dataset prevents

the inclusion of country fixed-effects in the models as an additional robustness check.

Chapter 4

1. Interestingly, many of the mutual aid societies opposed the social security fund on the basis that it would render them unnecessary (DeShazo 1983).

2. With employer agreement, bargaining could occur on an industry-wide basis. This happened in the textile, shoe, and garment industries. I thank J. Samuel Valenzuela for bringing these exceptional cases of industry-wide negotiation to my attention.

3. J. Samuel Valenzuela (2006) has pointed out that the expansion of existing labor laws to new sectors, rather than the design of new models of labor legislation, resulted in a tragic mismatch between needs and laws. He argues that the demand of *obreros* in Chile to share in the earlier established severance pay regime of *empleados*—rather than insisting on a solidaristic unemployment insurance system—undermined the achievement of meaningful protection against periods of unemployment.

4. Removal of the indemnity was phased in, such that it applied only to workers hired after the 1979 enactment of the measure, in order to diminish opposition.

5. These figures—which are the official measures released by the Chilean government—are calculated slightly differently from those in Figure 4.1, above. The earlier figure took as its denominator the entire economically active population (EAP), but this figure is expressed as a share of the occupied workforce (a subset of the EAP). Thus, these figures exclude workers who are unemployed, and are 1 to 2 percentage points higher than the earlier series. The Chilean government's Dirección del Trabajo also calculates the unionization rate as a percentage of workers eligible for unionization (private sector workers in firms large enough that unionization is permitted; public sector workers are not allowed to unionize). This results in unionization figures between 14 and 16 percent in the 2000s, after a high of 21.2 percent in 1991.

6. However, while these universalistic reforms were presented as an effort to achieve greater economic solidarity, they were also at least in part an implicit recognition of the shortcomings of the privatized pension system. Even before reform, 81 percent of pensions were being paid by the state, and 92 percent required some state contribution (Valenzuela 2006).

Chapter 5

1. Schneider and Karcher (2010) estimate that 65 percent of Peruvian nonagricultural employment occurs in the informal sector (632).

2. Collier and Collier (2002) place the incorporation period for labor earlier, in the 1940s, in the first APRA linkages to the labor movement. While

I agree that the 1940s were critical in laying the political relationships for later worker mobilization, I believe that the core features of Peruvian labor relations were set earlier (as outlined above). And I argue here and below that the key legal measures came later, in the second Prado Ugarteche government and, more important, in the Velasco Alvarado military regime.

3. The creation of "industrial communities" also allowed the state to co-opt and incorporate long-standing bases of union organization into the state. Among the most successful of the communities were the Comunidad Minera and the Comunidad de Compensación Minera, both of which drew on the pre-existing unions in the mining sector for their membership (Iguíñiz et al. 1985).

4. One commentator calls the rapid rise, and decisive power, of Fujimori, who had been a political outsider, the "tsunami Fujimori" (Tanaka 1998: 167).

5. The new modalities were for: beginning a new business or business activity; market necessities; reconversion of the business; short-term needs, including one-time, emergency, or supplementary needs; and characteristics of the work or service provided by the business, including specific, intermittent, or seasonal characteristics (Saavedra 2000: 392).

6. This dismissal of state workers not only affected them directly but also weakened the organizational potential of the labor movement around individual job protections in general. Survey data shows that state sector workers were better educated than private sector workers (Ruiz Pérez 1996: 222). The theory developed in Chapter 1 argues that these more skilled workers are key to union organizing and effectiveness, especially with regard to job stability provisions. By removing them from such positions, Fujimori transformed these workers from insiders into outsiders, and thus made them more likely to support his temporary hiring provisions in the long term.

7. In recent decades, Peruvian parties have become increasingly personalistic and short-lived rather than programmatic. Many are organized for the purposes of a single election, a practice followed by both Fujimori campaigns and Toledo's rise to power. Even APRA and Acción Popular, the parties with the longest histories in Peru, have largely become the vehicles of particular leaders in distinct periods of their existence.

8. I do not include a time-series for confidence in state-owned enterprises in Table 5.1 because Grupo Apoyo stopped including it in its polls in 1991.

9. A study of unions and their strategies in response to the Fujimori reforms (Mejía 1998) confirms many of the intuitions of the analysis to this point. One group of unions, including copper workers and some state workers, had leadership that remained intransigent and populist, and generally proved to be the biggest set of losers. Alternatively, many of the smallest and weakest unions turned to the CGTP as a source of material and organizational support, but given the diversity of these unions, the CGTP ended up fragmenting its lobbying efforts. And finally, the collapse of the political party system cut off

access to state institutions, in particular to Parliament and the Ministry of Labor (Mejía 1998: 35–37).

10. Another study in 2003 estimated permanent employment at 20.5 percent (down from 40.3 percent in 1990), temporary employment at 33.5 percent (up from 25.2 percent in 1990), and 46 percent of workers without employment contracts (up from 34.5 percent in 1990). The unionization rate was estimated at 8.3 percent (down from 39 percent in 1990) (Chacaltana 2005: 29).

11. Membership in the state-run National System of Pensions (*Sistema Nacional de Pensiones*) was 18 percent of the population, according to an Apoyo poll in June of 2003. Some 66 percent of the population reported that they were not covered by any pension program. The figure on confidence in the system comes from an earlier poll taken in 1999. While opinion may have shifted slightly over the intervening four years between polls, anecdotal evidence suggests that dissatisfaction with the private pension system remained high.

Chapter 6

1. Compliance with these measures varies significantly. A recent study of compliance with a set of six labor policies over the 1995–2002 period shows that minimum wage legislation stands out for 94 percent compliance, while maximum work hour legislation sees 84 percent compliance. Annual extra wages and mandated vacations see a much lower 58 percent compliance, and contributions to social security and health funds average 56 percent (Ronconi 2010: 723). This imperfect compliance is certainly a cause for concern, especially for the workers involved. Nevertheless, the relatively high level of compliance suggests that the legal mandates are not just words on paper, and that they have a significant effect in the economy.

2. Simplicity comes at a cost here, as the military governments mounted considerable challenges to Argentina's labor regulations, and Alfonsín (from the Radical Party) pursued a carefully constructed "concertation" between employers and workers even as he reinstated many of the classically Peronist labor laws.

3. As noted in Chapter 2, reliable unionization figures are extremely difficult to collect, especially across time and industries. Unions have incentives to overstate their membership numbers. And even when the unions or employers seek to provide accurate, honest figures, the flow of workers in and out of particular industries may make assembling data difficult. Nevertheless, the data in Table 6.1 can serve as a rough approximation of union affiliation in the 1936–2007 period. Indeed, to the knowledge of the author, the data presented here is the most complete quantitative time series of Argentine unionization available.

4. This discussion of Argentine individual labor laws draws on the summary of laws in Galiani and Gerchunoff (2003), 161–64.

5. Perón had initially sought ties with the Radical Party but was only able to attract the support of a dissident faction, the UCR-Junta Renovadora. The new Partido Laborista had greater "capacity to capture the votes of the other groups" already associated with Perón. Nevertheless, Perón incorporated various members of the UCR-JR into his early coalition, neutralizing the most strident demands of labor and preserving an electoral appeal to the middle and upper classes (Zarazaga 2004: 216–17).

6. Many unions also operated mutual aid societies, which gave them additional economic resources to bestow on their members and to use in courting favor with politicians. The societies spread through collective bargaining in the 1950s, and eventually in the 1980s developed into the *obras sociales* health care system. The later importance of the *obras sociales*—as a health care system and a source of power for unions—cannot be overstated. Through the system, both employers and affiliated employees make payments into a common *obra social* fund, administered by the union. As a result, the unions receive funds that are several times the size of their union dues. Historically, they have used these resources both to finance their health care plans and to promote union membership. Since union members are generally granted better privileges at health centers than their nonmember peers, there is an incentive for these nonaffiliates to join the union (Galiani and Gerchunoff 2003: 134). Further, the *obras sociales* offer more than simply health care, but also often include access to subsidized child care, discount tourism, and athletic facilities and theaters (Fescina 2004: 69). Juan Carlos Torre sums them up when he says they are an "enormous social patrimony" that confers remarkable power on the unions that administer them (Torre 2004: 10).

7. A minimum wage was established, as well, but the governing body responsible for its determination was not immediately created as the law required.

8. Galiani and Gerchunoff (2003) estimate that, in the early 2000s, this raised coverage of collective agreements from the roughly 45 percent of Argentine workers that are unionized to more than 50 percent.

9. Etchemendy and Collier (2007) point out that collective bargaining is asymmetric under Argentine law such that labor is structurally favored. While all workers in an industry are represented by only one actor—the monopoly union—employers may be represented by more than one employer's organization. Consequently, the union voice is more likely to be united while the employer position may be fragmented.

10. Figures on electoral outcomes and seats in the Chamber of Deputies and Congress are drawn from Mainwaring and Scully (1996).

11. The Peronist-worker alliance was not perfect, though, and it was severely tested when the PJ was not in power. Internally, competition for leadership emerged from communists and socialists, as well as from the industrial "62 Organizations" led by Augusto Timoteo Vandor (Godio 2000: 953, 955, 1040).

12. Employers wanted to keep wage agreements in check and limit union control of the *obras sociales* funds, while the CGT was unbending on these measures. In the end, however, it had to accept reduced social spending (Quiroga 2005: 39).

13. In a study of 1,300 manufacturing firms between 1990 and 1996, Mondino and Montoya (2004) find that the effects of Argentina's regulations "appeared regressive, limiting the opportunities of those worse off and protecting the jobs of those with higher human capital" (387).

14. Following the lead of Chile, whose privatization of its pension system had reduced the fiscal burden on the state, Menem sought to place the highly expensive pension system in private hands. Some commentators have questioned whether Argentina was in a position to enjoy the same benefits of pension privatization as had Chile. Chile undertook its reform at a time of budget surplus, allowing it to finance the enormous transfers of state pension funds into the private system. Argentina, on the other hand, undertook its privatization in a period of fiscal crisis.

15. Menem also acted shrewdly in dealing with the unions representing state workers. This sector is the only one in the economy in which monopoly union status is not granted; rather, the government tolerates (and perhaps even encourages) competition among two main bodies representing state employees. In pushing through his reform agenda, which included a number of union-weakening measures, he won the support of the larger, CGT-affiliated Unión del Personal Civil de la Nación (UPCN) by awarding it the administration of the *obra social* for state workers (called Unión Personal), which is among the largest *obras sociales* in the country. The dissident Asociación de Trabajadores del Estado (ATE) considered this decision an effort to make it "disappear," since many of its members were effectively co-opted into the UPCN and would need to make use of its *obras sociales* (Menéndez 2005: 186–87).

16. However, unions could in their collective bargaining agreement negotiate a maximum probationary period of up to six months.

17. Several other candidates also received substantial numbers of votes: Ricardo López Murphy (16.8 percent), Elisa Carrió (14.4 percent), and Adolfo Rodriguez Saá (13.4 percent) (Godio 2006).

18. The Central de los Trabajadores Argentinos (CTA) formed in 1991 after the CGT fractured in response to the early reforms of Menem; its early membership was drawn largely from dissident state workers in the Asociación de Trabajadores del Estado (ATE). It has been continually blocked from receiving *personería gremial*, and thus remains substantially weaker than the CGT. Unlike other Argentine labor confederations, it allows direct affiliation of members (rather than through member unions), and these members need not presently be employed.

19. The *obras sociales* by law must use 80 percent of their resources for health

services. The remainder is used both for administration and other union activities, so increasing the funds available to *obras sociales* effectively offers more political resources to the unions. In this decree (24 January 2008), Cristina Kirchner increased the maximum required monthly contribution to the *obras sociales* by the wealthiest workers. This measure could be justified on the grounds that health-care contributions had not kept pace with pension-plan contributions and that social equity required that the rich pay more to help their poorer compatriots. However, many commentators saw the marks of a politically motivated move to cement union support of the new Kirchner government as well as bolster Hugo Moyano, who was facing challenges from within the CGT.

20. According to Law 23,551, the secretaries general of labor unions were permitted to be re-elected indefinitely.

21. "Jamás voy a votar una ley contra los trabajadores." These words were spoken in reference to a proposal to reform the nation's labor codes during the presidency of Nestor Kirchner.

22. "Quiero agradecer en nombre de todos los argentinos el esfuerzo que los dirigentes sindicales están haciendo para darle sustentabilidad al modelo de desarrollo económico y social."

References

Acemoglu, Daron. 1998. "Why Do New Technologies Complement Skills? Directed Technical Change and Wage Inequality." *Quarterly Journal of Economics* 113 (4): 1055–89.

Adsera, Alicia, and Carles Boix. 2002. "Trade, Democracy, and the Size of the Public Sector: The Political Underpinnings of Openness." *International Organization* 56 (2): 229–62.

Alemán, Jose A. 2010. *Labor Relations in New Democracies: Latin America, East Asia, and Eastern Europe.* New York: Palgrave Macmillan.

Alexander, Gerard. 2001. "Institutions, Path Dependence, and Democratic Consolidation." *Journal of Theoretical Politics* 13 (3): 249–70.

Alexander, Robert J. 1962. *Labor Relations in Argentina, Brazil, and Chile.* New York: McGraw-Hill.

Almeida, Rita, and Pedro Carneiro. 2007. "Inequality and Employment in a Dual Economy: Enforcement of Labor Regulation in Brazil," Discussion paper 3094. Bonn, Germany: Institute for the Study of Labor.

Alonso, Guillermo V. 2000. *Política y seguridad social en la Argentina de los '90.* Buenos Aires: Miño y Dávila.

Altamirano, Carlos. 2001. *Bajo el signo de las masas (1943–1973).* Biblioteca del pensamiento argentino. Vol. 6. Buenos Aires: Ariel.

Angell, Alan. 1972. *Politics and the Labour Movement in Chile.* London: Oxford University Press.

Angell, Alan. 1979. "Peruvian Labour and the Military Government since 1968." Working paper no. 3. London: University of London, Institute of Latin American Studies.

Anner, Mark. 2008. "Meeting the Challenges of Industrial Restructuring: Labor Reform and Enforcement in Latin America." *Latin American Politics and Society* 50 (2): 33–65.

Anner, Mark. 2011. *Solidarity Transformed: Labor Responses to Globalization and Crisis in Latin America.* Ithaca, NY: ILR Press, an imprint of Cornell University Press.

Arias, Luz Marina. 2011. "Analytic Narratives." In *International Encyclopedia of Political Science*, edited by Bertrand Badie, Dirk Berg-Schlosser, and Leonardo Morlino. Thousand Oaks, CA: Sage Publications.

Barría, Jorge. 1971. *Historia de la CUT.* Santiago, Chile: Editorial Prensa Latinoamericana, S.A.

Barro, Robert J., and Jong-Wha Lee. 2000. "International Data on Educational Attainment: Updates and Implications." CID working paper 42. Cambridge, MA: Center for International Development at Harvard University.

Basualdo, Eduardo M. 2006. *Estudios de historia económica argentina: desde mediados del siglo XX a la actualidad.* Buenos Aires, Argentina: FLACSO: Siglo Veintiuno Editores.

Bates, Robert, Avner Greif, Margaret Levi, and Jean-Laurent. 1998. *Analytic Narratives.* Princeton: Princeton University Press.

Beccaria, Luís, and Roxana Maurizio. 2005. *Mercado de trabajo y equidad en Argentina.* Buenos Aires: Prometeo Libros.

Berg, Janine. 2006. *Miracle for Whom? Chilean Workers under Free Trade.* New York: Routledge.

Berg, Janine, Christoph Ernst, and Peter Auer. 2006. *Meeting the Employment Challenge: Argentina, Brazil, and Mexico in the Global Economy.* Boulder, Colorado: Lynne Rienner Publishers.

Bergquist, Charles. 1986. *Labor in Latin America: Comparative Essays on Chile, Argentina, Venezuela, and Colombia.* Stanford: Stanford University Press.

Bernedo, Jorge. 1990. "Empleo y crisis: una visión general." In *El empleo en el Perú: diagnósticos y propuestas*, edited by Jorge Bernedo. Lima, Perú: ADEC-ATC Asociación Laboral para el Desarrollo.

Birdsall, Nancy, Nora Lustig, and Darryl McCleod. 2011. "Declining Inequality in Latin America: Some Economics, Some Politics." Working paper 251. Washington, DC: Center for Global Development.

Blofield, Merike. 2011. "Feudal Enclaves and Political Reforms: Domestic Workers in Latin America." *Latin American Research Review* 44 (1): 158–90.

Blofield, Merike. 2012. *Care Work and Class: Domestic Workers' Struggle for Equal Rights in Latin America.* University Park: Pennsylvania State University Press.

Bombardini, Mathilde, Giovanni Gallipoli, and Germán Pupatoz. 2012. "Skill Dispersion and Trade Flows." *American Economic Review* 102 (5): 2327–48.

Botero, Juan C., Simeon Djankov, Rafael La Porta, Florencio Lopez-de-Silanes, and Andre Shleifer. 2004. "The Regulation of Labor." *Quarterly Journal of Economics* 119 (4): 1339–82.

Brass, Tom. 1999. *Toward a Comparative Political Economy of Unfree Labor: Case Studies and Debates.* London: Frank Cass and Co.

Bronstein, Arturo. 1990. "Protection against Unjustified Dismissal in Latin America." *International Labour Review* 129 (5): 593–610.

Bronstein, Arturo. 1995. "Societal Change and Industrial Relations in Latin America: Trends and Prospects." *International Labour Review* 134 (2): 163–86.

Brooks, Sarah. 2009. *Social Protection and the Market: The Transformation of Social Security Institutions in Latin America*. New York: Cambridge University Press.

Buchanan, Paul G. 2008. "Preauthoritarian Institutions and Postauthoritarian Outcomes: Labor Politics in Chile and Uruguay." *Latin American Politics and Society* 50 (1): 59–89.

Burgess, Katrina. 2004. *Parties and Unions in the New Global Economy*. Pittsburgh: University of Pittsburgh Press.

Calvo, Ernesto, and Maria Victoria Murillo. 2004. "Who Delivers? Partisan Clients in the Argentine Electoral Market." *American Journal of Political Science* 48 (4): 742–57.

Cameron, David R. 1978. "Expansion of the Public Economy—Comparative Analysis." *American Political Science Review* 72 (4): 1243–61.

Cameron, Maxwell A. N.d. *Workers and the State: Protest and Incorporation under Military Rule in Peru, 1968–1975*. Mimeo., Department of Political Science. University of California, Berkeley.

Campero, Guillermo. 2000. "Union Organization and Labor Relations." In *Chile in the 1990s*, edited by Cristián Toloza and Eugenio Lahera. Stanford: Stanford University Press.

Campero, Guillermo, and José A. Valenzuela. 1984. *El Movimiento sindical en el regimen militar Chileno: 1973–1981*. Santiago, Chile: Instituto Latinoamericano de Estudios Transnacionales.

Caraway, Teri L. 2007. *Assembling Women: The Feminization of Global Manufacturing*. Ithaca, NY: ILR Press, an imprint of Cornell University Press.

Caraway, Teri. 2012. "Pathways of Dominance and Displacement: The Varying Fates of Legacy Unions in New Democracies." *World Politics* 64 (2): 278–305.

Carnes, Matthew E. 2014. "Hooking Workers and Hooking Votes: *Enganche*, Suffrage, and Labor Market Dualism in Latin America." *Latin American Politics and Society* 56 (2).

Carnes, Matthew E., and Isabela Mares. 2007. "The Welfare State in Global Perspective." In *Handbook of Comparative Politics*, ed. Carles Boix and Susan Stokes. New York: Oxford University Press.

Carnes, Matthew E., and Isabela Mares. 2013. "Measuring the Individual-Level Determinants of Social Insurance Preferences: Survey Evidence from the 2008 Argentine Pension Nationalization." *Latin American Research Review* 48 (3): 108–29.

Carnes, Matthew E., and Isabela Mares. 2014. "Coalitional Realignment and the Adoption of Non-Contributory Social Insurance Programs in Latin America." *Socio-Economic Review*. doi: 10.1093/ser/mwt024.

Castiglioni, Rossana. 2005. *The Politics of Social Policy Change in Chile and Uruguay: Retrenchment versus Maintenance, 1973–1998.* New York: Routledge.

Castro Rivas, Víctor Manuel. 1981. *Evolución histórica de la legislación sobre estabilidad laboral en el Perú, 1901–1981: Organización Internacional de Trabajo.* Centro Interamericano de Administración del Trabajo. CIAT/DT/81/19.

Chacaltana Janampa, Juan. 2005. *Programas de empleo en el Perú: racionalidad e impacto.* Lima, Perú: Centro de Estudios para el Desarrollo y la Participación: Consorcio de Investigación Económica y Social.

Chang Rodríguez, Eugenio. 1958. "Chinese Labor Migration into Latin America in the Nineteenth Century." *Revista de Historia de América* 46: 375–97.

Chor, Davin, and Richard B. Freeman. 2005. *The 2004 Global Labor Survey: Workplace Institutions and Practices around the World.* NBER working paper Series, no. 11598.

Collier, David, and Ruth Berins Collier. 1977. "Who Does What, to Whom, and How: Toward a Comparative Analysis of Latin American Corporatism." In *Authoritarianism and Corporatism in Latin America,* edited by James M. Malloy. Pittsburgh: University of Pittsburgh Press.

Collier, David, Jody LaPorte, and Jason Seawright. 2012. "Putting Typologies to Work: Concept-Formation, Measurement, and Analytic Rigor." *Political Research Quarterly* 65 (2): 217–32.

Collier, Ruth Berins, and David Collier. 1979. "Inducements versus Constraints—Disaggregating Corporatism." *American Political Science Review* 73 (4): 967–86.

Collier, Ruth Berins, and David Collier. 2002. *Shaping the Political Arena: Critical Junctures, the Labor Movement, and Regime Dynamics in Latin America.* Notre Dame: University of Notre Dame Press.

Colomer, Josep. 2004. "Taming the Tiger: Voting Rights and Political Instability in Latin America." *Latin American Politics and Society* 46 (2): 29–58.

Contreras, Carlos, and Marcos Cueto. 2000. *Historia del Perú contemporáneo: desde las luchas por la independencia hasta el presente.* 2nd ed. San Miguel, Lima, Perú: Pontificia Universidad Católica del Perú, Universidad del Pacífico and Instituto de Estudios Peruanos.

Cook, Maria Lorena. 2007. *The Politics of Labor Reform in Latin America: Between Flexibility and Rights.* University Park: Pennsylvania State University Press.

Coppedge, Michael. 1997. "A Classification of Latin American Political Parties." Notre Dame University: Kellogg Institute working paper no. 244. November.

Coppedge, Michael. October 1998. "The Dynamic Diversity of Latin American Party Systems." *Party Politics* 4 (4): 547–68.

Córdova, Efrén. 1972. "Labour Legislation and Latin American Development: A Preliminary Review." *International Labor Review* 106 (5): 445–74.

Córdova, Efrén. 1986. "From Full-Time Wage Employment to Atypical Employment:A Major Shift in the Evolution of Labour Relations?" *International Labor Review* 125 (6): 641–57.

Córdova, Efrén. 1993. "Some Reflections on the Overproduction of International Labor Standards." *Comparative Labor Law Journal* 14 (2): 138–62.

Cortázar, René. 1993. *Política laboral en el Chile democrático: avances y desafíos en los noventa*. Santiago, Chile: Ediciones Dolmen.

Cortés Conde, Roberto. 2005. *La economía política de la Argentina en el siglo XX*. Buenos Aires: Edhasa.

Cox Edwards, Alejandra. 1997. "Labor Market Regulation in Latin America: An Overview." In *Labor Markets in Latin America: Combining Social Protection with Market Flexibility*, edited by Sebastian Edwards and Nora C. Lustig. Washington, DC: Brookings Institution Press.

Crassweller, Robert. 1988. *Perón and the Enigmas of Argentina*. New York: W. W. Norton and Company.

De la O, Ana. 2013. "Do Conditional Cash Transfers Affect Electoral Behavior? Evidence from a Randomized Experiment in Mexico." *American Journal of Political Science* 57 (1): 1–14.

de Ramón, Armando. 2003. *Historia de Chile: desde la invasión incaica hasta nuestros días (1500–2000)*. Santiago, Chile: Catalonia.

DeShazo, Peter. 1983. *Urban Workers and Labor Unions in Chile, 1902–1927*. Madison: University of Wisconsin Press.

De Soto, Hernando. 1989. *The Other Path: The Invisible Revolution in the Third World*. New York: Basic Books.

De Soto, Hernando. 2000. *The Mystery of Capital: Why Capitalism Triumphs in the West and Fails Everywhere Else*. New York: Basic Books.

Dirección General de Estudios y Formulación de Políticas de Empleo. 2004. Buenos Aires, Argentina: Instituto Nacional de Estadísticas y Censos. Accessed at http://www.indec.gov.ar/.

Di Tella, Torcuato S. 2003. *Perón y los sindicatos: el inicio de una relación conflictiva*. Buenos Aires: Ariel.

Drake, Paul W. 1996. *Labor Movements and Dictatorships: The Southern Cone in Comparative Perspective*. Baltimore, MD: Johns Hopkins University Press.

Drezner, Daniel. 2001. "Globalization and Policy Convergence." *International Studies Review* 3: 53–78.

Durand, Francisco. 2006. "El problema del fortalecimiento institucional empresarial." In *Construir instituciones: democracia, desarrollo y desigualdad en el Perú desde 1980*, edited by J. Crabtree. Lima, Perú: Pontificia Universidad Católica del Perú, Universidad del Pacífico and Instituto de Estudios Peruanos.

Economist, The. 2006. "A Worrying Precedent: A Generous Pay Deal for Striking Miners Alarms Chile's Copper Producers." 7 September 2006.

Edwards, Sebastian. 2012. *Left Behind: Latin America and the False Promise of Populism*. Chicago: University of Chicago Press.

Edwards, Sebastian, and Nora Lustig. 1997. *Labor Markets in Latin America: Combining Social Protection with Market Flexibility*. Washington, DC: Brookings Institution Press.

El Comercio. 2006a. "Anteproyecto de la ley general del trabajo fue enviado al Congreso." Lima, Peru: 28 October.

El Comercio. 2006b. "Ley del Trabajo pasa al Congreso." Lima, Peru: 28 October.

El Comercio. 2006c. "PCM aprueba libre desafiliación de AFPs." Lima, Peru: 10 August.

El Comercio. 2007. "La CTP destaca que se priorice el debate de la Ley General del Trabajo." Lima, Peru: 13 November.

Engerman, Stanley L., and Kenneth L. Sokoloff. 2005. "The Evolution of Suffrage Institutions in the New World." *Journal of Economic History* 65 (4): 891–921.

Engerman, Stanley, Kenneth Sokoloff, and Elisa Mariscal. 2012. "The Evolution of Schooling: 1800–1925." In *Economic Development in the Americas since 1500: Endowments and Institutions*, edited by Stanley Engerman and Kenneth Sokoloff. Cambridge: Cambridge University Press.

Epstein, Edward C. 1979. "Control and Co-optation of the Argentine Labor Movement." *Economic Development and Cultural Change* 27 (3): 445–65.

Esping-Andersen, Gosta. 1990. *The Three Worlds of Welfare Capitalism*. Princeton: Princeton University Press.

Estevez-Abe, Margarita, Torben Iversen, and David Soskice. 2001. "Social Protection and the Formation of Skills: A Reinterpretation of the Welfare State." In *Varieties of Capitalism*, edited by Peter A. Hall and David Soskice. Oxford: Oxford University Press.

Etchemendy, Sebastian. 2011. *Models of Economic Liberalization: Business, Workers, and Compensation in Latin America, Spain, and Portugal*. New York: Cambridge University Press.

Etchemendy, Sebastian, and Ruth Berins Collier. 2007. "Down but Not Out: Union Resurgence and Segmented Neocorporatism in Argentina (2003–2007)." *Politics and Society* 35 (3): 363–401.

Falabella, Gonzalo. 1981. *Labor in Chile under the Junta, 1973–1979*. London: University of London, Institute of Latin American Studies working papers.

Ferrer, Aldo. 2004. "La economía argentina: desde sus orígenes hasta principios del siglo XXI." *Sección obras de economía*. Buenos Aires: Fondo de Cultura Económica.

Ferreres, Orlando. 2005. *Dos siglos de la economía argentina (1810–2004)*. Buenos Aires, Argentina: Fundación Norte y Sur.

Fescina, Andrés. 2004. "Las obras sociales en la Argentina: un testimonio." Buenos Aires, Argentina: Realidad Argentina.

Flores, Galindo Alberto. 1993. *Los mineros de la cerro de pasco 1900–1930*. Lima: Casa De Estudios Del Socialismo.

Frank, Volker Karl. 1995. "Plant Level Leaders, the Union Movement, and the

Return to Democracy in Chile." Ph.D. dissertation, Department of Sociology, University of Notre Dame, 1995.

Galiani, Sebastián, and Pablo Gerchunoff. 2003. "The Labor Market." In *The New Economic History of Argentina*, edited by Gerardo della Paolera and Alán M. Taylor. New York: Cambridge University Press.

García, Norberto E. 2004. *Políticas de empleo en Perú*. 2 vols. Lima, Peru: Consorcio de Investigación Económica y Social, Centro de Estudios para el Desarrollo y la Participación, and Instituto de Estudios Peruanos.

Garrido, Francisca, and Eduardo Olivares. 2008. "Cómo el sistema beneficiará a los más pobres, actuales cotizantes, mujeres, jóvenes, independientes, y la industria: guía de 50 respuestas para entender los cambios." *El Mercurio* Online, 17 January 2008.

George, Alexander, and Andrew Bennett. 2005. *Case Studies and Theory Development in the Social Sciences*. Cambridge: MIT Press.

Gerchunoff, Pablo, and Lucas Llach. 2003. *El ciclo de la ilusión y el desencanto: un siglo de políticas económicas argentinas*. Edited, corrected, and augmented edition. Buenos Aires: Ariel.

Gibson, Edward L. 1996. *Class and Conservative Parties: Argentina in Comparative Perspective*. Baltimore: Johns Hopkins University Press.

Gobierno de Chile, Dirección Nacional del Trabajo. 2011. *Compendio de Series Estadísticas, 1990–2010*. Accessed at www.direcciondeltrabajo.cl.

Godio, Julio. 2000. *Historia del movimiento obrero argentino: 1870–2000*. 2 vols. Buenos Aires: Corregidor.

Godio, Julio. 2006. *El tiempo de Kirchner: el devenir de una "revolución desde arriba."* Buenos Aires, Argentina: Letra Grifa Ediciones.

González, Marcela Fabiana. 2004. "The Politics of Labor Union Laws: Policy Making in Argentina." Master's thesis, Department of Sociology, University of Maryland, College Park.

Gonzalez, Michael. 1989. "Chinese Plantation Workers and Social Conflict in Late 19th Century Peru." *Journal of Latin American Studies* 21 (3): 385–424.

Govan, Fiona, Aislinn Laing, and Nick Allen. 2010. "Families of Trapped Chilean Miners to Sue Mining Firm." *The Telegraph*. London. 26 August 2010.

Greene, William H. 2003. *Econometric Analysis*. 5th ed. Upper Saddle River, NJ: Prentice Hall.

Greenhill, Brian, Layna Mosley, and Aseem Prakash. 2009. "Trade-based Diffusion of Labor Rights: A Panel Study, 1986–2002." *American Political Science Review* 103 (4): 669–90.

Groisman, Fernando, and Adriana Marshall. 2005. "Determinantes del grado de desigualdad salarial en la Argentina: un estudio interurbano." *Desarrollo Económico* 45 (178): 281–301.

Grupo Apoyo, S. A. Public opinion polls. Various years. Lima, Peru.

Guasch, J. Luis. 1999. *Labor Market Reform and Job Creation: The Unfinished Agenda in Latin American and Caribbean Countries*. Washington, DC: World Bank.

Haber, Stephen H. 1989. *Industry and Underdevelopment: The Industrialization of Mexico, 1890–1940*. Stanford: Stanford University Press.

Haber, Stephen H., Herbert S. Klein, Noel Maurer, and Kevin J. Middlebrook. 2008. *Mexico since 1980*. New York: Cambridge University Press.

Haggard, Stephan, and Robert Kaufman. 2008. *Development, Democracy and Welfare States*. Princeton: Princeton University Press.

Hall, Peter, and David Soskice. 2001. *Varieties of Capitalism: The Institutional Foundations of Comparative Advantage*. Oxford: Oxford University Press.

Heckman, James J., and Carmen Pagés. 2000. *The Cost of Job Security Regulation: Evidence from Latin American Markets*. NBER working paper no. W7773.

Heckman, James J., and Carmen Pagés. 2004. *Law and Employment: Lessons from Latin America and the Caribbean: A National Bureau of Economic Research Conference Report*. Chicago: University of Chicago Press.

Heritage Foundation and Dow Jones and Company. 2009. *Index of Economic Freedom*. Washington, DC: Heritage Foundation.

Hopenhayn, Hugo A. 2004. "Labor Market Policies and Employment Duration: The Effects of Labor Market Reform in Argentina." In *Law and Employment: Lessons from Latin America and the Caribbean*, edited by James J. Heckman and Carmen Pagés. Chicago: University of Chicago Press.

Horowicz, Alejandro. 1991. *Los cuatro peronismos: espejo de la Argentina*. Buenos Aires: Planeta.

Houtzager, Peter P., and Marcus J. Kurtz. 2000. "The Institutional Roots of Popular Mobilization: State Transformation and Rural Politics in Brazil and Chile, 1960–1995." *Comparative Studies in Society and History* 42 (2): 394–424.

Huber, Evelyne, and John D. Stephens. 2001. *Development and Crisis of the Welfare State: Parties and Policies in Global Markets*. Chicago: University of Chicago Press.

Huber, Evelyne, and John D. Stephens. 2012. *Democracy and the Left: Social Policy and Inequality in Latin America*. Chicago: University of Chicago Press.

Iguíñiz, Javier, Denis Sulmont, and Comunidad de Compensación Minera (Peru). 1985. *Comunidad minera: itinerario de solidaridad*. Colección Peruanicemos el Perú. Lima: ATC: COCOMI.

International Labor Organization. 1997. *World Labor Report 1997–1998: Industrial Relations, Democracy, and Social Stability*. International Labor Office. Geneva, Switzerland.

Irureta, Pedro. 2009. "Regulación de la Libertad Sindical entre 1973 y 1990." In *Libertad Sindical y derechos humanos: análisis de los informes del Comité de Libertad de la OIT (1973–1990)*, edited by Elizabeth Lira and Hugo Rojas. Santiago, Chile: LOM Ediciones.

Iversen, Torben. 2005. *Capitalism, Democracy, and Welfare*. Cambridge Studies in Comparative Politics. Cambridge: Cambridge University Press.

Kaplan, David S. 2008. "Job Creation and Labor Reform in Latin America." *Journal of Comparative Economics* 37 (1): 91–105.

Kaplan, Stephen B. 2013. *Globalization and Austerity Politics in Latin America.* New York: Cambridge University Press.

Katzenstein, Peter J. 1985. *Small States in World Markets: Industrial Policy in Europe.* Cornell Studies in Political Economy. Ithaca, NY: Cornell University Press.

Kaufman, Robert R., and Alex Segura-Ubiergo. 2001. "Globalization, Domestic Politics, and Social Spending in Latin America: A Time-Series Cross-Section Analysis, 1973–97." *World Politics* 53 (4): 553–87.

King, Gary, Michael Tomz, and Jason Wittenberg. 2000. "Making the Most of Statistical Analyses: Improving Interpretation and Presentation." *American Journal of Political Science* 44 (2): 347–61.

Kugler, Adriana. 2000. *The Incidence of Job Security Regulations on Labor Market Flexibility and Compliance in Colombia: Evidence from the 1990 Reform.* Research Network working paper R-393.

La Nación. 2008. "Cristina ratificó su alianza con el sindicalismo." *La Nación,* 4 March.

La Porta, Rafael, Florencio Lopez-de-Silanes, Andre Shleifer, and Robert W. Vishny. 1998. "Law and Finance." *Journal of Political Economy* 106 (6): 1113–55.

Laugé, Luis. 2008a. "Darán más fondos a las obras sociales sindicales." *La Nación,* 24 January.

Laugé, Luis. 2008b. "El camionero logrará la foto que busca." *La Nación,* 22 January.

Laugé, Luis. 2008c. "La CTA también quiere una audiencia." *La Nación,* 22 January.

Levi, Margaret. 2003. "Organizing Power: The Prospects for an American Labor Movement." *Perspectives on Politics* 1 (1): 45–68.

Levitsky, Steven. 2003. *Transforming Labor-based Parties in Latin America: Argentine Peronism in Comparative Perspective.* Cambridge: Cambridge University Press.

Levitsky, Steven. 2005. "Crisis and Renovation: Institutional Weakness and the Transformation of Argentine Peronism, 1983–2003." In *Argentine Democracy: The Politics of Institutional Weakness,* edited by Steven Levitsky and Maria Victoria Murillo. University Park: Pennsylvania State University Press.

Levitsky, Steven, and Kenneth M. Roberts, eds. 2011. *The Resurgence of the Latin American Left.* Baltimore: Johns Hopkins University Press.

Levy, Santiago. 2008. *Good Intentions, Bad Outcomes: Social Policy, Informality, and Economic Growth in Mexico.* Washington, DC: Brookings Institution Press.

Lewis, Paul H. 1990. *The Crisis of Argentine Capitalism.* Chapel Hill: University of North Carolina Press.

Lo Vuolo, Rubén M., and Alberto Barbeito. 1998. *La nueva oscuridad de la política social: del estado populista al neoconservador.* 2nd. ed. Colección Políticas públicas. Buenos Aires: Miño y Dávila Editores.

Lobato, Mirta Zaida. 1998. "La vida en las fábricas: trabajo, protesta, y política en una comunidad obrera, Berisso 1907–70." Ph.D. dissertation, Facultad de Filosofía y Letras, Universidad de Buenos Aires, Argentina.

Long, J. Scott. 1997. *Regression Models for Categorical and Limited Dependent Variables, Advanced Quantitative Techniques in the Social Sciences.* Thousand Oaks, CA: Sage Publications.

Lora, Eduardo. 1997. *A Decade of Structural Reforms in Latin America: What Has Been Reformed and How to Measure It.* Washington, DC: Inter-American Development Bank.

Lora, Eduardo, and Carmen Pagés. 2002. "La legislación laboral en el proceso de reformas estructurales de América Latina y el Caribe (1996 Version)." In *La reforma laboral en el Peru: el derecho del trabajo y la política laboral del estado*, edited by Luis Pastor Iturrizaga. Lima, Perú: Gráfica Horizonte.

MacIsaac, Donna, and Martín Rama. 2001. *Mandatory Severance Pay: Its Coverage and Effects in Peru.* World Bank Policy Research working paper no. 2626.

Madrid, Raúl L. 2003. *Retiring the State: The Politics of Pension Privatization in Latin America and Beyond.* Stanford: Stanford University Press.

Magaloni, Beatriz. 2006. *Voting for Autocracy: Hegemonic Party Survival and Its Demise in Mexico.* New York: Cambridge University Press.

Mainwaring, Scott, Daniel Brinks, and Aníbal Pérez-Liñán. 2000. "Classifying Political Regimes in Latin America, 1945–1999." Notre Dame, IN: Notre Dame University, Kellogg Institute working paper no. 280.

Mainwaring, Scott, and Timothy R. Scully. 1996. *Building Democratic Institutions: Party Systems in Latin America.* Stanford: Stanford University Press.

Mares, Isabela. 2001. "Firms and the Welfare State: When, Why, and How Does Social Policy Matter to Employers?" In *Varieties of Capitalism*, edited by Peter Hall and David Soskice. Oxford: Oxford University Press.

Mares, Isabela. 2003. *The Politics of Social Risk: Business and Welfare State Development.* Cambridge: Cambridge University Press.

Mares, Isabela. 2005. "Social Protection around the World—External Insecurity, State Capacity, and Domestic Political Cleavages." *Comparative Political Studies* 38 (6): 623–51.

Mares, Isabela, and Matthew Carnes. 2009. "Social Policy in Developing Countries." *Annual Review of Political Science* 12: 93–113.

Marshall, Adriana. 2002. "Transformaciones en el empleo y la intervención sindical en la industria: efectos sobre la desigualdad de salarios." *Desarrollo Económico* 42 (166): 211–30.

Marshall, Adriana. 2005. *Labor Regulations and Unionization Trends: Comparative Analysis of Latin American Countries.* Ithaca, NY: Cornell University, Visiting Fellow working papers, Paper 22. Accessed at http://digitalcommons.ilr.cornell.edu/intlvf/22.

Marx, Karl, Friedrich Engels, and Robert C. Tucker. 1978. *The Marx-Engels Reader.* 2d ed. New York: Norton.

Matsushita, Hiroshi. 1983. *Movimiento obrero argentino, 1930–1945: sus proyecciones en los orígenes del peronismo.* Buenos Aires: Ediciones Siglo Veinte.

McGuire, James W. 1997. *Peronism without Perón: Unions, Parties, and Democracy in Argentina.* Stanford: Stanford University Press.

Mejía, Carlos. 1998. *Trabajadores, sindicatos, y nuevas redes de articulación social.* Documento de Trabajo 88, Serie Sociología y Política, no. 10. Lima, Perú: Instituto de Estudios Peruanos.

Meltzer, Allan H., and Scott F. Richard. 1981. "A Rational Theory of the Size of Government." *Journal of Political Economy* 89 (5): 914–27.

Menéndez, Nicolás Diana. 2005. "ATE y UPCN: dos concepciones de pugna sobre la representación sindical de los trabajadores estatales." In *Estado y relaciones laborales: transformaciones y perspectivas*, edited by A. Fernández. Buenos Aires, Argentina: Prometeo.

Mesa-Lago, Carmelo. 1978. *Social Security in Latin America: Pressure Groups, Stratification, and Inequality.* Pitt Latin American Series. Pittsburgh: University of Pittsburgh Press.

Mesa-Lago, Carmelo. 1994. *Changing Social Security in Latin America: Toward Alleviating the Social Costs of Economic Reform.* Boulder, CO: Lynne Rienner.

Meyer, John W., John Boli, George M. Thomas, and Francisco O. Ramirez. 1997. "World Society and the Nation-State." *American Journal of Sociology* 103 (1): 144–81.

Ministerio de Trabajo, Empleo, y Seguridad Social (MTSS). 2003. "Recuperación y crecimiento del empleo." *Informe Anual.* Buenos Aires, Argentina.

Mondino, Guillermo, and Silvia Montoya. 2004. "The Effects of Labor Market Regulations on Employment Decisions by Firms: Empirical Evidence for Argentina." In *Law and Employment: Lessons from Latin America and the Caribbean*, edited by James Heckman and Carmen Pagés. Chicago: University of Chicago Press.

Monteón, Michael. 1979. "The Enganche in the Chilean Nitrate Sector, 1880–1930." *Latin American Perspectives* 6 (3): 66–79.

Montevideo-Oxford Latin American Economic History Database. Accessed at http://oxlad.qeh.ox.ac.uk.

Morales, Karina. 2008. "Cámera aprueba reforma previsional y gobierno destaca cumplimiento de compromiso." *El Mercurio Online*, 16 January 2008.

Morris, James O. 1966. *Elites, Intellectuals, and Consensus: A Study of the Social Question and the Industrial Relations System in Chile.* Ithaca, NY: New York State School of Industrial and Labor Relations, Cornell University.

Mosley, Layna, and Saika Uno. 2007. "Racing to the Bottom or Climbing to the Top? Economic Globalization and Collective Labor Rights." *Comparative Political Studies* 40 (8): 923–48.

Mosley, Layna, and Saika Uno. 2007. Replication Data for: "Racing to the Bottom or Climbing to the Top? Economic Globalization and Labor Rights." http://hdl.handle.net/1902.1/10502.

Müller, Katharina. 2003. *Privatising Old-Age Security: Latin America and Eastern Europe Compared.* Northampton, MA: Edward Elgar Publishers.

Muñoz Gomá, Oscar. 2007. *El modelo económico de la Concertación, 1990–2005: ¿reformas o cambio?* Santiago, Chile: FLACSO-Chile.

Murillo, Maria Victoria. 2001. *Labor Unions, Partisan Coalitions and Market Reforms in Latin America.* Cambridge Studies in Comparative Politics. New York: Cambridge University Press.

Murillo, Maria Victoria. 2005. "Partisanship amidst Convergence—The Politics of Labor Reform in Latin America." *Comparative Politics* 37 (4): 441–58.

Murillo, Maria Victoria, and Andrew Schrank. 2005. "With a Little Help from My Friends—Partisan Politics, Transnational Alliances, and Labor Rights in Latin America." *Comparative Political Studies* 38 (8): 971–99.

Murillo, Maria Victoria, Lucas Ronconi, and Andrew Schrank. 2011. "Latin American Labor Reforms: Evaluating Risk and Security." In *Oxford Handbook of Latin American Economics*, edited by José Antonio Ocampo and Jaime Ros. Oxford: Oxford University Press.

Navia, Patricia. 2008. "Pinochet: The Father of Contemporary Chile." *Latin American Research Review* 43: 3.

Neffa, Julio C. 2004. "La forma institucional de la relación salarial y su evolución en la Argentina desde una perspectiva de largo plazo." In *La economía argentina y su crisis (1976–2001): visiones institucionalistas y regulacionistas*, edited by Robert Boyer and Julio C. Neffa. Buenos Aires: Miño y Dávila.

Novick, Marta, and David Trajtemberg. 2000. *La negociación colectiva en el período 1991–1999.* Secretaría de Trabajo, Coordinación de Investigaciones y Análisis Laborales

Obarrio, Mario. 2011. "Se ahonda el malestar de la presidenta con Moyano." *La Nación.* 17 December.

O'Brien, Thomas F. 1996. *The Revolutionary Mission: American Enterprise in Latin America, 1900–1945.* Cambridge Latin American Studies. New York: Cambridge University Press.

Oficina Internacional del Trabajo. 1928. *Legislación social en América Latina.* Vol. 1. Ginebra: Organización Internacional del Trabajo.

Ortiz Letelier, Fernando. 1985. *El movimiento obrero en Chile (1891–1919): antecedentes.* Madrid, Spain: Ediciones Michay.

Pace, Thomas. 1939. "Chilean Social Laws." Ph.D. dissertation, Graduate School of Law, Catholic University of America.

Pagano, Marco, and Paolo Volpin. 2001. "The Political Economy of Finance." *Oxford Review of Economic Policy* 17 (4): 502–19.

Pagés, Carmen, and Claudio Montenegro. 1999. "Job Security and the Age-Composition of Unemployment: Evidence from Chile." Office of the Chief Economist, InterAmerican Development Bank. Working paper 398.

Paredes, Maritza. 2008. "Weak Indigenous Politics in Peru." CRISE working paper no. 33. Center for Research on Inequality, Human Security, and Ethnicity, Department of International Development, University of Oxford.

Parodi Trece, Carlos. 2000. *Peru, 1960–2000: políticas económicas y sociales en entornos cambiantes.* Lima, Perú: Universidad del Pacífico, Centro de Investigación.

Pasco Cosmópolis, Mario. 2002. "Balance de la reforma laboral." In *La reforma laboral en el Perú: el derecho del trabajo y la política laboral del estado*, edited by Luis Pastor Iturrizaga. Lima, Perú: Gráfica Horizonte.

Payne, James L. 1965. *Labor and Politics in Peru: The System of Political Bargaining.* New Haven: Yale University Press.

Perelman, Laura C. 2001. "El empleo no permanente en la Argentina." *Desarrollo Económico* 41 (161): 71–96.

Pierson, Paul. 1993. "When Effect Becomes Cause: Policy Feedback and Political Change." *World Politics* 45 (4): 595–628.

Pierson, Paul. 1994. *Dismantling the Welfare State? Reagan, Thatcher, and the Politics of Retrenchment.* New York: Cambridge University Press.

Piñera Echenique, José. 1990. *La revolución laboral en Chile.* Santiago, Chile: Editora Zig-Zag, S.A.

Piore, Michael J., and Andrew Schrank. 2008. "Toward Managed Flexibility: The Revival of Labour Inspection in the Latin World." *International Labour Review* 147 (1): 1–23.

Poblete-Troncoso, Moises. 1928a. "Labour Legislation in Latin America: I." *International Labour Review* 17: 51–67.

Poblete-Troncoso, Moises. 1928b. "Labour Legislation in Latin America: II." *International Labour Review* 17: 204–230.

Poblete-Troncoso, Moises, and Ben Burnett. 1960. *The Rise of the Latin American Labor Movement.* New York: Bookman Associates.

Polity IV database. Accessed at www.bsos.umd.edu/cidcm/inscr/polity.

Pollack, Benny. 1982. "Comentarios preliminares sobre el plan laboral y el nuevo sistema de pensiones en Chile: sus alcances como instrumento de control social." In *Sindicalismo y regimenes militares en Argentina y Chile*, edited by Bernardo Gallitelli and Andres A. Thompson. Amsterdam: Centro de Estudios y Documentacion Latinoamericanos (CEDLA).

Pribble, Jennifer A. 2013. *Welfare and Party Politics in Latin America.* New York: Cambridge University Press.

Przeworski, Adam, Michael E. Alvarez, José Antonio Cheibub, and Fernando Limongi. 2000. *Democracy and Development: Political Institutions and Well-being in the World, 1950–1990.* Cambridge: Cambridge University Press.

Quiroga, Hugo. 2005. *La Argentina en emergencia permanente.* Buenos Aires: Edhasa.

Rama, Martín, and Raquel Artecona. 2002. "A Database of Labor Market Indicators across Countries." World Bank, Development Research Group. Washington, DC.

Restrepo, Jorge Enrique, and Andrea Tokman R. 2005. "Labor Markets and Institutions." Series on Central Banking, Analysis, and Economic Policies. Santiago, Chile: Banco Central de Chile.

Roberts, Kenneth M., and Erik Wibbels. 1999. "Party Systems and Electoral

Volatility in Latin America: A Test of Economic, Institutional, and Structural Explanations." *American Political Science Review* 93 (3): 575–90.

Rodrik, Dani. 1998. "Why Do More Open Economies Have Bigger Governments?" *Journal of Political Economy* 106: 997–1032.

Romero Montes, Francisco Javier. 2002. "La reconstrucción del sindicalismo." In *La reforma laboral en el Perú: el derecho del trabajo y la política laboral del estado*, edited by L. Pastor Iturrizaga. Lima, Perú: Gráfica Horizonte.

Ronconi, Lucas. 2010. "Enforcement and Compliance with Labor Regulations in Argentina." *Industrial and Labor Relations Review* 63 (4): 719–36.

Ronconi, Lucas. 2012. "Globalization, Domestic Institutions and Enforcement of Labor Law: Evidence from Latin America." *Industrial Relations* 51 (1): 89–105.

Rosenthal, Howard, and Erik Voeten. 2007. "Measuring Legal Systems." *Journal of Comparative Economics* 35: 711–28.

Rudra, Nita. 2008. *Globalization and the Race to the Bottom in Developing Countries: Who Really Gets Hurt?* New York: Cambridge University Press.

Rueda, David. 2005. "Insider-outsider Politics in Industrialized Democracies: The Challenge to Social Democratic Parties." *American Political Science Review* 99 (1): 61–74.

Rueda-Catry, Marleen, Juan Manuel Sepúlveda-Malbrán, and María Luz Vega Ruiz. 1998. *Tendencias y contenidos de la negociación colectiva: fortalecimiento de las organizaciones sindicales de los países andinos*. Oficina Internacional del Trabajo, Organización Internacional del Trabajo. Documento de Trabajo 88.

Ruiz Pérez, José Luis. 1996. "El mercado de trabajo en el sector público peruano: 1991–1994." In *Caminos entrelazados: la realidad del empleo urbano en el Perú*, edited by Gustavo Yamada Fukusaki and Guillermo Felices Sasvedra. Lima: Universidad del Pacífico, Centro de Investigación.

Ruiz-Tagle, Jaime. 1985. *El sindicalismo chileno después del plan laboral*. Santiago, Chile: Editorial Interamericana Ltda.

Ruiz-Tagle, Jaime. 2009. "El sindicalismo chileno entre 1973 y 1990." In *Libertad sindical y derechos humanos: análisis de los informes del Comité de Libertad de la OIT (1973–1990)*, edited by Elizabeth Lira and Hugo Rojas. Santiago, Chile: LOM Ediciones.

Saavedra, Jaime. 1999. "Reformas laborales en un contexto de apertura económica." Unpublished manuscript. Lima: Grupo de Análisis para el Desarrollo.

Saavedra, Jaime. 2000. "La flexibilización del mercado laboral." In *La reforma incompleta: rescatando los noventa*, edited by R. Abusada, F. Du Bois, E. Morón, and J. Valderrama. Lima, Peru: Universidad del Pacífico.

Saavedra, Jaime, and Máximo Torero. 2002. "Union Density Changes and Union Effects on Firm Performance in Peru." Inter-American Development Bank, Latin American Research Network, Research Network working paper no. R-465.

Saiegh, Sebastian. 2011. *Ruling by Statute: How Uncertainty and Vote-Buying Shape Lawmaking.* New York: Cambridge University Press.

Schmitter, Philippe. 1979. "Still the Century of Corporatism?" In *Trends towards Corporatist Intermediation,* edited by Philippe Schmitter and Gerhard Lehmbruch. Beverly Hills, CA: Sage.

Schneider, Ben Ross. 2009. "Hierarchical Market Economies and Varieties of Capitalism in Latin America." *Journal of Latin American Studies* 41 (3): 553–75.

Schneider, Ben Ross, and Sebastian Karcher. 2010. "Complementarities and Continuities in the Political Economy of Labour Markets in Latin America." *Socio-Economic Review* 8 (4): 623–51.

Schneider, Ben Ross, and David Soskice. 2011. *The Low-Skill Trap: Latin America in the Global Economy.* Mimeo. Massachusetts Institute of Technology.

Schrank, Andrew. 2009. "Professionalization and Probity in the Patrimonial State: Labor Law Enforcement in the Dominican Republic." *Latin American Politics and Society* 51 (2): 91–115.

Segura-Ubiergo, Alex. 2007. *The Political Economy of the Welfare State in Latin America: Globalization, Democracy, and Development.* Cambridge: Cambridge University Press.

Sehnbruch, Kirsten. 2006. *The Chilean Labor Market: A Key to Understanding Latin American Labor Markets.* New York: Palgrave Macmillan.

Senén González, Santiago, Fabián Bosoer, and Hiroshi Matsushita. 1999. *El sindicalismo en tiempos de Menem: los ministros de trabajo en la primera presidencia de Menem: sindicalismo y estado (1989–1995).* Buenos Aires: Corregidor.

Sherwell, Philip, and Harriet Alexander. 2011. "Chile Miners One Year On: Over Half of 'Los 33' Want to Return to Work Underground." *The Telegraph.* London. 31 July 2011.

Sidicaro, Ricardo. 2002. *Los tres peronismos: estado y poder económico 1946–1955, 1973–1976, 1989–1999.* Buenos Aires: Siglo Veintiuno Editores.

Silva, Patricio. 1988. "The State, Politics and Peasant Unions in Chile." *Journal of Latin American Studies* 20: 433–52.

Skidmore, Thomas E., and Peter H. Smith. 2005. *Modern Latin America.* 6th ed. New York: Oxford University Press.

Solow, Robert M. 1956. "A Contribution to the Theory of Economic Growth." *Quarterly Journal of Economics* 70 (1): 65–94.

Stigler, George J. 1971. "The Theory of Economic Regulation." *Bell Journal of Economics and Management Science* 2 (1): 3–21.

Szusterman, Celia. 2007. "Argentina's New President: Kirchner after Kirchner." openDemocracy.net, 29 October 2007. Accessed 5 March 2008 at http://www.opendemocracy.net/article/democracy_power/argentina_kirchner_after_kirchner.

Tanaka, Martín. 1998. *Los espejismos de la democracia: el colapso del sistema de partidos en el Perú, 1980–1995, en perspectiva comparada.* Serie Ideología y política. Lima, Peru: Instituto de Estudios Peruanos.

Tanaka, Martín. 2005. *Democracia sin partidos, Perú, 2000–2005: los problemas de representación y las propuestas de reforma política.* Lima: Instituto de Estudios Peruanos.

Thelen, Kathleen. 2004. *How Institutions Evolve: The Political Economy of Skills in Germany, Britain, the United States and Japan.* New York: Cambridge University Press.

Thorp, Rosemary, and Geoffrey Bertram. 1978. *Peru, 1890–1977: Growth and Policy in an Open Economy.* The Columbia Economic History of the Modern World. New York: Columbia University Press.

Tomz, Michael, Jason Wittenberg, and Gary King. 2001. CLARIFY: Software for Interpreting and Presenting Statistical Results. Version 2.0 Cambridge, MA: Harvard University. Accessed at http://gking.harvard.edu.

Torre, Juan Carlos. 1972. *La tasa de sindicalización en la Argentina.* Documento de Trabajo no. 77. Buenos Aires: Centro de Investigaciones Sociales del Instituto Torcuato di Tella.

Torre, Juan Carlos. 2004. *El gigante invertebrado: los sindicatos en el gobierno, Argentina 1973–1976.* Colección Historia y política 4. Buenos Aires: Siglo Veintiuno.

Torre, Juan Carlos. 2006. *La vieja guardia sindical y Perón: sobre los orígenes del peronismo.* 2nd ed. Buenos Aires, Argentina: Editorial de la Universidad Nacional de Tres de Febrero.

Torres, Rubén. 2004. *Mitos y realidades de las obras sociales en la Argentina.* Buenos Aires: Ediciones Isalud.

Train, Kenneth. 2003. *Discrete Choice Methods with Simulation.* New York: Cambridge University Press.

Valenzuela, J. Samuel. 1979. "Labor Movement Formation and Politics: The Chilean and French Cases in Comparative Perspective, 1850–1950." Ph.D. dissertation, Department of Political Science, Columbia University.

Valenzuela, J. Samuel. 2006. "Diseños dispares, resultados diferentes, y convergencias tardías: las instituciones de bienestar social en Chile y suecia." In *El eslabón perdido: familia, modernización y bienestar en Chile,* edited by J. Samuel Valenzuela, Eugenio Tironi, and Timothy Scully, CSC. Santiago de Chile: Taurus.

Valenzuela, J. Samuel, and Jeffrey Goodwin. 1983. "Labor Movements under Authoritarian Regimes." Monographs on Europe 5. Cambridge, MA: Harvard University Center for European Studies.

Vega Ruiz, María Luz. 2005. *La reforma laboral en América Latina: 15 años después—un análisis comparado.* Lima: Organización Internacional del Trabajo.

Velásquez Pinto, Mario D. 2009. "Flexibilidad, protección y políticas activas en Chile." In *El nuevo escenario laboral latinoamericano: regulación, protección y políticas activas en los mercados de trabajo,* edited by Jurgen Weller. Buenos Aires: Siglo Veintiuno Editores, S.A.

Vilela Espinosa, Anna, Aldo Vértiz Iriarte, and Alfredo Chienda Quiroz. 2006. *Compendio laboral: edición 2006.* 2nd ed. Lima, Perú: Biblioteca AELE.

Walker Errázuriz, Francisco. 2003. *Derecho de las relaciones laborales.* Santiago, Chile: Editorial Universitaria.

Weyland, Kurt. 2002. *The Politics of Market Reform in Fragile Democracies: Argentina, Brazil, Peru, and Venezuela.* Princeton: Princeton University Press.

Weyland, Kurt. 2004. *Learning from Foreign Models in Latin American Policy Reform.* Washington, DC: Woodrow Wilson Center Press.

Weyland, Kurt. 2007. *Bounded Rationality and Policy Diffusion: Social Sector Reform in Latin America.* Princeton: Princeton University Press.

Wiarda, Howard. 1978. "Corporative Origins of the Iberian and Latin American Labor Relations Systems." *Studies in Comparative International Development* 13 (1): 3–37.

Wilensky, Harold L. 1975. *The Welfare State and Equality: Structural and Ideological Roots of Public Expenditures.* Berkeley: University of California Press.

Winn, Peter, ed. 2004. *Victims of the Chilean Miracle: Workers and Neoliberalism in the Pinochet Era, 1973–2000.* Durham, NC: Duke University Press.

World Bank. 2007. *World Development Indicators.* Washington, DC: World Bank.

Yepez del Castillo, Isabel, and Jorge Bernedo Alvarez. 1985. *La sindicalización en el Perú.* Lima, Perú: Fundación Friederich Ebert y Facultad de Ciencias Sociales, Pontificia Universidad Católica.

Zapata, Francisco. 1976. *Las relaciones entre el movimiento obrero y el gobierno de Salvador Allende.* Cuadernos del CES no. 4. Mexico City: Centro de Estudios Sociológicos, El Colegio de Mexico.

Zapata, Francisco. 1998. *Flexibles y productivos? estudios sobre flexibilidad laboral en México.* México, D.F.: El Colegio de México, Centro de Estudios Sociológicos.

Zarazaga, Rodrigo. 2004. *La pobreza de un país rico: dilemas de los proyectos de nación, de Mitre a Perón.* Buenos Aires: Fundación OSDE: Siglo Veintiuno Editores Argentina.

Zellner, Arnold. 1962. "An Efficient Method of Estimating Seemingly Unrelated Regressions and Tests of Aggregation Bias." *Journal of the American Statistical Association* 57: 348–68.

Index

Agricultural workers: in Chile, 109, 112, 134, 135; collective organization, 32; unskilled, 34

Alfonsín, Raúl, 174–76, 206n2

Alianza Democrática, Chile, 108

Alianza Liberal, Chile, 105

Alianza Popular Revolucionaria Americana (APRA), Peru, 129, 133, 138–39, 141, 143, 152, 155–56. *See also* García, Alán

Allende Gossens, Salvador, 109, 110–12, 115, 122, 123

Anarchism, in Argentina, 162

Anarcho-syndicalism, in Chile, 104, 108

APRA, *see* Alianza Popular Revolucionaria Americana

Argentina: Constitution of 1949, 167; economic policies, 174, 176, 178–79; economic problems, 180, 183; European immigrants, 60, 63–64, 162, 163; industrial development, 162–63; literacy, 60–61, 162; meat industry, 163; Menem government, 71, 175–80, 187, 208nn14–15; military governments, 171–72, 174, 187; Ministry of Labor, 181; organizational capacity of labor, 65, 163–64; pensions, 178, 182–83, 195,

208n14; political incorporation of labor, 166–69, 172; preincorporation period, 161–65; primary school enrollments, 60, 61 (fig.), 62, 63 (fig.), 162; Radical governments, 171, 172, 174–75, 187; urbanization, 162–63; vacations, 159–60. *See also* Peronist Party

Argentina, labor laws: collective dismissal notifications, 54; on collective relations, 160, 166, 167, 171, 175, 177, 178, 179, 181–82; compliance, 206n1; as corporatist regime, 160; enforcement, 202n5; fixed-term contracts, 51; flexibilizing, 176–79; by government, 188–90 (table); individual protections, 160, 163, 165, 167, 172–73, 176–78, 181, 206n1; job stability measures, 165, 173, 181, 183–84; under Kirchners (2002–present), 180–86, 187; maternity leave, 53; under Menem, 51, 57, 65, 71, 176–79, 187; minimum wage, 206n1, 207n7; origins, 161–65; overtime hours, 53; under Peronist governments, 165–71, 172–74, 175–80, 186, 187;

Literacy: in Argentina, 60–61, 162; in
Chile, 61; in Peru, 61, 134. *See also*
Education
Low-skill trap, 46, 78, 150

Manufacturing employment: in
Argentina, 62–63, 64 (fig.), 64–65,
65 (fig.), 162–63; in Chile, 63, 64
(fig.), 64–65, 65 (fig.), 111, 116;
in cities, 7, 32; declines, 7, 64–65;
growth, 7, 32, 34; organizational
capacity and, 62–64; outsourcing, 12,
120; in Peru, 63, 64 (fig.), 64–65, 65
(fig.), 135, 140
Market labor law regimes, 27–28,
29–30, 80, 90
Market reforms, 2–3, 38, 195, 196
Maternity leave, 52 (table), 53
Menem, Carlos, 51, 57, 65, 71, 175–80,
187, 208nn14–15
Mining: in Chile, 96–97, 98, 101–3,
111; organizational capacity and,
62; in Peru, 134, 136; safety, 96–97;
unions, 32, 34, 97, 103, 111
Morales Bermúdez, Francisco, 141, 155
Moyano, Hugo, 185, 186, 208–9n19
Mutual aid societies, 64, 103, 104, 134,
204n1, 207n6

Obras sociales (Argentina), 167, 171, 178,
185, 207n6, 208–9n19
Odria, Manuel, 138
OECD, *see* Organization for Economic
Coordination and Development
Organizational capacity of labor: in
Argentina, 65, 163–64; in case
studies, 60, 62–64, 196; in Chile,
122; definition, 21; as determinant
of collective labor relations laws, 20,
23, 38–40, 43–44, 47, 79–80, 83; as
factor in labor law development,
5, 22–23, 199; factors in, 79, 83;
feedback effects of labor laws, 45,
46–47; fluctuations, 22–23; formal

organizations, 37; importance, 5,
89; labor law reforms and, 93–94;
measures, 62–63, 83; in Peru, 65,
129, 136–37, 138–41, 147, 156;
realized, 83; structural economic
factors and, 37–38. *See also* Politics
and labor; Unions
Organization for Economic
Coordination and Development
(OECD), 48, 84
Outsourcing, 12, 120
Overtime hours per week, 51, 52
(table), 53

Partido Justicialista (PJ), Argentina, *see*
Peronist Party
Partido Laborista (PL), Argentina, 167,
169, 207n5
Parties, *see* Political parties
Partisanship, 84, 86, 88–89, 92. *See also*
Political parties
Pension privatization: in Argentina, 178,
208n14; in Chile, 114–15, 119, 195,
208n14; in Latin America, 195; in
Peru, 153, 206n11
Pensions: in Argentina, 182–83, 195; in
Chile, 1, 114–15, 119, 195, 204n6; in
Peru, 206n11
Perón, Evita, 168, 170
Perón, Isabel, 173
Perón, Juan: death, 173; economic
policies, 174; labor policies, 166–71,
172–73; military junta, 165–67;
political coalition, 207n5; presidency,
167–71, 172–73, 174
Peronist Party (Partido Justicialista):
divisions, 180; electoral strength,
160–61, 169–70, 172; labor laws and
policies, 160–61, 165–71, 172–74,
175–80, 186, 187
Peronist Party (Partido Justicialista),
relationship with organized labor:
"62 Organizations," 168–69, 207n11;
electoral competition as factor,

Printed and bound by CPI Group (UK) Ltd, Croydon, CR0 4YY

23/04/2025

14660939-0002